People Skills

for

Policy Analysts

Michael Mintrom

Georgetown University Press
Washington, D.C.

Georgetown University Press, Washington, D.C.
© 2003 by Georgetown University Press. All rights reserved.
Printed in the United States of America

10 9 8 7 6 5 4 3 2 1 2003

This volume printed on acid-free offset book paper.

Library of Congress Cataloging-in-Publication Data
Mintrom, Michael, 1963–
   People skills for policy analysts / Michael Mintrom.
      p. cm.
Includes bibliographical references and index.
   ISBN 0-87840-900-9 (pbk. : alk. paper)
  1. Policy sciences. 2. Communication in organizations. I. Title.
H97.M56 2003
320'.6—dc21

                                   2002013811

Contents

List of Figures and Table

Preface

Effective policy analysts need both sound technical skills and superb people skills. Over many years of teaching courses in public policy analysis, I typically have augmented my lectures on applied microeconomic analysis and other topics relevant to policy analysis with workshops on topics such as interviewing informants, working in teams, and giving presentations. The popularity of these workshops among students led me to solicit their ideas for additional topics to cover. It was through this process of offering workshops and inviting student feedback that I struck upon the idea of writing this book.

The actual plan for the book emerged during a series of conversations. I especially wish to thank Jacqui True, for her initial encouragement to write the book, and Richard Callahan, director of the University of Southern California's Sacramento Center, who provided invaluable comments on my early ideas. Gail Grella, at Georgetown University Press, also expressed considerable interest in the plan for the book and gave me continual encouragement during the writing process. I began writing the chapters in 2001, while on leave from Michigan State University and visiting the School of Policy, Planning, and Development at the University of Southern California, where I taught courses in public finance and intergovernmental management. I continued with this work while a program visitor in the political science program in the School for Social Science Research at the Australian National University later that year. The Department of Political Science at Michigan State provided a supportive environment for completing the project. I am grateful to my spring 2002 undergraduate and graduate public policy analysis students at Michigan State University. In both classes, teams of students presented material from draft chapters of this book, and many provided extremely helpful suggestions for how the chapters could be improved. My research assistant, Joshua Spaulding, read and commented on each chapter.

As the book progressed, I commissioned the set of statements from policy practitioners and scholars that are contained in the epigraphs to chapters 2–11. These statements reflect their own views. They do not represent the positions of the organizations with which the authors are associated. I would like to thank the authors for taking time from their busy schedules to make these contributions. I am proud to note that six of them are former students of mine. In several cases, the authors also provided insightful comments on the draft chapters. Finally, I wish to thank the anonymous reviewers of the manuscript for their enthusiastic responses and their helpful suggestions for improvements.

1
...

Policy Analysts and People Skills

People become policy analysts because they care deeply about society. They want to help improve how we live our lives. This book is designed to aid those training to be policy analysts, and junior practitioners, to become more effective at what they do. The focus of the book is people skills. People skills are habits we cultivate that allow us to make good use of our time, to work well with others, and to communicate our ideas so that they are influential. I hope to make policy analysts more self-conscious of their behavior and to encourage the widespread improvement of their people skills. Beyond the other direct and spillover benefits to be gained from well-developed people skills, becoming an effective people person can add immeasurably to the sense of fulfillment and the pleasure that policy analysts attain from their work.

Over the past few decades, the training of policy analysts has grown increasingly standardized and sophisticated. University programs in public policy, policy analysis, and public management routinely offer courses designed to ensure that their graduates are familiar with the microeconomic foundations of policy analysis and that they know how to utilize qualitative and quantitative research methods. In addition, students in such programs typically take courses drawing on insights from a range of academic disciplines that are designed to build their knowledge of, among other things, organization theory, the politics of policymaking, public finance, and program evaluation. Undoubtedly, these advances in how policy analysts are trained have raised the quality of the analytical work and advice that inform public policy decisions. Despite these positive developments, however, practicing policy analysts and policy scholars continue to lament the frequency with which policymakers in a wide variety of public contexts appear to pay little attention to the work of policy analysts when it is laid before them (Beam 1996; Mooney 1991; Shulock 1999; Weiss 1977). Can we do better?

Highly effective policy analysts display both superb technical expertise and excellent people skills. The premise of this book is that, although considerable strides have been made in the technical training that policy analysts receive, the task of guiding policy analysts in the development of their people skills has been all but ignored. This neglect works to the detriment of the policy analysts themselves and to that of policymaking more generally. Perhaps such neglect is inevitable. As a society we often discount the importance of people skills to the quality of our lives. We frequently assume that some people are just naturally gifted at getting along with others, managing their time, making presentations, working in teams, or networking. Sometimes, it is said that such skills need not be taught in university programs because smart people will pick them up on the job. Such discounting of people skills, and what it takes to develop them, serves to arbitrarily demarcate what sort of knowledge is most valuable for policy analysts.

Policy scholars and practitioners have long worked to develop technical approaches and procedures that can usefully inform the ways that policy analysts assess the feasibility and merits of alternative approaches to addressing policy problems. Likewise, many people have contributed ideas and suggestions for how we might improve our abilities to communicate and collaborate with others. Nevertheless, though many technical approaches and insights have been codified and integrated into the training of policy analysts, no such effort has been made to do the same with the disparate contributions that could inform how policy analysts interact with people around them.

Policy analysts are not born; they are made. Because we believe this, a great deal of thought has gone into the structuring of university programs on public policy, policy analysis, and public management so that technical skills are well taught. Yet, if we believe that good policy analysts are made, we should also pay closer attention to the relevance of people skills and think seriously about how to impart them. As to whether excellence in the use of technical skills requires more analytical sophistication than does excellence in the use of people skills, I have yet to make up my mind. For those who claim that technical skills are obviously the "hard stuff," I ask, "How so?"

This book has much to offer individuals seeking to increase their effectiveness as policy analysts. Just as many textbooks lay out how to analyze policy issues appropriately, here I provide guidance on how policy analysts might present themselves and their work so as to improve the likelihood that they will produce quality advice and receive a good hearing from others in the policymaking community. By placing the spotlight on people skills for policy analysts, I also hope this book will contribute to a rethinking of what we mean when we say someone is an excellent analyst and of how policy analysts are trained.

To develop the advice presented in the following chapters, I have drawn on ideas, insights, and suggestions offered by scholars and practitioners from a wide range of disciplines and social contexts. As the suggestions for further reading contained at the end of each chapter attest, many authors have already made important contributions to our understanding of the various people skills that I cover here. Until now, however, no one has synthesized these scattered ideas and insights and demonstrated their potential value to policy analysts. In this work, I identify a set of people skills that are highly relevant for policy analysts, explain why these people skills matter, and give advice on how policy analysts might work to develop these skills. In so doing, I hope to lower the barriers that have previously kept many policy analysts from building people skills that complement their technical expertise.

POLICY ANALYSTS AND THE POLICYMAKING PROCESS

There are no hard and fast definitions of what it means to be a policy analyst. Over time, our understandings of the roles played by policy analysts have tended to change (Radin 2000). Also, because policy analysts perform roles that share similarities with those of other actors in and around the policymaking process, it is often the case that individuals holding a broad range of positions can legitimately claim to be policy analysts (Weimer and Vining 1999).

I think of policy analysts mainly as people who, using their expert knowledge and skills, produce high-quality information and advice for elected and appointed government officials, with the purpose of increasing the capacity of those officials to make sound decisions on the public's behalf. In this definition, many policy analysts will be government employees, but they need not be. Policy analysts can also be employees of political parties, interest groups, think tanks, and foundations. In addition, many people who are employed by consulting firms, universities, or are self-employed often serve as policy analysts, producing policy reports and advice, on a contract basis, to government officials and their staffs. Increasingly, we find people trained as policy analysts also being employed by private corporations. Such individuals tend to serve as interpreters of government policy, analyzing new and current policies with the purpose of determining their implications for the business strategies of their employers. All of these individuals have one thing in common: they produce policy analysis and advice with specific clients in mind. This client orientation has often been noted as a core attribute of the policy analyst's role (Behn 1985; Weimer and Vining 1999). We might also think of many scholars and journalists as policy analysts, because they often produce careful studies of public policies and their implications for various groups in society. Of course, the policy analyses of those who work at arm's length from government and the day-to-day world of policymaking cannot be thought of as having the kind of short-term impacts on policymaking as analysts employed by governments. Nevertheless, there is evidence that work by those standing at the periphery of the policymaking process can, in the long-term, influence the making of public policy, often profoundly (Derthick and Quirk 1985; Kingdon 1995; Mead 1985; Nelson 1984; Weiss 1977).

When thinking about the role of policy analysts in the policymaking process, it is important to differentiate between policy advice and policy advocacy. I associate advice with the role of the policy analyst. In contrast, I associate advocacy with the role of the politician, interest-group lobbyist, or policy entrepreneur (Mintrom 2000). What makes for the difference here? Most importantly, I see the difference as having to do with who gets to set the agenda for policymaking. Agenda setting, the determination of what issues will receive the attention of policymakers, involves high levels of advocacy, what we might call politicking. Politicking inside and outside of government helps to shape the broad public agenda at any given time. Politicking inside of government, among politicians and their political advisors, shapes the actual government agenda (Cobb and Elder 1983; Eyestone 1978; Kingdon 1995). Policy analysts are not employed to engage in politicking. The advisory work of policy analysts should be based on analysis and expertise; advocacy of specific policy positions should be downplayed.

Although some basic theoretical and practical distinctions can be drawn between advice giving and advocacy, there remains a gray area where the practicalities of drawing those distinctions make it difficult, if not impossible, to do. For example, policy advocacy will often take the form of advice giving. Furthermore, policy analysts who have toiled long and hard to develop their advice for their clients might find it irresistibly tempting to use their advisory role as a platform from which to advocate the adoption of specific policy alternatives. For my part, I like to conceive of policy analysts as highly creative individuals who use both their technical and people skills to help government officials redefine policy problems, who explore new ways to undertake their investigative and analytical work, and who develop new realizations of the policy alternatives that are available.

Wildavsky's (1979) notion that policy analysts are people who "speak truth to power" continues to hold appeal. Yet, as Radin (2000, 51) has observed, the one-to-one relationship between the policy analyst and the policymaker implied by Wildavsky's phrase is rarely found in the policymaking process. The policy analysis profession has become highly variegated. In Radin's words, "We are a field with multiple languages, values, and forms and with multiple individuals and groups as clients for the analyst." In such an environment, what constitutes "truth" is open to serious debate, and the view that power flows inexorably from a fixed center is also cast into doubt. In light of the complexity of interactions that define the policymaking process, how might policy analysts act so as to increase the odds that public decisions are informed by sound, appropriate evidence and advice?

A provocative way to think about the motivations and actions of policy analysts in the policymaking process is to consider how they might differ from those of the intellectual in society, as described by Said (1996, 23):

> The intellectual . . . is neither a pacifier nor a consensus-builder, but someone whose whole being is staked on a critical sense, a sense of being unwilling to accept easy formulas, or ready-made clichés, or the smooth, ever-so-accommodating confirmations of what the powerful or conventional have to say, and what they do. Not just passively unwillingly, but actively willing to say so in public. This is not always a matter of being a critic of government

policy, but rather of thinking of the intellectual vocation as maintaining a state of constant alertness, of a perpetual willingness not to let half-truths or received ideas steer one along.

In light of my definition of the policy analyst, where might we want to draw the line between what is reasonable and appropriate behavior for such an individual and what is reasonable and appropriate behavior for an intellectual? First, unlike intellectuals, who are ultimately accountable to themselves for what they do and for what they say in public, policy analysts are accountable to those who employ them. Often the employers will be government officials. Thus, if a study of relevant facts leads a policy analyst to believe that he or she should be critical of government policy, that criticism should initially be voiced privately to the client. If the client considers the criticism to be valid and appropriate for sharing with a broader audience, it is the client's role to determine how the voicing of that criticism should be done.

Said suggests that the public intellectual should shun the roles of pacifier or consensus-builder in the interests of maintaining a critical distance from the behavior of others. This points to a second difference between how intellectuals and policy analysts might go about what they do. Policy analysts will no doubt also consider it appropriate at times to present evidence and make arguments that could create conflict. But having differences of opinion with others, even when those differences are sharp, is no reason to abandon efforts to be diplomatic in our interactions. Thus, I would suggest that policy analysts should think carefully about ways to maintain the peace and to work toward consensus with others in the policymaking process. This is where having excellent people skills is crucial. Policy analysts should seek to advise and persuade on the basis of the quality of their analytical work and the clarity of their thoughts concerning particular policy issues and the best ways to tackle them. When people are regarded by others as highly argumentative or as "hotheads," they are likely to gain fewer opportunities to engage in policy discussions than would otherwise be the case.

A third difference also exists between the intellectual, as defined by Said, and the policy analyst. The task of the intellectual is accomplished through public commentary and criticism. Such individuals face no obligation to support public efforts to bring new programs or projects to fruition. In contrast, policy analysts are expected to furnish analysis and advice that will contribute to the broader public good, understood by their clients. Argument and critique assuredly can add positively to policy discussions and debates, but where the task of the intellectual might approximate that of the house critic, policy analysts must search for ways to ensure that policy alternatives viewed favorably by decision makers are indeed able to be implemented. Useful policy analysis suggests ways to get beyond endless discussion and debate.

In light of what has been written here, policy analysts would do well to distinguish themselves from intellectuals with respect to the making of public pronouncements about government policy and how they raise their points of disagreement with opponents. There remains, however, merit in policy analysts seeing themselves as kindred spirits with intellectuals. Policy analysts should exhibit strong critical-thinking skills and be constantly alert to the ways half-truths and received ideas enter into the policy discourse. Raising difficult questions should be thought of as part of the job. It is part of being a valuable, faithful advisor. But searching for feasible solutions to pressing policy problems is another key aspect of the job, and none of this is easy. With respect to the role of the intellectual, Said suggested that it requires "a steady realism, an almost athletic rational energy" (1996, 23). If that is so for those whose raison d'être is question, critique, and confrontation, surely the role of the policy analyst calls for even greater intelligence and energy. That might be asking too much of some policy analysts. Yet, to be working with others on difficult policy questions, to be steeped in the literature, empirical evidence, and folklore surrounding specific policy issues, and to be pressing on to make a positive difference for society can be enormously exciting. At their best, policy analysts represent a force for clarity in the dense, murky policymaking process.

PEOPLE SKILLS AND TECHNICAL SKILLS

My effort to highlight people skills should not be viewed as an affront to the importance of technical competency among policy analysts. Excellent policy analysts need both kinds of skills. I highlight people skills here because they have mostly been ignored by authors of policy analysis textbooks, where the central purpose has been imparting technical skills. A shift of balance is in order. This does not mean there should be a retreat from teaching technical skills, but only that people skills should also be given the emphasis they deserve.

Shifting the balance in what we emphasize as important for the training of policy analysts would undoubtedly lead to a change in how technical skills are taught and used. Other things being equal, policy analysts with excellent people skills are better able than are their counterparts with less keenly developed interpersonal skills to make effective use of their technical skills. For example, when undertaking benefit-cost analysis, policy analysts can improve the quality of their work by taking deliberate steps to listen to stakeholders while developing their analysis. It is often only at the end of the technical analysis that voices are raised about what costs and benefits have been included and what ones have been excluded from a study. Without making consultation and discussion an integral part of the development of benefit-cost analyses, policy analysts can quite easily end up producing work that appears technically sound but that is judged to be flawed because relevant information has not been incorporated into the modeling work.

Changing how we utilize our technical skills, so that our people skills become integral to their application, could raise the overall quality and relevance of the technical work produced by policy analysts. Moreover, as we give more recognition to the value of people skills, it is likely that we will eventually come to change our sense of what it means to be a technically competent policy analyst. To my mind, such a change would be a good thing. It would likely lead to changes in the ways we teach technical skills for policy analysts. Such changes could help to make the acquisition of technical skills appear more relevant and, hence, more appealing to a full range of students in university programs.

PEOPLE SKILLS FOR DEMOCRACY

This book is motivated by the view that policy analysts exhibiting excellent people skills are likely to be more effective than others in their work and that they will have more influence in the policymaking process. But policy analysts with excellent people skills can also help to change the broader culture of policymaking. Through their efforts to better meet the needs of their clients, and to better engage with other members of the policymaking community, it is possible for policy analysis to contribute to the ongoing task of strengthening the democratic basis of society. As

Ingram and her colleagues have observed, the design of public policies can have profound effects on the democracy-affecting behaviors of citizens (Ingram and Rathgeb Smith 1993; Schneider and Ingram 1997). When public policies serve to empower, enlighten, and engage citizens, they also help to embed democratic practices in society. My interest lies in pursuing the possibility that, through their efforts to better communicate and collaborate with others in the policymaking community, policy analysts might also contribute to the strengthening of democratic engagement among citizens.

A fear long expressed by democratic theorists is that, as government activities grow in scope and complexity, experts might come to dominate the public decision-making process. Among policy scholars writing over the past few decades, similar fears have also been expressed on occasion (Goldhamer 1978; Haas 1992; Massey 1988). Increasing opportunities for citizens to participate in discussions of pressing public policy issues would be one way to help allay fears of domination by experts. Implemented carefully, such efforts could also raise the prospects of a diversity of citizens becoming more interested in contributing to the policymaking process and democratic politics more generally. Consider the following statement by democratic theorist Robert A. Dahl (1998, 187–88):

> One of the imperative needs of democratic countries is to improve citizens' capacities to engage intelligently in political life. I don't mean to suggest that the institutions for civic education developed in the nineteenth and twentieth centuries should be abandoned. But I do think that in the years to come these older institutions will need to be enhanced by new means for civic education, political participation, information, and deliberation that draw creatively on the array of techniques and technologies available in the twenty-first century. We have barely begun to think seriously about these possibilities.

Efforts by members of the policymaking community to reach out to citizens are never easily undertaken. When problems arise, sometimes the result is a move away from the pursuit of democratic ideals. It is difficult to say how greater citizen input into the policymaking process might be best achieved. Most likely, the details will have to be worked out on a case-by-case basis until a sufficient store of experience has been amassed to allow for systematic learning from the past. But one thing is certain. Policy analysts with excellent people skills can serve as important resources for helping to further democratize policymaking and increase citizen engagement in government and society.

Using This Book

This book is designed to be read by graduate and advanced undergraduate students in courses or programs on public policy, policy analysis, and public management and by practicing policy analysts—especially those new to the profession. After this introductory chapter, in each chapter I provide advice on how policy analysts might improve a specific people skill and, hence, their overall performance as professionals. Like any other book, the chapters are arranged so that the topics covered in each fall into a logical sequence. Those who read the chapters in the usual serial fashion will discover many ideas for how to improve their day-to-day practices. For readers digesting the book in this conventional way, my hope is that it will serve as a manifesto, a call to greater recognition of the value of people skills for policy analysts. An unbroken reading through the chapters should kindle a desire for improving how one interacts with other policy analysts, with others in the policymaking process, and with the public.

By the same token, this book need not be read chapter by chapter. It can also be thought of and used as a compendium of people skills for policy analysts. Every chapter is deliberately self-contained and can be read individually with no loss of value in the treatment of its specific topic. So, as an addition to the policy analyst's bookshelf, this book represents a resource that can be regularly consulted, when the need for brushing up a particular people skill is most pressing. For example, knowing that one has agreed to give a presentation in the near future, you can consult chapter 5, "Giving Presentations," which explains how to prepare for the event effectively and increase the likelihood of it being a success. Likewise, chapter 10, "Professional Networking," sets out practical advice for those who hope to make the most of attending upcoming, work-related social events or conferences. In this way, each of the chapters to follow offers guidance for building and using a specific people skill. The chapters end with skill-building checklists. These summaries of the key items of advice contained in each chapter, like the chapters themselves, can be read in a stand-alone fashion. Thus, once the contents of the book have become familiar to the reader, taking the time now and then to read the skill-building checklists associated with each chapter is a quick way to become reacquainted with these people skills and determine areas of current practice where taking the time to strengthen one or two specific skills would be worthwhile.

As an assigned university text, this book can serve multiple purposes. In my own teaching of undergraduate and graduate courses on topics such as policy analysis, public finance, and intergovernmental management, I have typically integrated workshops on people skills into the broader framework of the course. Thus, students in my courses have been introduced to some of these people skills at the same time as they have been introduced to aspects of applied economics and management theory. This approach has the merit of ensuring that students come to see the ways in which analytical skills and people skills complement each other. In my courses, we tend to have brief presentations regarding specific people skills. These are followed by small group discussions and report-back sessions. Once specific people skills have been highlighted in this manner in my courses, I like to find ways to give students regular opportunities in the classroom to practice and hone those skills. The contents of this book, and especially the discussion ideas presented at the end of each chapter, are designed to support classroom activities of this sort.

As these comments indicate, I see this book as complementing other, more technically oriented, textbooks in courses on policy analysis and related topics. For example, in either graduate or undergraduate courses on policy analysis, this book could be assigned along with some combination of Eugene Bardach's *A Practical Guide for Policy Analysis: The Eightfold Path to More Effective Problem Solving* (2000), Kenneth N. Bickers and John T. Williams's *Public Policy Analysis: A Political Economy Approach* (2001), Duncan MacRae, Jr., and Dale Whittington's *Expert Advice for Policy Choice: Analysis and Discourse* (1997), Michael C. Munger's *Analyzing Policy: Choices, Conflicts, and Practices* (2000), and David L. Weimer and Aidan R. Vining's *Policy Analysis: Concepts and Practice* (1999). This list of five works is only meant to be representative of the rich collection of textbooks available. Many other relevant works could be mentioned that cover aspects of policy analysis, the skills needed to produce high quality analytical work, the nature of policy dialogue, and the contexts within which policy analysis is produced and consumed.

Given the importance of people skills for policy analysts, directors of programs in public policy, policy analysis, and public management should consider offering a course specifically designed to cover the topics presented here. Were that to be done, a considerable effort would need to be made to avoid the pedagogical compartmentalization of people skills from the many other skills that are essential to the training and work of policy analysts. In programs where other considerations limit opportunities to dedicate a full course, or even portions of courses, to training in people skills, this book could still be used by students, serving them as a compendium of people skills, as noted earlier. No matter how the material covered in this book is introduced to policy students or practicing policy analysts, I contend that a greater awareness of the importance of people skills and how they can be improved will be of enormous benefit to individual policy analysts, to the policymaking community, and, more generally, to democratic government and politics.

BEYOND THE ART OF THE POSSIBLE

Throughout this book I show how policy analysts might improve their effectiveness by working on their people skills. Policymaking is a deeply social enterprise. That is why, when describing this enterprise, we talk in terms of policy communities, policy networks, interest groups, and advocacy coalitions. By improving their abilities to collaborate with others in the development of policy analysis and advice, and by improving how they communicate the results of their policy analyses to others, policy analysts can become more effective, influential, and respected members of the policymaking community. Surely that is a goal worth seeking.

As increasing numbers of other policy analysts recognize the benefits of improved people skills, the incentive will grow for all to work at this kind of self-development. That has been the story of how policy analysts, over the past few decades, have come to be better trained and more competent in their use of technical skills for policy analysis. The adage "If you can't beat them, join them" applies. The prospect of large numbers of policy analysts displaying excellence in their people skills is genuinely exciting. The spillover effects would inevitably change how policymaking occurs. I hope what I have to say here will catalyze such change. Of course, such change occurs one person at a time, but as policy analysts improve their people skills, their changed behavior will change those around them, in positive ways. I suggest that, as they build their people skills and change their daily practices, policy analysts should think of themselves as prefiguring what is possible, and the big changes yet to come.

One way to conceive of the policy analyst is as a technical problem solver. In this conception, policy analysts accept problems more or less as they are presented and inform their clients of the policy alternatives they face and the costs associated with each. By thinking of policy analysts in this way, treating them in this way, and training them in this way, however, we run the risk of foreclosing significant opportunities for policy discussion. We limit the potential for discovering new understandings of the policy problems that confront us. Scholars of the policy process and some of the major contributors to the making of policy analysis as a profession have long recognized and emphasized the potential breadth of the role of the policy analyst (Kingdon 1995; Lindblom 1968; Stone 1997; Wildavsky 1979).

I urge that we carry on the tradition of conceiving of the role of the policy analyst in broad terms. Such a conception recognizes the importance of both superb technical skills and highly developed people skills. Once we adopt a broad conception of the policy analyst, it also becomes possible to think of the policymaking process and, indeed, democratic politics in a somewhat more expansive, ambitious way. We move beyond a world in which we accept certain constraints as given and into one in which, through expertly informed dialogue, questions can be raised concerning the nature of those constraints. In this way, politics—the so-called art of the possible—might be transformed to allow better public policies to be adopted and greater numbers of citizens to be engaged in the determination of the rules we live by. Although people skills for policy analysts are not all that matters here, they can make significant differences to how policymaking occurs. As we build our people skills, we clear space for policymaking to move beyond the art of the possible.

DISCUSSION IDEAS

- Aaron Wildavsky, in the introduction to his path-breaking book *Speaking Truth to Power* (1979, 17), observed, "Policy analysis . . . is about relationships between people. . . . Thinking about analysis as relations between people much like us—not as strange symbols or desiccated dollar signs—is not only more humane but also more accurate." Reflecting on this statement, in small groups, try to formulate answers to the following questions: How well does Wildavsky's statement square with your understanding of the role of policy analysts in the policymaking process? How well does it square with how you have been—or are being—trained as a policy analyst?

- In the training of policy analysts, technical skills are often given the greatest emphasis, whereas people skills are given little attention. This book is motivated by the view that policy analysts with excellent people skills will be better able to use their technical skills to provide high-quality, usable advice to policymakers. In small groups, pick a traditional technique used to analyze policy proposals (e.g., the model of choice, decision analysis, cost-benefit analysis, the market-failure framework, the government-failure framework). Discuss and then write down how five of the people skills listed below could help policy analysts to improve how they apply one of those traditional techniques of policy analysis in their work.
  - Building expert knowledge
  - Interviewing informants
  - Giving presentations
  - Working in teams
  - Facilitating meetings
  - Writing for multiple audiences
  - Conflict management
  - Professional networking
- Policy analysts are frequently represented as people who provide expert advice to policymakers. In democratic nations, where we aspire to "government of the people, by the people, for the people," policymakers may develop a dependency on policy analysts for their policy advice. Potentially, such a dependency can pose a threat to democracy, but if policymakers pay more attention to the general public than they do to professionally trained policy analysts, it is possible that unsound policy choices will be made. How do policymakers balance expert advice with advice from the broader public? How could policy analysts adjust their practices to reduce the tensions between the views of the public and their own views? What obstacles could stand in the way of such efforts?

FURTHER READING

Dahl, Robert A. 1998. *On Democracy*. New Haven, Conn.: Yale University Press.

Radin, Beryl A. 2000. *Beyond Machiavelli: Policy Analysis Comes of Age*. Washington, D.C.: Georgetown University Press.

Said, Edward W. 1996. "Representations of the Intellectual." In *Representations of the Intellectual*. New York: Vintage Books, pp. 3–23.

Schneider, Anne Larason, and Helen Ingram. 1997. *Policy Design for Democracy*. Lawrence: University Press of Kansas.

Weimer, David L., and Aidan R. Vining. 1999. "What Is Policy Analysis?" In *Policy Analysis: Concepts and Practice*. 3d ed. Upper Saddle River, N.J.: Prentice Hall, pp. 27–57.

Wildavsky, Aaron. 1979. *Speaking Truth to Power: The Art and Craft of Policy Analysis*. Boston: Little, Brown.

2

Managing Your Resources

A manager once told me, "You are your greatest resource. Invest in yourself." Another advised, "Be prepared for opportunity." Great career opportunities sometimes come out of the blue, so you need to make yourself ready to grasp them. Another piece of advice I've been told is, "Make yourself visible." You can invest in yourself and prepare for opportunity through your formal education and through maximizing your work experience. This can be done by volunteering for special projects beyond the scope of your normal work, by gaining experience and learning as much as possible in every facet of your organization, and by expanding your horizons to gain a broader perspective on how your part of the policy community works. Understanding and respecting the political perspectives and priorities of people in other organizations will go a long way toward building mutual respect and cooperation. I think it is important to position yourself where you will receive lots of different assignments and get to participate on teams or task forces that offer new experiences and possibilities for exposure in the broader policy community. If we want to, we really can make many positive contributions over the course of our careers. Through self-improvement, hard work, and understanding others, you can make a difference in the world.

—Dawn Phillips, *Policy Analyst, Michigan Family Independence Agency, Lansing, Michigan*

One way or another, policy analysis involves thinking carefully about the management of resources in society. Typically, we assume that resources are scarce and consider ways that public policy might serve to make the best use of those that are available. Sometimes, questions to do with the appropriate management of resources might be quite readily answered, but more often resource management questions are fraught with conundrums. This should not be surprising. Most social activities represent instances of resource transformation and, as such, they serve to raise various political and economic issues. Taking a historical view, we see that the basis of social change over the centuries has been people coming to new interpretations of what constitute available resources and by thinking about how those resources might be managed to yield improved social outcomes. All the important developments that have changed how we live our lives have been driven by people thinking inventively about resources and how best to manage them.

In this chapter I discuss ways that you can most effectively manage the professional resources that are available to you as a policy analyst. My basic argument is that, by critically scrutinizing your day-to-day work practices, you can increase your productivity and, hence, your ability to contribute to social problem solving. At some level, what I have to say here could be dismissed as nothing more than common sense. I disagree. Yet even if I were to concede the point, I would want to know why so many policy analysts—and other professionals who think for a living—frequently inhibit their own productivity by acting in ways that are at odds with such apparently common sense. By taking the time to think consciously and carefully about how you manage your resources, you open yourself up to the possibility of experiencing moments of invention. Attending to how you manage your resources today lays the foundation for resource development. As a policy analyst, you want to be viewed by others as resourceful and inventive. You can develop those attributes in a variety of ways. Thinking about how you manage your resources is a good place to start.

MODELING YOUR CAREER

When asked to reflect on their careers, many highly successful people will oblige by trotting out a seamless narrative, noting how new opportunities arose and dwelling on the parts they played in critical events as if everything were predestined. Great careers, it seems, flourish as naturally as the leaves grow on trees. Actually, they don't. Great careers, like all successful careers, are carefully managed. And, on close inspection, many apparently great careers also contain their share of difficult, rocky times. Of course, when asked to talk about their careers, successful people will gloss over the rough patches. This is natural. None of us want to dwell on the difficulties we have experienced, and many people probably would feel quite embarrassed if asked to talk about them.

Here, I note some concrete actions that you can take to increase the likelihood that you will have a highly successful career. The phrase *modeling your career* is intended to convey two ideas. First, just as policy analysts routinely use models to characterize key aspects of social processes and to consider the likely effects of new policy interventions, I believe that we can gain important insights into the management of our careers though planning, scenario writing, and asking *what if?* questions. Modeling our careers can be empowering. Second, even though it is often difficult to ascertain all the details of other people's careers, I believe we can learn an enormous amount about successful career management by studying the career paths that others have followed. Just as we engage in comparative institutional analysis with the purpose of determining the critical levers of organizational effectiveness, so we can gain insights into effective career management by comparing and contrasting the careers of other policy analysts. Looking for role models, and learning more about the careers of people you admire, is an excellent way to demystify the steps through which good careers are transformed into great ones. Incidentally, we can also gain many insights from observing people's career upsets and by tracing the steps that led to those unfortunate situations.

Plan Your Career Steps

Most of us have reasonably clear notions about our general career plans. At the start of every course I teach, I ask students to break into small discussion groups and, among other things, take the time to listen to each other say where they would like to be in their careers in five years. Given this medium-term time frame, the students usually find it quite easy to say where they want to go with their careers, but it is usually a little more difficult to articulate the steps they will need to take to get from their present circumstances to where they want to be. For students in university courses, degree completion serves as an important and easily identified step. Also, students will often talk about the kind of first job, or next job, that they want to obtain as another step in the right direction. Can we say more than this?

The actual paths our careers take depend on two main factors. First, there is the deliberate planning and preparation on our part. Second, there is the chancelike timing by which key opportunities open up for us. We can have a great deal of control over how we plan our careers and the effort that we put into preparing ourselves for the future. In contrast, we pretty much have to accept that decision processes and events beyond our control determine the appearance of desirable opportunities. In light of how opportunities open up, must we resign ourselves to living with career uncertainty? Although we cannot change the timing by which opportunities emerge in a given context, we can exercise some level of control over the contexts into which we place ourselves. If a particular context appears unlikely to offer any opportunities for future career advancement, you should avoid it. If you find yourself in such a context, you should make plans to move elsewhere.

Because moving from context to context is costly in lots of different ways, when planning out our career steps, just as when we are working through any decision-making process, we should try as much as possible to "look forward and reason back" (Dixit and Nalebuff 1991). When you are thinking about enrolling in a degree program, it is important to ask questions about the placements of recent program graduates. (Ask about all graduates—don't be satisfied to hear stories just about the program "stars.") When you are thinking about accepting a new job, you should also think seriously about the kind of opportunities for career advancement that the job would offer. In all such cases, you should pitch such questions in comparative terms. Compared to other degree programs, what is the placement record of this one? Compared with other jobs that I could potentially be offered, what sort of long-term career trajectory is associated with this one? There is a simple piece of advice that implicitly forces you to ask comparative questions like this: take the option that will open up the most future options for you.

The chancelike timing by which particular positions open up reduces your ability to plan out your career steps perfectly, but this need not immobilize you. Rather, once you have identified a particular position that is highly desirable to you, find out as much as you can about the training and experience that is needed by viable contenders for such a position. With this information in hand, you can then work to build up your credentials and your experience with an eye toward the possibility that the position you would most like will open up at some point. Once it does, you want to be ready to jump for it. You want to be well prepared for the position. In fact, what you desire most is that, when members of the recruitment team review your file and when others who know you are asked about the fit between you and the position, the immediate response is "of course, great match!"

To the extent that you plan ahead in your career, you can come fairly close to making good things happen for yourself. You should not fixate on achieving one particular position. Keeping your options open is important, but you can always do that while still figuring out the kind of positions that you would most like to achieve one day.

Suppose that you have a clear sense of your longer-term career goals but can see that serious bottlenecks exist that will slow your progress toward achieving those goals. For example, you might be in an organization that you like very much and see that you could make a great career within it. At the same time, however, you can also see that few middle-level positions are opening up in the organization and this situation is likely to remain the same for some years to come. In this situation, you might consider making a *knight's move*, going to another organization where middle-level positions are opening up, with the goal of building knowledge and skills that could put you in contention for a higher-level position in your current organization at a later time. Taking this knight's move gives you an opportunity to get ahead in your career in a way that staying in the same context for a longer time would not.

Observing the careers of others is also extremely important. When you see someone whose work you admire and who appears to be in an enviable position, make the time to investigate—in a low-key way—what career steps the person took before getting there. Often, you will find that there are certain credentials that are important for helping candidates achieve particular positions. For example, by learning about the career paths of various people who have recently held positions as the heads of policy in social services departments, you might find that experience working in a more general advice-giving organization is a common factor in the backgrounds of almost all of them. Further, by looking for patterns in the careers of apparent rising stars in an organization, you might find that most of them have come to be well known and well liked through their work on special project teams. Perhaps attending particular training courses or holding particular fellowships represent stations on the successful career paths you have noted. For you, the key is to look for patterns and then think about what career choices you might make to improve the chances that you too can become a contender for the positions you most desire. None of this advice is meant to suggest that you should snoop into the careers and backgrounds of people. You can learn an awful lot by just paying attention to what is going on around you and by making sure to ask the right questions at appropriate moments.

Integrate Your Resumé into the Planning Process

For the most part, people think about their resumés (or curriculum vitae) only when they are applying for a new job. This is the time when you make sure that you have listed all your qualifications correctly, noted your past experiences, and highlighted various professional accomplishments. Often, people customize their resumés with the aim of making themselves look as close as possible to a good fit for the positions for which they are applying. I suggest that you *look often and look hard* at your resumé, even when there isn't a particular job that you are thinking about applying for. Ultimately, I suggest that you treat your resumé as a planning document.

Think about the kind of positions that you would like to be able to be in contention for in the coming years. Then look at your resumé and think about how the items on it now would help you achieve those desirable future positions. In addition, think about the gaps in your resumé. What additional items must be on your resumé that are not there now? What additional items would be desirable? Having considered these questions, you can begin to think seriously about what actions you can take to build your resumé in ways that will be as helpful as possible for you in the future. Because, as I have already noted, particular positions always open up in a somewhat chancelike way, you should avoid building your resumé in a manner that perfectly customizes it for one somewhat specialized position. Instead, you should identify items to add to your resumé that would seriously increase your credentials and put you in contention for a *class* of positions. Because you do not have time to do everything, choosing to add to your resumé in one way inevitably means forgoing opportunities to build it in others. You should adopt a choice strategy that minimizes future possible regrets. This is yet another way of suggesting the importance of keeping your options open. Take the actions that are likely to yield the most generalizable benefits for your career.

Take Stock of Past Events

Like it or not, we carry the past with us. The good news is that our past successes can often provide the foundations for future successes. The bad news is that often our past mistakes can come back to haunt us. That said, we have a considerable amount of control over the ways that past successes and failures serve to affect our current and future performance. The more effort we put into thinking carefully about our past actions and their effects, the more likely we are to learn about ourselves, to judge our strengths and weaknesses, and to anticipate the consequences of our future choices and actions.

It is useful to think of ourselves as being endowed with a portfolio of skills and knowledge. Like anybody who manages a portfolio—be it a financial one or an organizational one of responsibilities—we should strive to develop our own portfolio of skills and knowledge. Ultimately, we want to be in charge of a portfolio that generates consistently strong, high-quality performance. Taking stock of past events, carefully analyzing what we did right and what we did wrong, can provide important insights into how we might develop our portfolio of skills and knowledge to serve us well in the future.

The popular business strategy tool called SWOT analysis can be usefully applied for helping us to think about managing our careers and thinking about our portfolio of skills and knowledge. This approach implores organizational leaders to reflect on their internal *strengths* and *weaknesses* and external *opportunities* and *threats* (see Wright, Kroll, and Parnell 1998). In the organizational setting, when efforts have been made to identify these items, discussions can be used to explore how particular organizational strengths might be enhanced and how particular weaknesses might be downplayed or, perhaps, transformed into strengths. Strategies can also be devised to make good use of emerging opportunities, and additional actions might be identified with the goal of avoiding perceived threats, or at least negotiating with the operating context so as to reduce the potential damage such threats could cause. For organizational leaders, making good use of SWOT analysis requires that they be prepared to hear both good news and bad and that they be prepared to accept that some of their past decisions and actions might have been detrimental to the organization's effectiveness. Of course, the same holds true for us as individuals. To become effective managers of our own portfolios of skills and knowledge, we have to be quite self-disciplined about assessing ourselves and should try to do so in a manner that is as clear-eyed as possible. Often, that will mean turning to others and asking for their sincere judgments on our recent performance and requesting their advice about future actions.

Identify Weaknesses and Address Them

Just as we have strengths, as individuals, we all have weaknesses, although fortunately we differ in what they are. Likewise, as policy analysts, we all have weaknesses. This does not necessarily mean that our individual weaknesses will hinder our chances of having highly successful careers. Rather, we need to identify our weaknesses and find ways to address them. In some instances, this might mean that we should seriously consider avoiding certain kinds of work or certain kinds of interpersonal interactions. Inevitably, candid acknowledgment of our weaknesses might mean that we must rule out the possibility we will ever hold certain desirable positions in our careers. Although we could take this as devastating news, we need not. Throughout our lives—typically unconsciously—we make choices that rule out options for the future. In many cases, we would not actually want to pursue those options anyway.

To make the most of our careers as policy analysts, we must find ways to manage our weaknesses. We do not want to place ourselves in situations where we are always competing head-to-head with other people who seem better able to perform the actions we find most difficult to do well. The economic principle of comparative advantage suggests that we should each put our energies into those actions that have the lowest opportunity costs for us. If you are more productive as an applied econometrician than as a manager of a policy team, you should seek positions where your statistical skills are well utilized and leave the management

roles to those for whom the opportunity costs associated with taking
such positions are low. Of course, policy analysts perform a wide variety
of tasks, and it is likely that we will be strong in some areas and weak in
others. Rather than give up completely on developing our abilities in
areas where we are weak, we should make strategic decisions about those
weaknesses that we seek to address. In subsequent chapters of this book,
I will discuss a range of people skills that policy analysts would find
worthwhile to develop. For the most part, these are precisely the sort of
skills that we can work at and thereby turn from weaknesses into areas of
competence and, ultimately, into areas of personal strength. Working on
people skills is an obvious way that policy analysts can strengthen their
portfolios of skills and knowledge. But we can strengthen our portfolios
in many ways. We should always be thinking of ways to strengthen our
project-based knowledge and how we might treat new projects as opportunities for developing additional, transferable technical skills and substantive policy knowledge.

Play to Your Strengths

What are you good at as a policy analyst? What policy issues excite you?
Questions of this sort typically require you to do quite a lot of thinking
before you can provide coherent answers. Take the time to think about
projects that you have worked on in the past and list the things that you
felt you did best. Sometimes, managers or mentors will provide you with
feedback on your project work. Through conversations with those who
have monitored you and your work, you might come to some fresh insights about your abilities and your strengths as a policy analyst.

  For the same reason that you should avoid putting all of your effort into activities on which you are quite weak, you should try as much
as possible to play to your strengths. Playing to your strengths does not
mean putting little effort into what you do. Rather, it means identifying
what you are good at and then working hard to increase your abilities in
those areas. This is how you can most readily expand your portfolio of
skills and knowledge. For example, if you have developed a strong ca-
pability for gathering and synthesizing the analytical findings of others,
then you should continue to play to this strength. That does not mean
you should focus only upon doing this sort of work. Instead, you should
make the most of your skill in this area and use it as a foundation on

which to advance your knowledge and skills as a policy analyst. Notice that playing to your strengths is different from addressing weaknesses. If you play to your strengths, you will be able to determine what areas of weakness will be worth addressing. Playing to your strengths gives you the space to work strategically on a few of your weaknesses while simultaneously continuing to produce quality policy analysis.

Choose Projects Carefully

As policy analysts, our careers are defined to a large degree by the projects we work on. Although we do not always have control over what we can work on, we do have considerable control over how we shape those projects. Another way of saying this is that there is no such thing as a boring policy project. The challenge for us is to think about projects in ways that make them interesting, in ways that leverage particular issues into generalizable insights. Done well, we can use a given project as a way to highlight new areas requiring research and analysis. Well-managed, well-executed policy projects suggest possibilities for future work.

Every project is a potential line on your resumé. It is important to view your project work in this way. If you have been paying attention to policy developments, you will have a sense of how the particular project you are working on relates to general themes and issues that are currently gaining attention within your broader community of policy analysts. How can you strategically link what you are doing to current policy conversations? How might current questions help you to shape what you are doing? How might a project contribute in interesting ways to more far-reaching conversations? These are difficult questions to answer, ones that you will get better at answering as you gain more experience as a policy analyst. No matter where you are in your career, though, these questions are important to consider.

Project work can be characterized in a variety of ways. Academic researchers are sometimes divided into those who seek out and chart new frontiers (pioneers) and those who work to develop and refine the territories charted by others (settlers). From the perspectives of social science and policy studies, we see that both forms of activity are vital for the broader enterprise of thinking about social organization and the appropriate role that government can play in developing and regulating social interactions. One of the dangers of seeking to be a pioneer is that you might undertake project work that is viewed by others as esoteric at best and as irrelevant at worst. For this reason, it is probably important to begin your career as a settler, where there are more role models and the set of issues and problems to be worked on are more clearly defined. Over time, however, you should think carefully about ways that you can venture out from your efforts to work on problems defined by others and begin to work on problem areas that you have defined for yourself. Working on settled topics is not without its own set of drawbacks. One of the dangers of working on territories charted by others is that attractive new sites for study will quickly become popular and even overcrowded. When many people are working on aspects of the same problem, the competition will often grow intense. In such an environment, it becomes all the harder for any single analyst to shine.

So far, I have placed most emphasis on the need to think strategically about how you choose projects, but strategic matters should not be the only concern. No matter what your project work, you should strive as much as possible to enjoy doing it. Whenever we work on projects, times arise where the problems are difficult and where making progress seems almost impossible. During such periods, it is easy to become discouraged and perhaps even want to give up. Getting through these times is easier when you find the project topic inherently fascinating. You will always be able to find the energy needed to press ahead and make progress on a project when the topic excites you and you believe that what you are doing matters. This suggests that you should avoid the temptation to work on fashionable topics simply because they are fashionable. If you are not drawn intrinsically to such topics, you are likely to find your work being eclipsed in quality and impact by others who do feel a natural affinity with them. By choosing topics that you enjoy and by thinking about their linkages to broader policy conversations, you increase the likelihood that you will produce high-quality work that others will notice and appreciate.

Make the Most of Present Circumstances

In discussing ways to model your career, I have emphasized the need for you to be future-oriented, to do things today with an eye toward tomorrow. Of course, following such advice has the potential to make us feel frustrated in our current positions, as if we are stuck in a holding pattern, always waiting for brighter opportunities to open up. But we need not, and should not, view present circumstances negatively. If we think of ourselves as destined for bigger and better things than present circumstances permit, we should model our actions today as if we are already where we want to be. In other words, you should find ways today to build into your work habits *prefigurative forms* of how you intend to work in the future, when you have a more desirable position. Make the most of present circumstances to expand your portfolio of skills and knowledge and to strengthen your ability to produce excellent work. Real stars should be able to shine anywhere. Don't just do your present work well; strive to excel at everything you do. You have it within your power to manage your resources in this way. By actions, not by what you tell yourself and others, make it clear that you are on an upward trajectory in your career.

Interacting with Colleagues

Throughout this book, I will frequently discuss ways that you can make the most of your interactions with others in the world of policy analysis and public management. My purpose in this section is to emphasize how those around us represent important resources. By carefully managing our interactions with our colleagues, we can keep ourselves informed of broader policy developments, find out about emerging opportunities, learn tricks of the trade, and save ourselves time. Treating our colleagues as valuable resources, to be managed with care, is a good career strategy. But working hard to make the most of the interactions we have with others is also important at the human level. When everybody in an office or organization is on good terms, the work is much more enjoyable, and a lot more work gets done.

Your Organization Provides Resources

Many policy analysts work in relatively large organizations. Even if you work in an organization with as few as ten people, however, it is likely that on a day-to-day basis you will interact intensely with fewer than half of them. In light of this, it is easy for us to wind up defining our working environment in quite limited ways. I suggest that, as much as possible, you should strive to think of yourself in relation to the whole organization, not just in relation to those people with whom you interact most frequently. When people outside of your organization meet with you, when they hear about you, and when they see your resumé, they will identify you with your organization. Whether you like it or not, the impression that outsiders form of you will be heavily influenced by their knowledge of who you work for. Working in an organization with good name recognition and a solid reputation in the policy community gives you an enormous advantage. But no matter what your present circumstances, you should always look for the positive aspects of your organization. Further, when talking with others, if your organization becomes the topic of conversation, you should always play up its positive aspects. When people speak negatively about their organizations, it raises a question for the audience: "If it's so bad, why hasn't this person moved on?" Speaking ill of your organization or others in it reflects badly on you, even if your negative comments are justified. As I said before, stars should be able to shine anywhere, and you should always attempt to make the most of your present circumstances.

View your organization in resource terms. Even though your day-to-day activities in your organization will involve a limited number of interactions with others in it, you should think of ways to keep connected to the resources of the organization. Most organizations, no matter their size, will contain people or units that are responsible for human resources, computer support, and library resources or information management. You should not expect these people to know automatically how they can help you. Often, they will be following standard operating procedures, and it will be up to you to introduce yourself to them and to ask them for help. Whenever you join a new organization you should make the time to have an initial one-to-one meeting with these organizational support staff.

Staff in human resources departments will know what courses people in the organization have been attending lately. They will probably know about skill-building and knowledge-building courses and opportunities that you have not heard about. This could be important information for you. Computer support staff can be helpful for doing more than dealing with network problems or helping you when your computer malfunctions. Because computer support staff talk with a lot of people about their computers and because they monitor developments in the information technology industry, they are likely to be readily able to answer your questions about how to get the most out of particular software, or how new software can improve your productivity. Likewise, people in your organization's library can prove invaluable for helping you to locate information that can help you with your work. Although you do not have to meet with these people frequently in the course of your work, seeing them as important resources can be helpful. Try to keep on good terms with them. Often, in meeting with them over a pressing concern, you will be able to ask them questions about other issues that have occurred to you. Organizational support staff will often know things and be able to answer questions for you that will save you a lot of time.

Managers Are Resources

In most organizations, policy analysts work under the supervision of managers. These managers get to choose the projects or parts of projects that particular analysts will work on. They also work to set the broader parameters of those projects, usually in consultation with both the clients and the policy analysts who will be involved. In this setting, as a policy analyst you are highly dependent on your manager as the person most able to provide opportunities for you to develop your analytical skills and policy knowledge and to determine how much control you have over what work you produce and how you produce it. Since managers have reputations that they wish to both advance and protect, they face strong incentives to provide good quality guidance and mentoring to the policy analysts who report to them. The incentives faced by your manager and the incentives that you face are somewhat different, but they are usually mutually reinforcing. Managers want members of their staff to do good work that reflects well on them in the eyes of both their supervisors and the clients for whom the work is being done. For this reason, they will be interested in finding ways to bring out the best in analysts on their staffs. At the same time, you want to do good work that gives you room to grow as a policy analyst and to become someone others recognize as able to contribute to policy discussions.

These observations indicate that you should make every effort to develop a productive working relationship with your manager. You should seek opportunities to listen to your manager and to watch how he or she approaches the work to be done. Because managers typically have extensive experience as policy analysts themselves, they can bring insights to situations that you cannot. Learning about your manager's career and observing how your manager thinks about the broader policy-making terrain can be enriching for you. Inevitably, there will be times when managers are critical of the work you have done and will suggest revisions or entirely new starts. Although such criticisms can be hard to hear, rather than reject them or react badly toward critical comments, you should work at finding ways to calm down after hearing them and to think in a cool, clear-headed manner about their implications and how you might productively respond to them. Managers like to see their staff learn from mistakes. They like their staff to be ambitious and talented, but they do not react well to "hotheads."

Over the years, I have heard many horror stories about apparently bad managers. I have also heard of people who keep notes on the behaviors of their managers, with the goal of ensuring that when they become managers themselves some day they will not fall into the trap of taking similar actions. This is probably a good, low-key way to manage frustration. No doubt, there are times when criticisms of managers are justified. But it is also the case that managers often find themselves pressured by their supervisors and clients. Because of this, they must take actions to protect themselves and their staff. From the perspective of a policy analyst, whose job is typically less fraught with shifting political pressures and rapidly changing agendas, the actions of managers can at times appear capricious or even inept. My advice is to try as much as possible to keep your head down and do the work that is asked of you in the most competent fashion that you can. Whenever you can, try to place yourself in your manager's shoes. When appropriate opportunities arise, be candid and ask your manager what you can do in your project work to ensure that it will be well received by the people that he or she must satisfy. In fact, looking at things from the perspective of your manager is likely to improve the overall utility of your policy analysis (Leman and Nelson 1981).

Coworkers Are Resources

Policy analysts typically work in teams. They may not always be working together on projects, but they are often working alongside people who are undertaking similar projects and who have similar broader public policy concerns. Although there is a tendency for people to compete with their coworkers, competition need not be—and should not be—the dominant principle in the workplace. Competition and cooperation can coexist. How effectively the balance is struck between competition and cooperation will depend in large part on the formal and informal incentive structures established by organizational leaders. Although management may determine these structures, you have a great deal of control over the nature of your interactions with those around you. Without advocating that you set yourself up so that others around you gain at your expense, I do believe that we can gain much more in work environments by placing the emphasis on cooperation with coworkers as opposed to competition.

I suggest that you view your coworkers as resources. They will each bring to their positions different experiences, and each will have unique skills and knowledge. Talking with them frequently and informally about their project work and your own project work is likely to provide many opportunities for mutually beneficial learning. When you read newspapers and news magazines, or when browsing the professional journals, you should always keep an eye out for items that might be of interest and relevance to your colleagues as well as to yourself. If you make efforts to reach out to others in a cooperative spirit, it is likely that these efforts will be met with a degree of reciprocity. It might take longer than you would like for the work climate to change to one that exudes the virtues of high levels of cooperation, but you have to start somewhere. If you are to reap the benefits of your coworkers as resources, then you have to be prepared to act as a resource for them.

The benefits of developing good, mutually supportive relationships with your coworkers can be considerable. Through your coworkers, you are likely to learn new information about what is going on around you in the organization and in the broader policy community. Your coworkers can also be valuable as sources of information about career management. It is unlikely that they will all be at the same stage as you. Because of this, you will often be able to gain important insights into project management and career management from those around you. When you are having difficulty gathering information for a new project, or if some part of what you would like to do analytically seems intractable, having good colleagues you can talk with can save you an enormous amount of time. In suggesting that you develop good relations with your colleagues, I do not mean that you should strive to be the best of friends with them. Actually, mixing personal friendships with professional, workplace relationships is never easy, given the nature of careerism and the underlying competitiveness that often must exist among colleagues. That said, seeing your coworkers as potentially significant resources and treating them with respect can be personally and professionally rewarding.

Subordinates Are Resources

Because this book has been written for people who identify themselves primarily as policy analysts rather than as organizational managers, the term *subordinate* used here refers to support staff, not to more junior policy analysts. For the most part, these are the people in an organization who routinely engage in secretarial tasks, such as handling the mail, answering telephones, ordering supplies, photocopying, and routine filing. Sometimes policy analysts or people in other professional positions like to differentiate themselves from the support staff by adopting an air of superiority and acting towards them in a brusque, "managerial" manner. Don't do this. You do not know—and you do not need to know—the personal circumstances that have led support staff to be in those roles rather than in the roles of you and your colleagues. The key is to treat subordinates with the same respect that you treat everyone else in your organization. They have a vital organizational role to perform, and they do a lot to help you do your work better.

By building good, friendly relations with subordinates, you can do a lot to reduce the transaction costs associated with your work. Secretarial staffs have an uncanny knack for knowing the pulse of an organization. They can tell you about a multitude of "small" details that can improve your understanding of how the organization functions. For example, they can let you know good times and bad times to meet with managers. Or they can help you with the scheduling and arranging of events, like an in-house presentation of some of your project work. When you are on good terms with subordinates, when you have shown them that you respect them and value them, you can ask them to do favors for you—jump the photocopy queue, order supplies, track down a necessary piece of information—and they will do it. In contrast, policy analysts who treat subordinates as inferior human beings are likely to find themselves hugely frustrated when they are in panic mode and their reservoir of goodwill with subordinates has long since run dry. Building goodwill in the workplace is most effectively done by simply treating people with respect and showing a genuine interest in them. This is not too much to ask, but the payoffs can be considerable.

Managing Your Time

The time available to us is obviously a scarce resource, and one that needs to be carefully managed, but that does not mean that we have to transform ourselves into work machines. So let's right away set one matter straight. As a policy analyst, you should consciously try to avoid becoming one of those hideous, self-important people who rush their lives away and who seek verbal doggy biscuits by telling everyone how busy, busy, busy they are. I am not convinced that such people really add a whole lot to the effectiveness of the workplace. Even if they do get a lot done, it is often at the detriment of the productivity of those around them. I suggest that we think about time management somewhat differently.

The goal of time management should be that you are readily able to determine the right amount of time to allocate to tasks so that you will deliver them when promised while meeting or exceeding people's expectations concerning quality. The more carefully you manage your time, the more able you will be to get things done as anticipated and enjoy the process. Through effective time management, you will also be able to ensure that your interactions with those around you are productive and pleasurable for everyone. As a good manager of your own time, you will come to seem like a naturally competent, accomplished professional. If you can do this while having a calming effect on those around you, all the better.

Make "To Do" Lists

Making "to do" lists is an essential part of effective time management. You can work with several lists at the same time. For example, you can have a to do list for the year, laying out key tasks to be performed over the course of several months. Then you can have monthly and weekly to do lists. Finally, you can construct daily to do lists. (You should write these daily lists at the end of each day; taking time to figure out the structure of the following day.) The trick of using these lists is to ensure that there is consistency across them, so that by accomplishing the tasks on your weekly lists you will eventually accomplish the goals for the year as well.

When working with "to do" lists, you should try to set realistic goals for yourself. As you get into the habit of working with daily lists, judging what you can actually achieve in a day will become much easier. Check off items on your list as you accomplish them (don't erase them). At the end of the day (or week) you can readily see what was done and what wasn't. Several software packages are available to help you organize your time. Ask other people what packages they have found most helpful.

Batch Routine Tasks

Our plans for the day can often be dashed because of interruptions. Common interruptions come from the telephone or e-mail, but we can control these interruptions. I suggest that you set aside regular blocks of time each day for dealing with routine tasks. These tasks might include reading and replying to mail and e-mail and checking and responding to phone messages. You should work hard to avoid handling mail and e-mail more than once. Get into the habit of quickly determining what needs to be dealt with and when. Don't waste time reading and thinking about things that you do not intend to completely deal with there and then.

Prioritize

There are some tasks that we have to attend to immediately and others that can wait. It is wise to get into the habit of asking questions about tasks as they come in. Do I have to respond to this? Must I respond today? What is the deadline? Thinking in terms of your workspace (including your computer screen), these questions suggest that you should set work into three groups: high priority, pending, and no deadline.

Think about Opportunity Costs

The time you spend working on one task is time that you cannot spend working on another. In general, when you are deciding what to work on next, you should think in terms of opportunity costs, that is, you should always seek to put your energies into that activity having the lowest opportunity cost at that time. A simple example can prove the point. A chief executive officer of an organization should avoid doing his own photocopying. Others are paid far less than he to do such work. The chief executive officer is paid to engage in decision making and organizational outreach activities that will improve the overall performance of the enterprise. Likewise, you should avoid putting your efforts into activities that have little payback and that cut into the time that you would otherwise spend on making serious contributions.

Think in Marginalist Terms

The most effective way to manage your time in accordance with the opportunity cost principal is to do so by thinking in marginalist terms. For example, suppose that you have one hour left at your office before a lunch meeting. Instead of jumping to respond to the latest request that has been made to you, ask a simple question: given the things that are most important to my work, what is the best use of this next hour? It might take two minutes of conscious thought to ask and respond to this question. Yet, by consciously thinking about how to best use your time, you avoid the possibility of squandering the next fifty-eight minutes of quality time on activities that could be left until later in the day when you are too tired to engage in serious intellectual work, but when you still have the energy for doing a range of lower-level, but necessary, tasks.

Set Aside Blocks of Quiet Time

What we most want to do in our work life is set aside quality, quiet time to spend on important intellectual tasks. I am a big advocate of doing one thing at a time. I also think it is vital for us to avoid appearing rushed when we are around other people. Try to organize your time in ways that allow you to have the quiet time you need for getting quality work done. Try to ensure that you are in a good frame of mind when you have such times. Over the years, I have come to find that mornings are a great time for writing and thinking. I work to protect this time, because I know that, if I attend to a range of small tasks beforehand, it is hard to get back into the state of peace that I need to do serious thinking work. According to Dixit (1994), the times that work best as quality periods for writing often change as a person ages. Once you have determined the times you want to set aside for yourself as quiet periods, make others around you aware of your work patterns. You want others to respect the time that you need to complete serious work. As you work toward determining how to set aside and protect your blocks of quiet time, it might help to keep a list of the factors that cause interruptions during these periods. Having a list like this is the starting point for better management of your time in the future.

Manage "Down" Time

Sometimes it is just very hard to work. We get cranky, or our interactions with other people upset us, and so on. My first response to this is to say, "It's OK to give yourself space. Many things that seem pressing can actually wait." But it is also true that doing at least a bit of work when we are cranky or depressed can be quite uplifting. If you have a list written, you can look down it and pick out tasks that must be accomplished and that you could work on, even in the present state of mind. Maybe they are tasks that are not especially urgent, like filing, or going to the library, or shopping, and so on.

When you are cranky or upset, it is vital that you avoid letting this affect your relations with others. If you find an interaction with someone else upsetting, walk away before conflict starts. If you are upset by some news, tell people that you need time to think it over before providing a response. This advice is not "time management" advice of the usual sort, but if you are seeking to manage your time effectively, you should also be seeking to find productive ways to structure the time you spend with others. It is acceptable to ask for time from others, just as it is acceptable to say "no" when people make requests. The key is to do so in a way that is respectful, rather than upsetting or annoying, to others.

Reflect on Recent Events

Your time is a scarce resource and one that you should take care to manage. As a policy analyst, you need to manage your days and weeks so that you can free up quality, quiet blocks of time to devote to the intellectual work that is central to completing your projects and delivering high-quality results. In addition, because your work as a policy analyst often takes place in an organizational setting, you always must be conscious of the ways that you interact with others. No matter what position you hold, you do not want to get a reputation for being stressed out or for making bad decisions because of stress. Overall, I believe that, if you manage your time well, you will be a much better on-the-job performer, with respect to both getting your work done and managing your relations with those around you. I suggest that, as much as possible, you should set aside an hour at the end of a project or at the end of a busy week to reflect on how you have been managing your time and how you might improve your productivity. If you have made to do lists to work from, you can use them when you are reflecting on your past performance. Think about how much time you anticipated spending on a given project and how long you actually took. Consciously reflecting on matters like this will help you to budget your time more appropriately in the future. Likewise, if you have made a list of the interruptions that you had to your schedule, you can begin to think about ways to better protect your time in the future and to avoid the possibility of surrendering the management of your time to others.

Organizing Your Workspace

Taking time to organize your workspace carefully and keep it tidy can help to save you a lot of time. Keeping a tidy workspace also makes you feel better about starting new tasks and gives other people the impression that you are a well-organized, reliable person. Here I suggest some of the key things that you can do to ensure that your workspace provides you with an effective environment in which to do quality work and from which to build your career.

Streamline Your Office Space

In setting up your office space, think carefully about how, and how frequently, you make use of various items within it. You should arrange your office around a simple principle: maximize access to the things you use most. Find ways to conserve the amount of energy you use on routine tasks. In addition, you should set up your office space so that you feel comfortable working in it. Think about ways you can arrange the lighting, your chair or chairs, and your desk so that it is a pleasure to be in your workspace. If you feel physically strained and tired during the workday, think carefully about the features of your workspace that might be sapping your energy. If you can identify useful changes, implement them as soon as possible.

Arrange Your Files

As policy analysts, we have been trained to be highly systematic thinkers, but this thinking is typically done in association with documents. Hence, we should find ways to organize our documents into files in ways that reflect and support systematic thought. As a starting point, you should arrange your files (both physical files and files on your computer) so that the ones you make use of most are the easiest to retrieve. Arranging your files neatly and making use of color coding can reduce retrieval time. In addition, building a close relationship between the organization of your electronic files and the organization of your physical files can help to reinforce the psychological associations that you draw between items and where they are stored. If you find yourself each day engaging in one or two searches for items that take more than five minutes, chances are you could increase your productivity by spending a few hours bringing greater order to your filing system.

A simple and low cost way to begin doing things more productively might be to establish a new set of files for each new project that you begin. Slowly, as your project grows more complicated, you can expand the files in ways that are most logical, given your retrieval needs. Most projects draw on both general knowledge and information and case-specific materials. You should organize the project-based files in ways that allow you to separate the general materials from the specific materials rapidly, once the project is completed. Most likely, at that point, you would move the specific items to an archive and add the more general items to other general items in your filing system.

Customize Your Computer

Consider how much time we save by making use of the speed-dial buttons on our telephones. It is such a simple thing. Just as you can save time by customizing your telephone, you can save enormous amounts of time for yourself by customizing your computer. Find ways to rapidly access the software that you most frequently use. Make sure that you organize your files in systematic ways. You can save a lot of time by routinely transferring incoming e-mail messages into appropriate categories. You can save time searching the Internet by making good use of the bookmarks feature on your web browser. You should not spend large chunks of time perfecting your retrieval systems, to the point where you never actually get much serious work done. It is important, however, that you think of straightforward ways to customize your computer so that it is a highly efficient tool.

Build Links to the Broader Organization

As a policy analyst, you want to be aware of relevant developments in the world around you. This suggests that you should set up systems that ensure a flow of useful information continuously comes your way. A starting point for this is to see yourself as part of something more than your immediate work environment. If you work for a government agency, you should make sure that you have information on broader developments both within the organization and within the overall governmental organization. You can set up your computer so that you receive information from various organizations about upcoming events. You can place yourself on mailing lists and other circulation lists so that you are kept informed of what is going on around you. In building these links to the broader organization, you should be somewhat judicious. You do not want vast quantities of marginally useful information coming across your desk or your computer screen. Sample what is out there and, after a while, settle for making regular use of the information sources that you find most consistently relevant to your interests.

At the End of the Day

At the end of the day, people are mostly keen to end their immediate task and quickly head for home. Although I do not advocate lingering at the office, it is worth setting aside ten minutes as deliberate *winding-down* time. During these minutes, you should figure out your to do list of tasks for the following day. You should also take the time to clear your workspace so that it will be a welcome sight the next morning. Cluttered offices and desks are depressing places to work. It is natural that during the day you will amass a variety of materials on and around your workspace as you concentrate on your project work, but you do not want things to get out of hand. As much as possible, you should organize things so that there is a place for everything and, at the start and the finish of the day, everything is in its place.

Keeping your workspace clear is important for other reasons beyond having an efficient environment to support your intellectual work. First, if something comes up in your home life and you cannot make it to your office as planned, by having a clear, organized workspace, it will be easy for you to direct others to particular items, should they be needed. Second, a clear workspace makes it easier for you to find things when you are doing your work. Cumulatively, people waste a great deal of time searching for various items in their offices. This is time worth saving. People also have a tendency to lose track of items and then make new copies of them. Although this saves having to engage in an extensive search for particular items, it is wasteful. Such waste can be avoided by keeping things in their place. Third, it is important for security reasons that you keep your workspace clear. Some organizations make it mandatory that confidential files be locked away at night, but keeping items in their place is also likely to reduce the risk that things will be lost due to unforeseen events like office fires, or flooding, or overzealous cleaners mistaking items on the floor for trash.

At the End of the Year

The end of the year is a good time to reflect on the organization of your workspace. Because things typically slow down for policy analysts in late December, this is a time when you can make structural adjustments to your filing systems with few disruptions. You can think about what items you have not used over the past year and how you might move them so that you can free up the most accessible filing space for the most frequently used items. This is also a good time to change, or make adjustments to, the filing system on your computer. You can place a lot of files into archives, reduce the number of e-mail messages you have in various mailboxes, and so on. The end of the year is also an opportune time for working with new software and making changes to the array of items that you routinely work with during the busier times of the year. Just as we often make New Year's resolutions, it is good to take the time to clear the clutter of your workspace once a year. The time needed to do this will not be great, but it can boost your productivity when things start getting busy again.

SUMMARY

The work of policy analysts typically involves exploring the efficiency and effectiveness of actual or proposed government interventions in society. Here I have suggested that we should apply some of our analytical thinking to assessing how well we manage our own resources. Just as gains can come from reinventing government (Osborne and Gaebler 1992) and reengineering corporations (Hammer and Champy 1993), so too can we benefit from thinking strategically about how we do what we do. We might have the tidiest desks around, but if we are not thinking carefully about where we are going with our careers, we might be missing important opportunities. We might have a reputation for scrupulously managing our time, but if we treat others in a brusque, uncaring manner, we might well be undermining our personal effectiveness. I suggest that policy analysts should carefully manage their personal resources. By doing so, we allow ourselves to dedicate the bulk of our time and effort to the major project tasks that we are expected to complete. Managing your career, managing your time, thinking of your colleagues as resources, and organizing your workspace are people skills. How well you succeed at managing your resources will have a material bearing on how effectively you can work with others to make a positive difference to society. When you develop routine strategies for carefully managing your resources, you will open yourself to finding opportunities for improving your productivity and your overall effectiveness. In this way, other people will come to see you as an inventive and resourceful colleague. By maximizing your personal effectiveness, you will be less likely to be rushed and more likely to have time to spare for those around you. Because of this, they will respect you and value your presence in the organization. There is little more that you could ask for from colleagues.

SKILL-BUILDING CHECKLIST

- In managing your career, look ahead to where you want to be, and then reason back to identify the steps you will need to take to realize your goals.

- Think of yourself as a portfolio of knowledge and skills. Strive to expand your portfolio through carefully chosen project work and formal or informal training.
- Recognize that other people will identify you with the organization you work for. Your organization is a resource for you. Always be positive about it and make the most of your time there.
- Treat your colleagues as resources and strive to build relationships with them that are professional, personable, and highly productive.
- Devote your energies to producing high-quality project work and maintaining effective relationships with others inside and outside your organization. Look for ways to save time on routine tasks and eliminate time-wasting activities.
- Make routine time to keep your workspace tidy. If you frequently find yourself losing items relevant to your work, look for ways to improve the organization of your workspace and your computer.

DISCUSSION IDEAS

- In a small group, tell each other where you would like to be in your careers in five years. Try to answer these questions: How many people do you know personally who are now where you would like to be five years from now? Have you talked to them about your career? What steps do you think you need to take to get to where you want to be in five years?
- When asked how things are going, many professionals will tell you how busy they are. In fact, often people appear to want to be in competition with each other to determine who is the busiest. In a group, come up with answers to these questions: Is being busy necessarily an indicator of a person's importance? What interpersonal tensions can being "too busy" cause? How could you organize your time so that, when you interact with others, you can avoid the appearance of being "rushed" or "self-important"?
- Individually, reflect on the way that you have organized one of the following: your office files, your document files on your computer, the bookmarked pages on your web browser, your e-mail folders. In a small group, share with others your answers to these questions: What is the logic of your organization scheme? How often

do you "lose" items? Is there a pattern to how you "lose" items? How would you like to change your present filing system?

FURTHER READING

Carnegie, Dale. 1937. *How to Win Friends and Influence People.* New York: Simon and Schuster.

Dixit, Avinash K. 1994. "My System of Work (Not!)" *American Economist* 38:10–16.

Fox, Jeffrey J. 1998. *How to Become CEO: The Rules for Rising to the Top of Any Organization.* New York: Hyperion Press.

Gleeson, Kerry. 2000. *The Personal Efficiency Program: How to Get Organized to Do More Work in Less Time.* 2d ed. New York: Wiley.

Heller, Robert. 1999. *Achieving Excellence.* New York: DK Publishing.

3

Building Expert Knowledge

One of the great things about being a policy analyst is the opportunity it gives you to work on diverse issues throughout your career. So far, I have worked in many areas including transportation, technology, the national election process, and government contracting. As analysts, we learn and use skills that allow us to elicit the best decision out of all possible options. In my experience, the more complete my understanding of the issue, the better my ability to recommend the decision that is most likely to produce the best outcomes. To understand and evaluate various policy options, you must be able to build expert knowledge about the problem or the issue area. Building expert knowledge is achieved through obtaining good information, discussing the most important aspects of each issue with involved stakeholders, and critically thinking through available options. Of course, to be a successful policy analyst you need to do more than build expert knowledge. You also need to communicate your findings and demonstrate that your recommendations are supported by sound reasoning. But building expert knowledge is vital, and I have also found it to be an extremely interesting and challenging part of my work.

—Michelle Dresben, *Analyst, United States General Accounting Office, Los Angeles, California*

Expert knowledge is central to what policy analysts bring to the policy-making community. During policy discussions and debates, the more pertinent, original, and deep the knowledge that you can share with others, the more valued you will be as a policy analyst. The reason is straightforward. Policymakers seek to avoid trouble and embarrassment. They are risk-averse. Thus, when it comes to adopting new policies or changing established ones, policymakers want as much reassurance as possible that the choices they make will be sound ones. As a policy analyst with expert knowledge of the policy issues at hand, you can do a lot to help policymakers work through the decisions before them. Through your efforts to build expert knowledge about specific policy issues and the context in which they have arisen, you reveal your seriousness of purpose. In this way you also show your respect for the policymakers you seek to advise and for the people who will be directly affected by any policy change. In return, your knowledge, and the manner by which you present it to others, will greatly affect the credibility that is accorded to you and to the organization you represent.

It seems hardly controversial to suggest that the quality of your expert knowledge and how you share it will affect your interactions with others in the policymaking community. But does this necessarily mean that building expert knowledge is a people skill? In contrast to the other skills discussed in this book, building expert knowledge can be done quite well in a solitary manner. When we read, when we search databases, when we create and analyze datasets, and when we build files, we typically do so alone. What's more, we can engage in all of these efforts to build our expert knowledge simply for our own edification and sense of purpose. But I consider building expert knowledge to be a people skill, because, as policy analysts, we engage in it with the primary goal of improving our ability to contribute to policy discussions and to persuade others that our ways of thinking about issues hold merit. In this chapter, I focus on the recognizably people-oriented aspects of building expert knowledge.

The Merits of Thinking Like a Journalist

Consider the differences between how journalists and policy analysts approach policy issues. Journalists are distinguished from other professionals by their ability to tell a story about an issue or event, the background to it, the personalities involved, and the politics of the situation. Journalists seek to understand how particular individuals or groups view issues, and they try to account for why these views might differ.

This is how journalists often come to pinpoint the sources of conflict over policies long before those conflicts actually rise to the surface in debates. To do their work well, journalists need excellent people skills, because they rely on others to give them information and direct them to other relevant information sources. Thus, the best journalists nurture long-term relationships with informants, or organizational "worms," who are well situated to be able to answer their queries and provide off-the-record information on an ongoing basis.

In contrast to journalists, policy analysts are distinguished from other professionals by their ability to analyze information in ways that generate new insights into the nature of policy problems and the alternative ways that those problems might be addressed. Policy analysts engage in a variety of technical activities, including dataset construction and model building. Policy analysts often place too much store on their technical expertise, playing down the relevance of other types of expert knowledge, like the background knowledge on issues and people that journalists work hard to acquire. Excellent and relevant technical work is best undertaken and interpreted by policy analysts who come to their task with strong substantive knowledge of the issues at stake, the players involved, and the likely sources of policy conflict. In other words, policy analysts should strive to have as much substantive knowledge of policy issues as any top-flight investigative journalist would want to have before writing a story. There are no shortcuts. Policy analysts who want to have something interesting, original, and important to say should first strive to be at least as well-informed about policy issues as other actors involved in the relevant policy discussion. Good technical skills, while critical for producing good policy analysis, are no substitute for a sound knowledge of how a given issue has arisen and why other people view it as important. When policy analysts combine the skills of the investigative journalist with excellent technical skills, the result is likely to be very insightful, helpful policy advice.

THE COSTS OF BUILDING EXPERT KNOWLEDGE

Whenever we put time into one activity, we need to think carefully about the opportunity costs involved. What better use could I be making of the time I am spending on this task? The issue of opportunity cost is particularly apt when we think of building expert knowledge. We do not want to waste time acquiring irrelevant knowledge, but sometimes we will be unsure even of what is relevant and what is not. In this chapter, I note how we can reduce the risk of spending time chasing up false leads or learning facts that, while interesting, are not critical to the completion of pressing project work. In general, the opportunity costs associated with building expert knowledge can be viewed from the perspective of both the short term and the long term.

Taking the short-term perspective, we should remember that almost always, policy analysts face deadlines. As Weimer and Vining (1999, 34) have pointed out, "The advice of policy analysts, no matter how sophisticated and convincing, will be useless if it is delivered to clients after they have had to vote, issue regulations, or otherwise make decisions. Rarely will it be the case of better late than never." In light of this, policy analysts always need to weigh the merit of acquiring additional expert knowledge against the risk of missing a deadline, although it is also true that the time pressures faced by policy analysts tend to ebb and flow over the course of a year. This suggests that there will be times when a reasonable degree of effort can be put into building expert knowledge that may or may not be linked to a specific project. Appropriately directed, such effort can have large pay-offs later, in terms of equipping the policy analyst with valuable insights that can be drawn on quickly, and to good effect, when the deadline pressure is on.

Taking the long-term perspective, as a policy analyst you need to think carefully about how much highly specific expert knowledge you want to acquire. Clients often benefit from analysts who hold a wealth of specific policy knowledge. Likewise, organizations benefit from staff who have been around a long time and who have developed detailed institutional knowledge. In either case, you need to be careful that the client or organization you work for does not come to exploit you because of the specificity of your policy knowledge. The danger of exploitation arises when your knowledge becomes so specific to your current position that it seriously limits your prospects for finding employment elsewhere. In this chapter, I emphasize the importance of linking general knowledge and particular knowledge. When you strive to do that, you inevitably reduce the risk of building too much narrow expert knowledge. By remembering that some forms of specific knowledge can be a curse as well as a blessing, you are more likely to make the right assessments about when to continue building such knowledge and when to stop.

I do not want to emphasize the potential costs of building expert knowledge to the point that we lose sight of the benefits involved. Aside from the important professional benefits that can come from building expert knowledge, it is useful to bear in mind the personal rewards that come from it. The more you throw yourself into building expert knowledge of the relevant policy area, the more likely you are to gain pleasure from your work. And, of course, if you use every position you have as an opportunity to extend your expert knowledge, it is likely that others in the policymaking community will come to value you highly for your contributions. Thus, the personal rewards of building your expert knowledge can be both intrinsic and extrinsic. Plus, the adage "knowledge is power" holds here. Policy analysts who have high levels of relevant expert knowledge, and who know how to use it effectively, can be formidable assets to their clients during policy discussions and debates.

LINKING GENERAL AND PARTICULAR KNOWLEDGE

Most people who are drawn to the policy analyst profession bring a general knowledge of government, politics, and society. Along with this general knowledge, people often come with more specific policy interests. So it is common to hear people say that they enrolled in a program in public management, public policy, or policy analysis because of their interests in particular areas of policy, such as health care, environmental management, criminal justice, or government regulation of business. Also, through time spent in junior positions or internships in government agencies, nonprofits, or businesses, people often develop specific interests that they subsequently seek to build on through additional training. Even before we become professional policy analysts, therefore, all of us possess some mixture of general and particular knowledge. Here I discuss how we can systematically and productively build on this knowledge.

Start with a Specific Project

Working on a specific, tightly focused project is the best way to build expert knowledge in an area of public policy that is new to you. This is the case no matter whether you are at the start of your career as a policy analyst or have vast experience working on policy issues. The tight focus ensures that you have something to work on that, while stretching, will not overwhelm you. It also gives you an opportunity to become acquainted with some of the broader questions and concerns associated with the field of policy you are working in.

Suppose you were asked—or you chose—to develop a policy report assessing the implications of expanding a long-established state park. This would appear to be a manageable task for most people who have at least some understanding of the rudiments of policy analysis. But, done well, work on such a project would lead you to ask questions about the environmental, social, political, and financial implications of the park expansion. You would want to have a sense of the history of the issue, the people and groups involved, and where people's views conflict over the expansion. Even if you were to only touch on some of these questions in your final report, having thought about them would surely improve the quality and value of your work. More importantly, working on this tightly focused project would give you an opportunity to begin thinking about broader issues having to do with the role of government in supporting the recreational activities of citizens and the various trade-offs involved. This specific project, while narrow in scope, could provide a starting point for building your expert knowledge in a variety of ways.

Having something specific to think and write about provides an excellent way to become acquainted with new issues and new literatures. All of us could choose to read widely and think about issues to do with recreation policy—or any other policy—regardless of whether we have a specific project to work on. That reading would be unfocused, however, and we would have little incentive to draw direct connections between what we were reading and its practical implications. Wildavsky (1993, 33) has observed, "I cannot recall a subfield of study, other than a new language or extensive history, that takes more than six weeks to three months to master." In making this statement, Wildavsky could be accused of discounting the effort that is required to build expert knowledge. But that would be unfair. Wildavsky understood that building expert knowledge is always easier when you are doing so to answer specific questions. Inevitably, the specificity of the task before you will lead you to ignore a lot of interesting literature. But you can come back to that for further reading and review once the immediate project work has been done. More importantly, you probably would not have even come across a lot of that interesting literature in the first place had it not been for the motivation created by the specific task lying before you.

Question and Be Curious

Whenever we begin working on a specific analytical project, there are several questions we can ask that will help us to better frame and think about the topic. In standard textbooks on policy analysis, we are sometimes encouraged to begin by determining whether a policy problem has arisen because of market failure or because of government failure. Sometimes, we are told to quickly achieve a sense of the money at stake—where it is coming from and how it is being spent. Although, undoubtedly, these are key issues to be addressed by policy analysts, if we focus upon them too quickly, we run the risk of making our analysis unduly narrow and ignoring other relevant matters. I suggest that, as a way to begin thinking about policy problems, we should ask the following questions: What is going on here? Who are the main actors involved? How have they defined the problem? Why has this issue come up now? What makes this issue similar to others? What makes it unique? To answer questions like this, you will need to consult a variety of information sources, including other people working in this area of policy, policy reports produced on similar or related issues, and newspaper archives. As you work to find answers to such questions, you will gain many insights into the problem you are addressing.

Eventually, as you work on any project, you will be required to dig deep for data, to engage in a variety of analyses, and to produce new, relevant, and helpful knowledge for the people you seek to advise. But it would be foolish to try to undertake that work before you have achieved at least the same level of general understanding of the policy issue as that already possessed by other interested policy actors.

Arrange a Site Visit

If you were working on a project assessing the implications of expanding a long-established state park, a good way to begin building your expert knowledge would be to actually visit that park. By making such a visit, you would get a sense of the surrounding area. What is the land bordering the park being used for? What parts of the area around the park would be taken over by the expansion? Of course, you could answer these questions by talking to others who are already acquainted with the park and the expansion plan, but a visit to the site can be helpful in allowing you to picture the place and to get a firm sense of what the expansion would involve. If you plan ahead for the site visit, it is likely that you will be able to arrange for a member of the park staff to take you on a tour. You should also try to prearrange meetings with some of the people who would be most affected by the park expansion. These do not have to be formal meetings, although it could be useful to treat them as interviews.

The main point of the site visit is to engage in familiarization and fact collecting. But, in addition, taking the time to make a site visit can be good for boosting your credibility as a policy analyst. Engaging in a site visit shows that you care about the issue you are working on. It signals to the people that you meet that you are seriously interested in producing a well-informed policy report. Further, if you have taken a site visit and met a few people, it becomes much easier for you to get back in touch with those people later to ask for more information or to check on facts as your work moves forward.

Work on policy issues that involve land use, like the expansion of a state park, lends itself to undertaking site visits. When you are working on issues such as proposals for change in the financing of public schools, or the deregulation of the trucking industry, the prospects for a site visit will not present themselves so readily. Wherever possible, though, making some kind of relevant site visit or visits will work powerfully to increase your understanding of the issues at stake. Over the years that I have worked on various policy issues, I have almost always engaged in site visits of one sort or another. Often, driving to meet with people, I have wondered whether I am wasting time that could otherwise be spent on other aspects of the project. Yet I can think of no occasion where I have subsequently regretted the site visits that I have made. More frequently, I have come away from those visits with new insights into the relevant enterprise and of the people who will be affected by policy changes. Having this deeply grounded knowledge can be a great stimulus to bolstering the knowledge of the issues that you can gain through such means as literature searches and reading. At a personal level, relevant site visits can help you clarify why you are doing this work and what sort of contribution you seek to make to policy-making on this issue.

Draw Broad Connections with Other Issues

When studying a particular behavior or event, good social scientists ask, What broader phenomenon is this an instance of? The task of the social scientist, after all, is to reveal interesting and important patterns in society, and then develop causal explanations for the existence of such patterns or regularities. Many intriguing things happen in society, but this does not make them worthy of study by social scientists. For such scholars, isolated events and actions become seriously interesting only when plausible linkages can be drawn between them and what is known about similar events and actions elsewhere. Mills (1959) suggested that good social scientists link the particular and the general through exercise of "the sociological imagination." Mills was describing what all social scientists look for: theoretically interesting ways to compare and contrast across cases.

Policy analysts engage in work that is quite distinctive from that of social scientists. Nonetheless, thinking like a social scientist, invoking the sociological imagination, can help you to gain fresh insights into policy problems. As a policy analyst, you can do well to try to draw connections between the particular problem you are working on and other kinds of policy problems. Bardach (2000, 11) makes this point when he suggests that policy analysts make use of analogies. "Sometimes it pays to gather data about things that are, on the surface, quite unlike the problem you are studying but that, under the surface, show instructive similarities. For instance, your understanding of how a merit pay plan for compensating managers in the public sector might work could perhaps be improved by seeing how similar schemes work in the private sector." Thus, even as you work on specific policy projects, you should think consciously about how to draw connections between your project topics and other issues, emphasizing the broader implications that make those connections meaningful.

Two main benefits can come from seeking to draw broad connections between what you are working on and other policy issues. First, by thinking about how your project topic fits into the wider context, you are likely to identify ideas and approaches that you potentially could adapt to help you produce helpful, creative policy advice. Inevitably, such an effort will also lead you to identify other people with whom you could talk about your project work. Second, by seeking to link general and particular knowledge in this manner, you can become more adept at developing your work and talking about it in ways that allow other people to see its broader relevance. This can be important for helping you to gain a better sense of how your work contributes to the policy community of which you are a part. In turn, it can help other people understand where your work fits into the big picture. That can be important for allowing you to make more professional contacts and, thus, join in more conversations about policy problems and potential solutions.

As you gain a sense of what people know and what they do not know about specific policy problems, you can begin spotting gaps in policy knowledge. This can be a starting point for you to draw connections between what you know and what others need to know. Like everyone else, you will often have to work on just small portions of the broader public policy jigsaw puzzle. But standing back now and then to assess the big picture can be clarifying. This is how you can come to see how you could best make productive contributions through your current and future work.

Remember Your Long-Term Goals

As a policy analyst, your biggest asset is your reputation for producing excellent, knowledge-based policy advice. The best way for you to build this reputation is to deliver consistently high quality work—not quantity, but consistent high quality. Given this, as you work on each project, you should have a clear sense of how it is allowing you to develop as a policy analyst. As a check on the link between your day-to-day work and your long-term goals, consider these questions: How can I make my present project as relevant and insightful as possible for my client or immediate superior? What new knowledge could I build through this current work? In the best-case scenario, what career benefits could come to me from producing excellent work here? Wherever possible, you should strive to use each project as an opportunity to get better at what you do, and to build your general and particular policy knowledge.

Learning from the Past

All policy issues come with a history. Individuals and groups who have vested interests in an issue will be well acquainted with that history. Thus, if you are to add fresh, relevant ideas to the present policy conversation, you will need to be familiar with the history of the issue as well. Working to understand the history of an issue will help you gain insights into its present manifestation. To learn from the past, you need to develop appropriate strategies for gathering and organizing relevant information. Each issue that you work on will no doubt require you to use somewhat unique approaches to make sense of its history. The steps suggested here, however, should help you build your expert knowledge in ways that will improve the value to your client of your policy analysis and advice.

Establish the History of Policy Activity

Let us return to the example where you are to assess the implications of expanding a long-established state park. Piecing together the history of policy discussions and activity concerning the park and its expansion is a useful way for you to get acquainted with a wide variety of relevant issues. Looking at historical records, you should be able to determine when and why the park was established. In this way you might also be able to determine whether park expansions have occurred in the past and what issues were raised at those times. To build this historical record, you can look at local newspaper archives, the annual reports of the relevant government department, and any legislative records that might pertain to the park and its expansion. Increasingly, information of this sort is able to be located by use of Internet resources. Work of this sort represents microhistory. The insights you gain from it might be quite helpful to building your expert knowledge of the park expansion issue. Most importantly, such work will give you a sense of the policy context and the issues that have been raised previously. It can be helpful for you to become familiar with the interests that have been at stake before and the arguments that people have made in the past to support their positions. As a policy analyst, this information will allow you to anticipate the sort of concerns that might be raised in current discussions and how your policy analysis might most effectively serve to enlighten the policymakers involved.

In general, when working on a policy topic, I suggest that you seek to establish a history of policy activity, beginning at the microlevel and then extending outward. Start by tracking the history of the issue within your own jurisdiction. If you are studying a local-level policy, trace the history of the relevant debates that occurred there and the decisions that were made by local politicians. If you are studying a state-level policy, try to trace the history of state policy controversy over the issue and the relevant actions of state legislators, governors, and judges.

If you have the time, it can sometimes be beneficial to trace the history of activity on the policy issue of interest both in your own jurisdiction and elsewhere. Ideas for policy change often diffuse from place to place. In the United States, it is common to observe many cities and states adopting similar public policies all within just a few years of each other. Often, the policy debates and the broad outlines of the policies under discussion will be much the same from place to place. Interesting differences also arise across jurisdictions now and then, however, so that particular policy ideas can be seen to change as they diffuse. Working to trace the consideration and adoption of similar policies across several jurisdictions can be an especially rich way to gain insights into the variety of policy alternatives that might be adopted to address a particular policy problem. Interest groups and think tanks increasingly go to great lengths to document the history of specific policy issues across multiple jurisdictions. Looking at the websites of such groups can be a good way to begin learning about the history of policy activity elsewhere.

Of course, as well as being absorbing and a potential gold mine for gathering policy ideas, work of this sort can take up a lot of precious time. Comparative work of the sort I have mentioned here is probably best undertaken during periods when you are not facing deadline pressure.

The discipline required to establish the history of policy activity can be very rewarding in terms of the insights that you can gain into your policy topic. This sort of work will help you to establish why policymakers in the past believed that particular actions had to be taken, and why those actions took the form they did. But this is another way of saying that an investigation into the background to a present policy issue will help you to understand its current manifestation, why particular individuals and groups view it in particular ways, and so on.

It would be easy to devote a great deal of time to work of this sort. Thus, discretion is called for. It should not take you too long to trace in broad outline the previous decisions that have been taken that are directly relevant to the topic you are working on. No matter how extensive or how brief your work on previous policy activity, it is important that you take the time to write up a narrative that pulls together the information that you have acquired. Often, tables, charts, and flow diagrams can help you to make sense of this kind of information. For some useful ideas in this regard, see Miles and Huberman (1994) and Tufte (1983, 1990, 1997). Writing your narrative while still undertaking your investigative work can be clarifying, helping you keep track of what you have learned and spot gaps in your knowledge.

Like a lot of the work that you will do to build your expert knowledge, it is unlikely that you would present much of the history of a policy activity in your policy reports (although tabular summaries and so on might be included in appendices in some cases). This does not mean that such work is a waste of time, or that few others will see it. If, over the course of working in a particular policy area for several months, you develop a detailed narrative that is unique from anything else that you have come across in your searches for relevant information, you might desire to provide copies of it to other people who share your policy interests. Meanwhile, engaging in this work will have helped you to build your expert knowledge in important ways.

Review Relevant Literature

The exhortation to review relevant literature conveys the sense that there is a great deal of information relevant to your policy project—whatever that project might be—and that, having located that literature, enlightenment will soon follow. But things are not that simple. The problem we all face is that the most formal and systematically organized literature of relevance to policy issues rarely addresses policy concerns with the same level of detail or specificity that is found in unpublished policy reports. Journal articles and books treating policy topics are typically designed to address general policy questions or concerns, even though they will usually contain empirical explorations of particular cases. Here we bump up against the issue of different audiences having different concerns. All journals—both popular and scholarly—seek to be of general appeal to the members of their target audience. Thus, they tend to treat policy issues and concerns in somewhat general ways. In contrast, as a policy analyst, you typically write for a more focused audience. Having thought about the audience concerns of various authors, you will get a better sense of the strengths and weaknesses of particular literatures, given your particular concerns.

In working to establish the history of policy activity relating to your policy project, you will already have started to engage with relevant literature in the form of departmental reports, newspaper articles, trade journals, studies undertaken by interest groups, and so on. A good way to extend your search for relevant information and ideas involves simply building on what you already have. For example, if a particular trade journal has been the source of highly relevant information, it might be useful to extend your search of that source, looking for other articles on related topics.

As a policy analyst, you usually want to be able to give advice indicating the likely impacts associated with particular policy choices. Often, general theories about how people respond to policies can help you assess likely future scenarios. But learning from the past can also be instructive here. It would be particularly helpful if you could track down evidence produced by program evaluations. You might be lucky; however, it is often the case that the impacts of particular policies are never reviewed in systematic ways. Even when you can find evaluations, they are unlikely to address the particular questions that you have in mind. This is why you need to continually find ways to link the specifics of your project to more general policy concerns. Taking this approach, you are more likely to track down the results of program evaluations that, while not directly related to your interests, offer insights that are relevant to your project.

What about working with the scholarly literature? Journals, especially those that are targeted at people with policy interests, will contain much that is potentially relevant to your project. But, in searching through and working with the articles contained in such journals, you should expect them to be most useful not for their substantive focus but for the theoretical frameworks they develop or the methodological strategies they document. By browsing through the titles and abstracts of scholarly articles, you should be particularly alert to how the various theoretical and methodological contributions contained within them could help guide the ways that you choose to approach and analyze the problem that you are working on. For example, it is unlikely that you will find much in the way of scholarly articles addressing a topic as specific as the expansion of state parks. You will, though, find plenty of articles that cover topics such as the definition and redefinition of property rights and the relationship between property rights and effective resource management. You might also find that reading a few articles on topics such as public-private partnerships will give you some new insights into how the park expansion could be most effectively undertaken.

As you begin to review relevant literature, you will quickly find that you could read far more material than you will ever have time for. I do not suggest that you respond to this by engaging in speed-reading. Rather, you should develop your ability to rapidly scan a large amount of material. Look at the titles of articles. If they seem vaguely relevant, read their abstracts. Having done that, you should be able to see whether an article is likely to help you build your expert knowledge in relevant ways. Reserve the time you spend for careful, close reading to focus on those ten to twenty items that appear most promising for helping you think about your policy topic. You might also find books that are relevant to your work. Again, be highly judicious in what items you choose to read. Scanning widely is vital. But you need to develop a sound way to select from the items you scan. Ultimately, close reading of a few excellent, relevant articles or books will be much more useful to you than trying to skim read a lot of material.

Listen to Seasoned Policy Actors

Documents are not the only means by which you can learn from the past. People can also be extremely helpful. Well-informed people in particular can save you a lot of time, by referring you to documents of the most relevance to your project or to other people who might be able to offer valuable insights into the policy topic. Like working with documents, you need to be careful how you spend your time when deciding whom you will talk to about your project. It is much better to talk to two highly knowledgeable people than to talk to ten whose knowledge is not so relevant to your project. Who would be good to talk with? I suggest that you keep this question in mind as you initially work with documents to establish the history of policy activity. It is also important that you take care to gain a reasonable understanding of key aspects of the policy issue and its background before you approach people and ask to speak with them. People with deep, relevant knowledge are much more likely to share it when they can see that you have already made an effort to gain insights about and understanding of the issue.

TRIANGULATING FROM DIFFERENT INFORMATION SOURCES

Discussion and debate about policy issues can often grow contentious. As a policy analyst, it is important that you do as much as possible to anticipate policy disagreements. It is especially important that you conduct and present your work in ways that reduce the likelihood that you will unwittingly fuel contention. Therefore, it is useful to remember that good policy analysis should clarify policy discussions, not cause confusion. Other people might call your analysis into question, and it is quite legitimate for them to do so, but by making appropriate efforts to ensure that your knowledge of the policy issue is sound you can reduce the possibility of receiving unnecessary challenges. Further, if you anticipate challenges to your work, you can take steps in the development of your work that will preempt criticisms or—if they still come—can rapidly and satisfactorily respond to them. This is where the notion of triangulation can be particularly helpful for a policy analyst.

When you triangulate, you consciously make use of multiple and independent sources of information to help you verify an observation or set of observations concerning an event or phenomenon. As you strive to build your expert knowledge on a policy issue, as you conduct your policy analysis, and as you write up your policy report, there will be many instances where conscious effort on your part to triangulate and, hence, verify the validity of your observations will be beneficial to both you and your audience.

When efforts to triangulate go as anticipated, you should discover a degree of convergence in what your distinctive information sources tell you. But efforts to triangulate might not be reassuring. For example, there might be times when each source of information points to different interpretations of an event or phenomenon. Divergence like this should force you to reexamine the conclusions you have drawn from a given information source. If you can achieve an explanation of divergence, or revise your interpretations so that you begin to see convergence, you will put yourself on stronger ground than if you had never thought to engage in a triangulation effort. It is better to go through this self-questioning as you work than to be forced into rethinking your understanding of an issue only after others have read and called into doubt the contents of your policy report.

Assemble the Fragments

As you seek to build your understanding of a policy issue, you will amass a large amount of information from a variety of sources. During the tracking down and gathering of information, you will inevitably begin to acquire a range of insights about the issue. You will also probably begin to interpret informally what the information is telling you. At some point, however, you will have to formalize the gathering of information. I think of this as assembling the fragments. This is where you attempt to lay out and make sense of what is before you. There are many questions that you can ask to begin the sense-making process. Perhaps two of the most important are "How does all this stuff fit together?" and "What is this information telling me about the policy issue?" I suggest that you try to assemble the fragments of your information searches at regular intervals, starting fairly soon after you begin the search.

Taking the time to scrutinize what you have amassed will help you to build your knowledge, even as your search for information is continuing. Most importantly, this effort to make formal sense of the information you have been gathering will help you see where your search is leading to overlaps and where gaps in your knowledge need to be filled. Taking stock of what you have while you are still searching will help you to determine the highest priorities for the ongoing process of filling gaps. As you seek to assemble the fragments, it might be helpful to develop tables, charts, and diagrams that allow you to visually display and summarize the information you have gathered.

Assembling the fragments on a regular basis will help you to identify the information sources that have so far been most fruitful in helping you to build your knowledge of the policy issue. Suppose you find a particularly helpful report written by another policy analyst a few years ago. If the report seems more useful than anything else that you have read, you might consider contacting the author to discuss the policy issue. If you find that there was a large amount of discussion about this same policy issue a few years ago in another jurisdiction, you might try to isolate the best sources of information about that episode. Think about who were the main actors to participate at the time. What arguments did they make? What evidence did they use? You should think carefully about the insights that you could get from that episode to help you with your own work.

In general, as you work to assemble the fragments, try to think in terms of the most relevant information, the sources of that information, and how you might fruitfully build on the information that you have already obtained. Also, be aware that all searches will always lead to a few dead ends. When you see that a particular line of inquiry does not seem to be yielding much in the way of useful information, switch your efforts to more promising leads.

Once you have a sense of the background to the policy issue that you are working on, scanning the main chapters of a good policy analysis textbook can be one of the best ways to clarify your thoughts. At this point, you can come back to asking, As a policy analyst, what value-added can I bring to thinking about this issue? Policy analysis textbooks such as Weimer and Vining's (1999) *Policy Analysis: Concepts and Practice* present basic frameworks and approaches for application in analyzing specific policy problems. The combination of expert knowledge regarding the substance of the issue you are working on and the systematic application of well-established analytical frameworks will take you a very long way toward developing a high-quality policy report.

The discipline of having to account for how you spend your time can be particularly helpful when you are trying to build your knowledge of a new area of policy. Even if you do not have to write a report for a superior, it is a good idea for you to write notes for yourself as you search among information sources. Part of assembling the fragments should be the writing of brief narratives for your own use. They should state what information you have gathered so far, what information appears most useful for helping you to build your knowledge, and what gaps you still need to fill. Reading over these narratives will give you a sense of accomplishment, but, more importantly, they should help to guide the remainder of your search.

Play the Skeptic with Your Evidence

When you seek to triangulate with your evidence, you force yourself to confront alternative ways of thinking about the issue at hand. In a sense, then, this strategy leads you to be skeptical of initial findings, or to play the devil's advocate against the argument that you would otherwise make. Doing this is likely to lead you to be a better policy analyst, one who is surer of the reasonableness of his or her analysis and arguments. It should also make you better at anticipating the kind of questions that others might raise in response to what you have to say. Of course, one can go too far with questioning and self-doubt. As in other activities, setting priorities is important. First, try to isolate the evidence that is most central to the interpretations that you are developing of the policy issue. Second, think carefully about the possibility that, considering the same evidence, someone else could come to exactly the opposite interpretation. Is there a reasonable way that this could happen? Third, think about alternative means of generating evidence pertinent to the issue at hand. Could you obtain such evidence?

Sometimes, people involved in policy disputes stake out positions that are supported primarily by their ideological beliefs or by their beliefs about where their particular interests lie. As a policy analyst, you might also hold strong beliefs, but if such beliefs lead you to give policy advice that is simplistic, or that is not based on appropriate investigation of the relevant evidence, you will not be especially helpful for your client or the broader audience for your work. Being skeptical about evidence and its interpretation—especially your own—helps you build your expert knowledge. It also helps you become a better policy analyst.

Creating Files

At the most general level, your files are the practical manifestation of how you make sense of the policy issues on which you work. Here, I will briefly discuss the ways that you might organize your files to support the building of your expert knowledge. It is highly likely that much of your filing will be done on your computer. Nevertheless, you will still require physical files, and the organizational principles that I will mention apply to all filing systems, be they physical or electronic.

When you begin a new project, you should dedicate specific file space to it. One way to do this would be to start with a file dedicated to background on the issue, another dedicated to previous policy activity, another to notes from your site visits, and another for related documents and literature. As the project develops, you might want to add files on particular people and groups. These files would each contain information and documents relevant to these people and groups, and how they view the policy issue you are working on. As you work on a specific project, your system of filing should serve to support your knowledge creation. The act of assembling the fragments should begin with your files. At these times, you can systematically review what is in your files and how information within each of them is helping you to make sense of the policy issue. During your review of your files, you will often find that the contents of certain files can be merged, while other files have been growing so large that you need to divide them.

Over a sufficient amount of time, say a year or more, you will most likely develop sets of files relating to several distinct policy projects. As you switch from working on one project to working on another, you will often find that material you collected to help you work on the first project will be relevant to the second. This suggests that what you really need to do is develop a set of files that are general in nature and that do not relate to any particular project. You will still want to maintain your project files, although obviously the most important of these will always be the ones that relate to your current project. In addition, I suggest that, over time, you work to build sets of general files. Useful categories for these files would include, "Master Bibliographies," "Articles and Book Chapters," "News Clippings," "Issues," and "People."

MAINTAINING AND EXPANDING YOUR KNOWLEDGE

Since our expert knowledge is of most value when we use it to shed light on specific policy issues, one might think that building expert knowledge is something we do only while working on discrete policy projects. I prefer to view building expert knowledge as a continuous activity, one in which we strive to link our general understandings of government, politics, and society with our insights concerning specific policy issues. You can maintain and expand your expert knowledge through a number of activities that I see as distinctive from those that might be associated with working on a particular project.

Reading habitually is essential. As a policy analyst, you should always read at least one daily newspaper. At least one of these newspapers should be a high-quality source of information on a broad range of political and policy issues, such as the *New York Times*. You should also read at least one good news magazine that routinely covers policy issues. *The Economist, Business Week*, and *The Atlantic Monthly* are good examples of such magazines. Increasingly, it is possible to belong to news groups on the Internet that will channel relevant information to you. Asking other policy people about their reading habits is a good way to get a sense of the sort of information sources that are out there that will be of relevance to your work. Reading good newspapers and news magazines should keep you informed about emerging policy issues beyond the issues that you are working on directly. These sources are also helpful for keeping you informed of new books and reports that might provide insights for your project work or that might simply be of general interest.

To further support your reading habit, it is useful to make regular visits to a good library, such as a university library or a main city library. Despite making increasing use of electronic resources and catalogues, I continue to find it valuable to actually go to the library, especially to scan the shelves of the current periodicals section and the new books section. Even if these visits result in you reading the abstracts of just two articles, they can be helpful for keeping you up to date on how people are thinking about policy issues. Good bookstores are also great resources for keeping you up to date with new and recent books relating to politics and policy. Because Internet book merchants now offer a large amount of useful information on the titles they stock, and the software encourages browsing of related titles, spending time checking book information at those websites can be very helpful.

Belonging to one or two professional associations is another way to maintain and expand your policy knowledge. Most associations of this sort, such as the Association for Public Policy Analysis and Management, have their own journals and they hold annual conferences. Thus, membership in a professional association will lead you to mix with other policy people, attend functions where policy issues are discussed in serious ways, and receive access to state-of-the-art scholarly thinking on policy issues.

Finally, I suggest that you keep a notebook or a journal to support and document your efforts to maintain and expand your expert knowledge. When you attend conferences or talks, you should take this notebook with you so that you can write down interesting or important information. Having a notebook close by while you read the newspaper or news magazines will allow you to jot down the names of new books or articles that appear relevant to your work. It is a simple way to keep a record of some of the items and information that you come across in your reading and your conversations that you could benefit from tracking down. Just as I have suggested that you should review your project files on a regular basis, I suggest that there is considerable value to be had from reviewing your notebook or journal at regular intervals. Often, we record items only to forget about them in the rush of other pressing issues. It is good to take some quiet moments now and then to determine what items you might follow up on. Combining this sort of reflection with library visits can be particularly helpful.

MAPPING CONTEMPORARY ISSUES AND PEOPLE

As policy analysts, we build our expert knowledge to better serve our clients and, more generally, to improve our ability to make high-quality contributions to policy discussions and debates. Aside from the knowledge-building efforts that I have mentioned so far, it is important that policy analysts continually seek to make sense of the contemporary policy scene. When working on a specific project, you should make it a top priority to learn the key players who will be involved in making any policy change. You should also work to build your understanding of the positions being taken and arguments being made by the major interest groups and citizen coalitions whose interests are at stake. Beyond this, if you expect to spend the medium term conducting policy analyses within a specific policy area, it is essential that you find ways to identify and keep track of the major issues at stake and the main players in policy debates.

Depending on the size of the jurisdiction within which the policy decisions relating to your work are made, the number of issues at stake and players involved could range from a handful to several dozen. You cannot expect to know everything that matters about these issues and people, but having a sense of what the "hot topics" are and who's who will be helpful to your work. In particular, your knowledge of big issues and key players will help you to better tailor your advice so that it addresses the kind of concerns that are most likely to arise in discussions of the particular policy issue you are studying. Obtaining various organization charts, lists of legislators, and the names of people on important committees or boards is a way to begin this kind of mapping. You can add information as you come across it in newspaper reports, conversations, and so on. The point of such mapping is not to develop something elaborate. Rather, it is to develop something that readily summarizes your knowledge and is as easy as possible to access. Where visual displays of such information would make sense, you might try to develop them.

The suggestions I have made here represent ways to answer two questions: Who says these issues matter? and Why do these people get to speak? But such questions can be answered in different ways, ways that can also be important to helping you think about the work you do. Selection processes are always at work in politics and society. Among other factors, these processes influence how some issues get politicized and receive attention while others do not. If you seek to improve your understanding of a particular policy issue, looking for the absence of concerns and people to express them can also be important. Because it is always easier to respond to people who are present and issues that have been raised, looking for absences requires a deliberate attempt to break from instinctual behavior. One way to do this is to begin by thinking about the consequences of a policy change and listing systematically all the groups in society who would most likely to be affected by it. Rather than thinking in broad terms such as "winners" and "losers," start with particular groups. Individuals in society can be categorized in a variety of ways. Think about people in different age categories. How might policy affect each age group differently? Think about people in different income categories. What about people living in different places? What about differential impacts on men and women, or on people from different racial groups? You might also improve your analysis by thinking about the indirect impacts of a policy change in other areas we care about. What might be the overall fiscal impact of this policy change? How might this policy affect the environment? How might it affect civic participation? Could it bring people closer to government, or could it alienate people?

Sitting at your desk, you could probably develop some plausible responses to questions of this sort. Many of these questions, however, can also be thought of as prompts to consider how other people, especially those who will be affected by a policy change, think about an issue. As always, the pressure to produce your work in a timely fashion might lead you to overlook the kind of concerns these questions raise. Yet paying attention to the silences, the otherwise unheard voices, can be an excellent way for you to identify knowledge gaps within the policy conversation. In turn, this can open possibilities for you to suggest policy alternatives that serve to address aspects of the issue that others have not thought about.

Consider the following anecdote. A school district in a poor part of Los Angeles had a serious problem with truancy. The superintendent's office thought about a variety of measures that could be taken to stem the problem. Most of them involved punishing the students involved or their parents. The principal of one school, however, had been talking with members of her staff, who noticed patterns to the truancy. For example, children from one family would appear to rotate the days that they attended school. After some further observation and talking with some of the students involved, the teachers and principal decided that installing a laundry in the school could address the truancy problem. A laundry? One of the common reasons why students regularly stayed away from school was that they did not have enough clothes at home to ensure that all of them could attend school everyday in clean, comfortable clothes. In some families, children shared their school clothes. Installing a laundry at the school, so that clothes could be washed at the end of the day, made a considerable dent in the school's truancy figures. This change of practice in the school was unconventional, but it helped address a major problem. The change occurred because the people involved in policymaking actually cared about the children and families concerned. By listening to the issues raised by people who would otherwise have remained silent, a creative solution was found to a pressing and troubling issue. This anecdote contains a lesson about expert knowledge and the places we might look to find it.

SUMMARY

Policy analysts are most useful when they help clarify the thinking of others in the policymaking community, but you cannot help others if you know less about the issues at stake than they do. Therefore, policy analysts must continually strive to build their expert knowledge. In a sense, every new project forces you to confront your own ignorance. As a policy analyst, you are continually being thrown into the deep end of the pool, forced to rapidly find ways to make sense of new policy issues. This is the case even when many aspects of your present knowledge will serve to help you work effectively on your next project. In this chapter,

I have suggested a few strategies that should help you to build your expert knowledge of a new policy issue, so you can quickly turn from being a knowledge consumer to a knowledge producer. I have also tried to be honest about the messy nature of the process we go through when we strive to build expert knowledge. Mistakes are made, and rarely do we know as much as we would like. Recognizing these limitations is a good thing. At a minimum, it should lead us to have respect for others engaged in particular issues who do know more than we do. Better still, a sense of humility about our knowledge should lead us to strive continually to learn more and to be somewhat skeptical about the veracity of the answers we give ourselves.

SKILL-BUILDING CHECKLIST

- Treat tightly focused projects as opportunities to develop your expert knowledge. Such projects will allow you to engage with new concepts, analytical techniques, and evidence without becoming overwhelmed.

- Begin thinking about policy problems by asking the sort of questions investigative journalists ask: What is going on here? Who are the main actors involved? How do they define the problem? Why has this issue come up now? What makes this issue similar to others? What makes it unique?

- Explore ways to build relevant site visits into your early work on new projects. List questions you would like to answer, documents you would like to obtain, and people you would like to meet through such visits.

- While you work on your specific projects, think consciously about how to draw connections between the problems you are wrestling with and other contemporary policy issues.

- To gain insights into present issues, trace related policy activities of the past. By studying the history of an issue, you can come to appreciate why earlier policymakers took the actions they did and see how particular arguments were used in particular ways.

- As you assemble information about policy issues, try to triangulate across those information sources. Look for instances of convergence and divergence. To avoid jumping to easy interpretations of evidence, deliberately play the devil's advocate.

- Build into your daily and weekly routine good reading habits that will keep you well informed about a broad range of contemporary developments in politics and policy. These habits will help you to integrate your general and particular policy knowledge.

DISCUSSION IDEAS

- Over the course of a week, collect together four or five brief newspaper articles that report on aspects of current policy issues. Divide into groups of three or four people. Each group should take one of the newspaper articles and read it through. Following this, group members should imagine that they have been asked to write a policy report documenting the lead-up to the current situation. In your groups, try to answer the following questions: If you were to undertake a site visit or set of visits to help you build your expert knowledge of this policy issue, where would you go? Why? What documents do you think would help you to trace the history of policy activity relating to this issue? Report your answers back to the full group and discuss the similarities and differences across your responses.

- Think of a policy issue that is of interest to you or on which you have begun to do project work. Sometime this week, use a library catalog to locate a journal article published within the past three years that, from its title and abstract, appears relevant to this issue. Skim read the full article and have a close read through the references listed in it. After this, note five ways that this exercise has been helpful in contributing to your knowledge of this policy issue. In small groups, report back on the success of your search and what you learned. Reflecting on your various experiences, collectively list how you think journals and journal articles can be most productive for helping you as you work on policy projects.

- Take some time to list the ways that you currently keep track of contemporary issues in politics and public policy. What newspaper do you read? What news magazines do you receive? Do you belong to any Internet-based discussion groups? If you could do two things to improve your ability to keep track of contemporary issues, what would they be? Having written out your answers, discuss them with two or three other people who have also written out their responses. On the basis of your sharing of notes and ideas, what daily or weekly habits would you like to develop to help you build your general knowledge of politics and policy?

FURTHER READING

Bardach, Eugene. 2000. "Gathering Data for Policy Research." In *A Practical Guide for Policy Analysis: The Eightfold Path to More Effective Problem Solving*. New York: Chatham House, pp. 47–70.

Patton, Carl V., and David S. Sawicki. 1993. "Crosscutting Methods." In *Basic Methods of Policy Analysis and Planning*. 2d ed. Englewood Cliffs, N.J.: Prentice Hall, pp. 74–146.

Weimer, David L. and Aidan R. Vining. 1999. "Gathering Information for Policy Analysis." Appendix 10A in *Policy Analysis: Concepts and Practice*. 3d ed. Upper Saddle River, N.J.: Prentice Hall.

Wildavsky, Aaron. 1993. "Reading with a Purpose" and "Why It Is Necessary to Read Real Science in Order to Understand Environmental and Safety Policy and Politics." In *Craftways: On the Organization of Scholarly Work*. 2d ed. New Brunswick, N.J.: Transaction, pp. 25–40 and 149–56.

Yin, Robert K. 1994. *Case Study Research: Design and Methods*. 2d ed. Thousand Oaks, Calif.: Sage.

4
...

Interviewing Informants

Interviews can provide policy analysts with a wealth of information not available elsewhere. Unlike quantitative data, the qualitative nature of interviews allows the policy analyst to ask "why" and "how" questions. Interviews enable policy analysts to examine the chronology of events, or obtain point-of-view perspectives from multiple players and then tease out the implications. In my experience, preparation is the key to good interviews. I like to begin with a series of questions that lead easily from one another. This helps the interview flow well. Moreover, I often have different sets of questions for different types of informants. For instance, when I am interviewing people who are extremely busy I ask fewer questions, and I make those questions short and to the point. I have also found that the first question used in an interview may be the most crucial. The first question in many ways sets the tone of the interview. Typically, I ask the informant to tell me about herself, how long she has been in her current position, about her professional background and academic work. These kinds of questions are easy to ask and they help draw out an informant. An informant will begin to relax and feel she can trust you. And of course, most people love to talk about themselves!

—Dr. Susan Silberman, *Research Analyst, American Association of Retired Persons, Washington, D.C.*

As policy analysts, the greatest contributions we can make to the policy process involve clarifying the nature of problems, summarizing the issues at stake, and explaining how particular policy changes might serve to alleviate (or, in some instances, worsen) those problems. Good policy analysts, then, perform an enlightenment function. Yet, in saying

this, I could very easily be misconstrued as suggesting that policy analysts are special beings—the inherently enlightened ones—who now
and then venture down from on high to lead the lost and the blind from
harm's way. I view the enlightenment function differently. To perform it
well, policy analysts must be adept social actors, people who construct
relevant knowledge not in isolation but through their high-quality interactions with other members of society.

Perhaps the most critical insight emerging from the scholarship on
social networks and the network society is that knowledge is typically
located in disparate clusters across the social terrain. Thus, those who
seek to develop new understandings of problems and how they might be
addressed must be prepared to reach beyond their familiar social settings
to connect with and learn from others who have different knowledge
and who can offer the new insights that they need. This poses difficult
social challenges for us. We have to be very good at finding mutually
comfortable ways to interact with others who have quite different life experiences from our own and who view the world differently too. Even
as we speak the same language, we are likely to use and hear unfamiliar
words that create barriers to mutual understanding.

To enlighten ourselves about policy issues, we must be prepared to
pay close attention to the thoughts and ideas of various people who have
"situated knowledge," that is, knowledge specific to a given context.
Over the course of our careers, it is likely that we will meet a vast number of people like this. Usually, our interactions with them will be tran-
sitory. We will determine that we should talk with them and will locate
them, ask questions, listen, and learn. And then we will move on. If we
ask the right questions and listen carefully, through these interactions
we will gain knowledge and insights. By listening to others, and blend-
ing what we know with the thoughts and information that they have to
offer, we can develop deeper understandings of policy issues.

At every stage of working on a policy project, there will be moments when you run into problems or barriers simply because there are
things you do not know or do not understand about an issue. In those
moments, it would be great if you knew someone you could immediately reach, pose your questions to, and receive answers from. Sometimes, you will be able to do this. But when you reach that person, you
will not want to engage in a formal interview. Instead, you will want to
have something approaching a normal conversation, albeit one where

you do little of the talking and most of the listening. As a policy analyst, your low-key conversations with informants will probably far outnumber the occasions where you want to have more formal interviews. Regardless of the formality of your interactions with informants, you should seek to put your informants at ease and find ways to elicit precisely the kind of information you need.

ASSESSING YOUR INFORMATION NEEDS

Interviewing takes a lot of time and can often be expensive. Hence, whenever you are thinking about conducting interviews, you should think carefully about both the direct costs and the opportunity costs involved. You must be able to convince yourself that interviewing informants represents the best use of your time, in view of where you are with your work. Therefore, as well as taking the costs of interviewing into account, you must think carefully about your information needs. Are interviews absolutely necessary? What information could you obtain through interviews that you could not obtain through other, lower cost research and information-gathering strategies?

Look Forward and Reason Back

When you are considering setting up some interviews, it is a good idea to think in terms of the outcome you most desire. When you have completed the interviews, what sort of information and documents would you most like to have at your fingertips that you do not have now? This question is critically important to ask. The answer you give will help you determine the people you should interview, the appropriate way to conduct the interviews, and how best to record them. Consider two scenarios.

In the first scenario, you are working with a team of policy analysts who are preparing a report on state health expenditures and the possibilities that exist for reallocating resources among current programs. You have been asked to investigate how local health clinics have changed their practices in response to budget cuts made several months ago. You are expected to write a paper on this topic that will be used as the basis for a section of the broader report. Interviewing top administrators of several local health clinics could yield useful information. Further, these people might be able to refer you to one or two other people in each clinic who could give you more information. Given your brief, your ideal outcome would be a descriptive list setting out each of the ways that clinics have changed their practices. You would also want to give a sense of the scope of these changes and the extent to which separately and in combination they have produced negative or positive effects. It is unlikely that you would want to quote directly any of your interview subjects. The knowledge and impressions obtained in the interviews should be sufficient for you to summarize and give assessments of the changed practices. The necessary interviews can be conducted either by telephone or in person. In view of your informational needs, taping and transcribing the interviews would probably not add much value to the exercise and might be a waste of time.

In the second scenario, you have been asked to write a policy report documenting the ways parents of children with special needs organize their time and coordinate visits to specialists and other service providers. The report has been commissioned because some health professionals have observed that appointments for these children are often missed or that parents bring their children late. Here, your ideal outcome would be to have sufficient evidence to be able to give your readers a clear sense of the lives of parents of special-needs children. Meeting with the parents, and interviewing them face-to-face, would give you more insights into their lives than would a telephone interview. Taking notes while the parents talk could be distracting and lead you to miss some of the nuances of their responses to your questions. Thus, having transcripts of your interviews with, say, ten parents would provide a rich source of information for you to draw on. Being able to directly quote from the parents would give your report depth, and it would allow you to illustrate common problems that you heard about. Your information needs here suggest that taping and transcribing the interviews would contribute greatly to the project.

FIGURING OUT THE LOGISTICS

Before you begin a series of interviews, there are a number of matters that you should focus on. Regardless of whether you are conducting interviews by telephone or in person, you will need to pay attention to a variety of logistical issues. They include thinking about the people you would like to interview and how you will go about making contact with them. You should also think about how to collect background information that will help you to ask the right questions of the right people. Finally, you should carefully consider the amount of time you can devote to interviewing and the period of time over which you can conduct the interviews. Interviewing can often take a lot of time, not because you spend long in the actual interactions but because it takes time and patience to locate people and to then establish a mutually agreeable time to talk.

Identify Potential Interviewees

By the time that you have decided that there is value in conducting interviews, you will likely have amassed a fair amount of information on the topic of interest to you. If your work has been thorough, it will help you identify people or organizations to approach with the goal of setting up interviews. Once you begin to get a sense that interviews might be helpful for your work, start making a point of asking potentially knowledgeable people for suggestions about who you might begin with. The more accurately you can target the people you seek to interview, the better. You do not want to waste time interviewing the wrong people. It is usually good to begin your interviews with the most accessible people, sequencing your interviews with the intention of interviewing the busiest—and, perhaps, most senior—people only after you have acquired a lot of basic knowledge from others. Regardless of the particular order, the overriding concern should be to interview people who can give you the information you need in the most accurate way.

Often, you will need to rely on the "snowball" technique to identify potential interviewees. This involves asking people who you are interviewing to recommend other people you should talk with. As with building a snowball, you need to have some material—some interviewees—to start with. But once you begin asking for referrals, you will quickly build a larger interviewee pool.

When you first make contact with potential interviewees, you should give them a sense of how long the interview will last. Typically, interviews should last no longer than about forty-five minutes. Since this is a fair amount of time out of anyone's day, you should always offer to conduct your interviews at times that are most suitable for the interviewees.

Build Interview Files

Before you talk to anyone, you should try to obtain appropriate background information on them or the issues that you wish to speak with them about. It is useful to place this information in files, one each for every person to be interviewed. Of course, you could readily get ahead of yourself here, and spend too long on acquiring background information instead of setting up and conducting the actual interviews. But you can save time in the interview and focus on obtaining the right information from your interviewees if you have previously familiarized yourself with readily available information that is pertinent to the issues you intend to cover and the questions you plan to ask.

Establish a Time Line

If it matters a great deal that you speak to specific individuals, then you should expect that it might take up to three weeks before you will get a chance to talk with any one of them. Sometimes you will be lucky and people will be able to meet with you, or talk with you on the telephone, right away. But often it takes a while to set up an interview, simply because everyone is busy. Given this, you should avoid trying to conduct interviews when you have a pressing deadline. By giving yourself a few weeks over which to space your interviews you are more likely to get to talk with the people you have targeted. Giving yourself some lead time also opens the possibility that you will be able to arrange your interviews in clusters, so that you can conduct three or four per day over a period of two to three days.

QUESTION DESIGN AND SEQUENCING

The quality of your questions will dictate the quality of your interviews. No matter how well everything else goes, if you ask the wrong questions, you might as well not have conducted the interviews. Therefore, you must develop a well-planned interview guide.

Prioritize

You should think carefully about the set of questions you wish to cover in your interviews. Once you have made a basic list, you should go over it, figuring out which questions are the most important and which are the least important. In most interview situations, you will not get a chance to ask more than six to ten questions designed to evoke a reasonably complex response. Given that, you should make sure that the interview guide is organized in a way that ensures that the most important questions will be asked.

Write Short Questions

Interviews are built around six questions: who, what, when, where, why, and how. Often *how* and *why* questions are the most important. You should avoid situations where you find yourself mixing questions with explanations. I suggest that you write short questions. In some instances, you will need to preface your question with an explanation or a description of a situation you would like to ask about. That is fine, so long as these perfunctory comments are also brief. You should never ask two questions at the same time. Getting into the discipline of writing short questions will help you to avoid confusing the interviewee. Confusing questions are likely to lead to confusing responses. You do not want that.

Sequence Your Questions Carefully

Interviews work best when you follow a simple pattern. Think of the interview as being divided into three sectors: the first quarter, the middle half, and the final quarter. You should plan to start with easy questions. For example, ask people how long they have been in their current positions and what positions they held before; that is a good way to ease them into the interview. Once you have asked these straightforward, factual questions, move on to more substantive questions that constitute the heart of the interview. Often, you can improve the quality of the responses you obtain by ordering your topics so that they stimulate people's memories in logical ways. For example, if you want to know the history of the implementation of a particular policy reform, you might ask, "When did you and your colleagues begin to implement the new screening process?" You might then ask, "What problems did you encounter in that early stage?" Next you might ask, "What stands out as the next milestone in the implementation process?"

In general, you should reserve the middle half of the interview for all your major questions. If you have questions that are likely to be sensitive and make the interviewee uneasy, push them closer to the end of this section. By doing this, you are likely to reduce the possibility that the interviewee's reactions to them will influence his or her responses to other key questions. In addition, leaving them until later in the interview gives you an opportunity to capitalize on the rapport that you will have established earlier. A question that would evoke a bristly response at the start of the interview might evoke a more measured one toward the end. Plan to keep the final quarter of the interview for lighter questions and efforts to bring the interview to a satisfactory close.

PREPARATION

Beyond setting up the interviews and determining the questions that you will ask, there are a variety of details to attend to before every interview. Some of these details may seem minor or trivial, until you forget about them and problems arise. Because you can never tell in advance exactly how an interview is likely to go, you should strive to eliminate as much uncertainty as possible by attending to those details that are within your control.

Prepare Your Interviewees

Before you conduct each interview, you should make sure that the interviewee has a clear sense of the sort of questions you will be asking. You should also tell people why you have selected to interview them in particular. The more that the interviewee knows in advance, the better able he or she will be to think about the issues at stake and the kind of answers and information that could be of most value to you. Sometimes, it will make sense to share the interview guide, or a version of it, with your interviewees ahead of your interviews.

Create an Interview Kit

No matter whether you are conducting telephone or in-person interviews, it is important that you have a kit of items ready in advance. You should have your question guide ready at hand, plenty of notepaper, and all necessary items for recording the interview. For each interview, you should have a separate sheet of paper listing the name of the person to be interviewed, the time and place of the interview, and all relevant contact details.

Check Details

Before every interview, take time to check that you are thoroughly prepared. If you have to go some distance to meet a person, be sure to give yourself plenty of time to get there. Plan to arrive early, so you can locate the exact meeting place and still have time to relax and collect your thoughts before the interview. Even if you are conducting telephone interviews, there are details to check in advance. For example, you might be planning an interview with someone who is in a different time zone. It is important that you allow for this. Calling someone an hour late is not a great way to start things off. Because of the ease with which we can now send messages and share documents by e-mail, we can readily check details with people before an interview takes place.

The Interview

Though all interviews are different, you can do a number of things in all your interviews to increase the likelihood that they will go well. Near the end of this chapter, I discuss several strategies that you can use to improve your conversation skills and, hence, make the most of all of your interactions with others, regardless of whether you are in a formal interview setting. But for now, I will discuss more procedural matters. Most of these apply to both telephone and in-person interviews.

Set the Scene

Although you will have previously given your interviewees a sense of the topics to be covered, when you are in the interview situation it is important to begin with a brief overview of what you want to know and why you want to know it. Taking a minute or so to cover these matters is a way for you to put yourself at ease in the new situation and also to help the interviewee prepare mentally to answer your questions. At this scene-setting stage, also make sure to do all you can to make yourself and the interviewee comfortable. That means you may want to ensure that you are in a private space where interruptions will be minimized. During this time before the interview begins you should tell the interviewee what you intend to do with the information you obtain. You should state whether you plan to record the interview. You should also advise the person whether you intend to quote the interviewee directly. If you offer confidentiality, explain how you will guarantee it.

Follow the Question Guide

Try to follow your question guide fairly closely during your interviews. At the start, ask questions that the interviewee can readily answer without much effort. Once you have the person talking, you may want to diverge from the order of the question guide if you assess that the responses you are getting are useful and worth pursuing. It is important, however, to keep the interview on track, and that means pulling the interviewee back to your questions when you get a sense that he or she is drifting off subject.

Following the question guide is also critical for ensuring that you ask every important question. This might sound odd, but it is surprising how often interviews will move along in ways that make it hard for you—the interviewer—to keep control of the content and to keep track of what questions are yet to be asked.

Probe for Clarification

Often a question will elicit a relatively short response where a longer response is desired. This situation might arise because the interviewee is uncertain as to how much information you actually want. At these times, you will have to ask a subquestion, or a probe. For example, suppose you ask the administrator of a local health clinic a broad question: "How have your staff responded to the recent budget cuts?" She might respond, "Well, none of them have been happy about this, but they have been coping." At this point, you should probe for clarification by asking, "What would be some examples of the ways they have been coping?" As the responses are given, you might probe further by asking, "Do you have any other examples?" Or you might find one of the examples particularly intriguing and state, "That last example suggests that people have been learning from each other. Can you think of other examples of that?" Clearly, you will want to limit the amount of effort you put into squeezing out answers to each of your questions. Probing for clarification, however, is an important way to keep the interview going and to ensure that you gain the kind of information that you are seeking.

Sometimes there is merit in returning to a question later in the interview that you first asked near the beginning. For example, if you think that the initial response to a question was somewhat inadequate, you might seek to gain a more thorough response by approaching the question in a different way once you have established more rapport with the interviewee.

Let the Interviewee Do the Talking

The interview is a valuable opportunity for you to acquire information. Although you should strive to develop a good rapport with the interviewee, do not do this by talking at length yourself. The interview is of most value to you when the interviewee is doing the talking. Your task is to elicit and guide the talk. Silences can be an important part of the process, providing spaces for your interviewees to collect their thoughts. A good rule of thumb is to strive toward having the interviewee talk for about 80 percent of the time, while you talk for 20 percent. Obviously, there is no hard-and-fast rule here, but you should try to monitor the situation and limit what you say, without making the interviewee uncomfortable.

Keep an Appropriate Record

How you choose to record the interview will depend greatly on the use you plan to make of the information that you acquire. At a minimum, you should strive to make good notes. In some instances, you will want to use a tape recorder or even a video recorder. The quality of the record you keep will ultimately dictate the value that you derive from the interviews. At the same time, you should ensure that your method of recording or taking notes does not detract from the quality of your interaction with the interviewee. If recording makes the interviewee nervous and less inclined to talk, try to work without it. If taking copious notes limits your ability to make eye contact with the interviewee and ask coherent questions, using a tape recorder is definitely advisable.

Know When to End

When you judge that you have acquired all the information that you need from an interview, stop asking questions. There will be times when you have an interviewee who is quite content to keep talking for a while. In such instances, try to find ways to bring things to a close. Because interviewing is time consuming, there is no point is stretching it out unnecessarily. At the end of each interview, always make a point of thanking your interviewees for making the time to talk with you and for sharing their knowledge, experiences, and thoughts with you.

Capture "Free" Information

Interviewees often will offer additional information once the interview has come to a close. You should listen closely for such "free" information. It is also a good idea to end your interviews by asking, "Is there anything that I forgot to ask?" or "Can you think of anyone else I should talk to about these issues?" People will quite frequently offer helpful answers to these questions, pointing you in the direction of issues worth pursuing and people worth contacting.

AFTER THE INTERVIEW

The actions you take following an interview will have a considerable bearing upon the value you derive from it. Typically, you should expect to spend a lot more time on postinterview activities than on conducting the interview itself.

Work with Your Notes and Recordings

Depending on the goal of the interview, at the end you will have some combination of notes and a recording to work with. The next task is to take that material and transform it into a coherent text. What you plan to do with the interview material—how you see it informing your broader project work—will dictate your approach to preserving it.

If you conducted the interview without recording it, it is vital that you immediately take time to review your notes and begin filling in the inevitable blanks in your written record. In many cases, you will find it helpful to type up notes, adding to them from memory as you go. One way to structure the write-up is to use your questions as headings for each section of text. When you are working from notes, strive to develop an interview report that conveys the general sense of what the informant said. With good notes, you can train yourself to recall a fair amount of the subject matter of the interview.

If you recorded the interview, you can follow one of two strategies. The first is simply to transcribe the entire interview verbatim. This is particularly important when you want to compare across interviews and when you expect to quote liberally from what the interviewee said. Transcribing an interview, however, can be extremely time consuming if you do it yourself and expensive if you have somebody else do it for you. If you are going to engage in full transcription, you should have a clear rationale for doing so. Once the transcribing has been done, review the record to check for errors. Think also of adding notes from your written record, so the transcript contains as much useful information as possible.

A second strategy for working with the recorded interview involves treating it as an aid for the production of notes that summarize the information obtained. When you work in this way, you might still transcribe quotes from the interviewee. You would do so selectively, however, with the purpose of illustrating the broader summary points you are making. If you do not intend to use direct quotes from your interviewee, this approach to working with the recording is taken primarily to ensure that your summary of what you learned in the interview is as accurate as possible.

Thank Your Interviewees

Interviewing requires time and energy on your part, but good interviews also take their toll on the interviewees. Therefore, it is important that you acknowledge their efforts. Of course, you can do this as you are concluding the interview, but, wherever possible, you should also take the time to follow up in the week after the interview. Sending an e-mail message or a brief letter is all that is required. You never know if you might need to be in touch with the person again. Aside from that, though, showing appreciation to the people who help you with your work is just good manners. Sometimes, the people you interview will ask to see the outcome of your work. Where possible, think of ways to share your findings with them. When you do this, you should think of their needs, which might be quite different from your own or from those of your immediate client. A brief summary of your findings would suffice for most people.

Assess Your Questions and Your Interviewee Selection Criteria

Once you have produced your interview notes or transcription, review it with the purpose of evaluating the overall quality of the information that you obtained. During this process, you will become aware of what questions elicited too little or too much information. This awareness is useful for helping you to make a conscious effort to pursue particular topics—and, perhaps, skip others—in subsequent interviews.

When you have a clear sense of the information you were seeking from your interviews, it is easier for you to determine how much value you have obtained from each one. Suppose you have conducted three good interviews and obtained a great deal of relevant information. If the subsequent two interviews yield no new information, you should stop the interview phase of your work. Alternately, if you find that some interviewees appear much more informative than others, try to develop ways of judging who are likely to be the best informants in the pool of people yet to be interviewed. At this point, try to rank the people you are yet to interview and make it your top priority to get interviews with those who you judge likely to be the most informative. Of course, you do not want to annoy people by canceling interviews at the last minute, but if you really judge that more interviews will be a waste of your time, canceling is the right thing to do.

CONVERSATION STRATEGIES

Although interviews represent a distinctive—and quite formal—type of interpersonal communication, we can improve our interviewing style by making ourselves more self-conscious of some of the actions we can take to promote good conversation. As an interviewer, you want people to feel at ease sharing information with you. Therefore, you need to find effective ways to get people to talk. Formulating your questions in the right way, practicing active listening, and showing understanding are the three most important ways to keep people engaged and willing to talk with you.

Ask Questions That Get People Talking

The key to getting people to talk is to ask them questions. It is important, however, to distinguish between closed-ended and open-ended questions. Closed-ended questions call for short responses, like "yes" or "no." When you begin talking to someone, avoid asking too many closed-ended questions. Of course, you will need to ask some, but try to intersperse them with open-ended questions. Questions that are open-ended cannot be answered with a simple "yes" or "no."

For example, suppose that you want to get somebody to talk with you about his or her work on health care policy. You understand that they have been involved recently in exploring state efforts to ensure insurance coverage for all children. A closed-ended way to start a conversation would go like this: "So, am I right in thinking that you are working on health insurance for children?" Unless the other person takes your cue to talk, his response could be just "yes" or "no," and you both might feel rather awkward. In contrast, consider this open-ended starter question: "So, what policy issues are you working on at the moment?" The question is quite broad, requiring something other than a one-word response. If you are interested in learning more about the person's work on health insurance for children, you can easily narrow the focus of the conversation with follow-up questions. Without saying too much, open-ended questions can quickly get people to talk with you about topics that interest them. A simple *why?* often evokes long responses.

Practice Active Listening

If you want people to talk to you, you need to be a good listener. One sign of being a good listener is making meaningful eye contact. As someone speaks to you, nod your head as a sign of understanding and occasionally signal that you are following what is being said by uttering "yes" or "uh-huh." Try to avoid interrupting people or finishing their sentences for them. Not only is that frustrating for the people speaking to you, but it means that you stop them from saying what might really have been on their mind. Often, when people are speaking to us, we let our internal tapes begin to play. That means, while others are talking, we are focusing not on what they are saying but what we want to say in response. It is better to try to hear someone out. Only when they have finished speaking should you begin to formulate your response. If you need to stall for time, you can begin by making a statement such as, "I like the way you've described that . . ." or, "Yes, I can see your point of view." As an interviewer and as a conversationalist, you can gain a lot from others by paying attention to what is said, encouraging exploration of a topic, observing, asking clarifying questions, and taking the time to paraphrase what has been said.

Show Understanding

People are most likely to open up to those who they perceive as being genuinely concerned with what they have to say. To show understanding, you must demonstrate that you can see the situation from the other person's point of view. Active listening is an important prerequisite for showing understanding. For example, by listening carefully to what somebody else has to say, you will find yourself in a position to give responses that show a genuine effort on your part to see their point of view. You can express understanding by responding to statements with comments beginning with phrases such as these:

- Could it be that . . .
- Maybe I'm wrong, but . . .
- I get the impression that . . .
- You're thinking that . . .
- From your point of view . . .
- So you figure that . . .

Listening closely to what others have to say and then responding with an effort to summarize what you have heard indicates that you are seriously interested in understanding what has been said. Practicing this skill will help you become a better interviewer. It will also help you to become a better colleague and associate, someone with whom others enjoy engaging.

Summary

As policy analysts, we often find ourselves needing to interview informants in order to tap their situated knowledge. This process can create anxiety and be both frustrating and laborious. In the midst of conducting a series of interviews, it is difficult to devote quality time to other tasks. This is why you should interview only when you are certain that it is the best way for you to acquire the information you need. Even then, you should be careful not to set overly high expectations as to what you can achieve through interviewing. Wildavsky (1993, 58) has suggested that interviewing can never be done perfectly. "The best that can be expected is not too bad or better still, not so bad as before." Of course, there is much we can do to improve the ways that we conduct interviews. In this chapter, I have set out some guidelines that should help you make the most of the interviews that you conduct. The better we get at interviewing, the better the quality of the information that we will have to work with. And sometimes we will be surprised. With good questions and articulate interviewees you can strike gold, obtaining insights that will do much to build your expert knowledge and improve your policy advice.

Skill-Building Checklist

- Interviewing is time consuming and can often be expensive. Before conducting interviews, you must convince yourself that this would represent the best use of your time and resources, in light of where you are with your work.
- As you plan your interviews, think in terms of the outcome you most desire. At the end of the process, what information and documents would you most like to have at your fingertips that you do not have now? Your answer to this question will determine the people you should interview, how you should conduct the interviews, and how best to record them.
- For each interview you should have an interview guide, setting out the questions you plan to ask. In creating the interview guide, you

should determine what questions are most important to ask and how best to sequence them.

- You should strive to develop a good rapport with your interviewees, but not by talking at length. Interviews are of most value when the interviewees do most of the talking.
- You can improve your interviewing style by learning strategies for promoting conversation. Formulating open-ended questions, practicing active listening, and showing understanding are the three most important things you can do to keep people engaged and willing to talk with you.
- With a clear sense of the information you are seeking, and by evaluating the quality of the information you have acquired so far, you can determine how much value you have obtained from your interviewing efforts. You should also always assess whether additional gains from further interviewing are likely to be large or small and then plan further work accordingly.

Discussion Ideas

- We can learn a lot by listening. By developing our listening skills, we can become better at having quality conversations with others. Good listening skills can also improve our ability to make the most of interviews. Individually, list some specific qualities that you associate with good listeners. Then, working in a small group, compare your lists and make a composite list. Next, develop examples of how you might use these good listening skills to prompt an interviewee to share knowledge with you in an interview situation. Finally, develop a response to the statement "Good listening is really all about asking good questions."
- You have begun work on a project designed to identify the ways that a city of 300,000 people funds local arts and cultural activities and to determine the value for money that citizens receive from this funding. The project manager has suggested that it would be helpful if you could "do some interviews" to gain more insights into the issue. Working with two or three other people, develop a plan that you could follow to increase the likelihood that this interviewing work will be highly beneficial to the broader project. Pay specific attention to issues of gathering background in-

formation, subject identification, and establishing contact with the subjects.

- Some authors argue that all interviews should be recorded and transcribed. Others argue that it is better to make notes at the interview and to follow up by writing up an interview narrative. List the benefits and costs associated with each strategy for preserving the information obtained in an interview. With one or two others, discuss instances where one approach would be preferred over the other. Write brief explanations for your group decisions.

FURTHER READING

Barker, Larry, and Kittie Watson. 2000. *Listen Up*. New York: St. Martin's Press.

Dilley, Patrick. 2000. "Conducting Successful Interviews: Tips for Intrepid Research." *Theory into Practice* 39:131–37.

Gorden, Raymond L. 1998. *Basic Interviewing Skills*. 2d ed. Prospect Heights, Ill.: Waveland Press.

McCracken, Grant. 1988. *The Long Interview*. Newbury Park, Calif.: Sage.

Wildavsky, Aaron. 1993. "The Open-Ended, Semistructured Interview: An (Almost) Operational Guide." In *Craftways: On the Organization of Scholarly Work*. 2d ed. New Brunswick, N.J.: Transaction Publishers, pp. 57–102.

5
...

Giving Presentations

In reflecting on what it takes to give really good presentations, I have come to realize that every time you interact with colleagues, clients and other professionals, you are actually making a type of formal presentation. I think this is an important insight, although it is not especially comforting. Those people we all admire, the ones who stand up and give off-the-cuff comments with comfortable glibness and precision of speech, are those who know that the formal presentation on a podium merely anchors one end of a spectrum of ways to communicate policy ideas. The next time you see people giving engaged, powerful presentations, try to keep an eye on them for a while after they have finished, when they're no longer on the podium. My bet is that you'll see them talking over and over about the topic of their presentation. One reason why these people are so relaxed yet so precise on the podium is that they have already made the very same policy points with the same effort at persuasion in many less formal encounters with their colleagues. In my view, this kind of constant practice, coupled with an approach to the craft that recognizes that every professional interaction is a presentation upon which we are judged, is the key to successful communication of policy ideas.

—Dr. Gregory Cline, *Program Director, Michigan Public Health Institute, Okemos, Michigan*

People often fear public speaking. We experience angst about it because, more than anything, we seek to avoid making fools of ourselves in front of others. As policy analysts, giving presentations is an important part of what we do. It is important, yet it is often underrated as an aspect of our work, and I suspect that this underrating occurs because giving presentations is viewed as something that most of us do infrequently. Ask most policy analysts how often they give presentations, compared to how often they write memos or engage in data analysis, and it is likely that they will report that they devote a comparatively limited amount of time to preparing and giving presentations. Nevertheless, the frequency with which we give presentations should not be regarded as the basis for judging the importance of this aspect of our work. To have impact, policy analysts must develop skills as excellent public speakers. Doubtless, even the most experienced policy analysts will still exhibit anxiety before giving important presentations. The good news is that we can do a lot to reduce the possibilities of things going wrong in our presentations. With sufficient practice, many people even come to *seek out* opportunities for speaking in public.

Here, following the lesson contained in Erving Goffman's pathbreaking sociological work, *The Presentation of Self in Everyday Life* (1956), I suggest that as policy analysts we should become much more conscious of the ways in which we routinely present ourselves to those around us and of how others judge us by our presentations. Most policy analysts are unlikely to give more than a handful of formal presentations each year. These presentations include public lectures or conference presentations, where we stand at the front of a room and all eyes are upon us. Aside from these really significant presentations, there are many times when we present ourselves to others in more or less formal ways. How well we prepare and deliver these presentations can have a considerable bearing upon how others think about us, the seriousness with which they engage our ideas, and, in the end, the influence that we can hope to have upon the policy debates that we care about.

It is common for people to view their oral presentations as subordinate to their written work. Such a way of viewing things is intuitively reasonable. After all, many of our oral presentations do involve introducing others to topics or to analytical investigations and findings that we have previously devoted a lot of time to working on and writing about. At academic conferences, I have seen seasoned policy scholars give presentations where their "speaking notes" consisted of the full text of their conference papers, strategically marked up with highlighter.

Here, the connection between the written work and the oral presentation is obvious, but I consider this to be a poor approach to preparing for a presentation of your work. Although it is true that many of our presentations will draw on material contained in our written work, it is vital that we treat preparing notes for a presentation and writing the text of a paper or a report as fundamentally different activities. Simply extracting a paragraph here or there from our written work does not produce effective presentations. To the extent that people do this, they seriously underestimate the thought, preparation, and practice that must go into developing a captivating oral presentation.

To introduce you to the people skill of giving presentations, I first review the elements of communication. Following that, I discuss effective ways of going about developing a formal talk, such as a lecture or a conference presentation. Even though many policy analysts will present themselves and their work more often in less formal ways, I believe that taking the time to think seriously about the elements of an effective formal presentation is an excellent starting point for considering how to give a broad range of presentations. Ultimately, I want to suggest that there are some very good reasons why, as policy analysts, we should treat most of our interactions with others as instances where we are presenting ourselves and, hence, giving presentations. Reporting back information in a meeting, introducing ourselves to clients, and interviewing people are all instances where attending to our personal presentation style can have important consequences for our ongoing effectiveness as policy analysts. How well we perform in these situations and when giving formal presentations will depend a lot on how much time we have given to reflecting on the nature of the situation and appropriately preparing ourselves for it.

Maybe some lucky individuals have sufficient personal savoir faire to give effective presentations without premeditation. For the rest of us, I contend that the effectiveness of our presentations will always be improved through careful forethought and preparation. What we would most like, of course, is for observers of our carefully planned presentations to judge them as both seemingly effortless and superb. How might we increase our prospects of achieving that outcome? On this we can do no better than to subscribe to the mantra of all stellar performers, be they musicians, cooks, sports players, or speakers. *Practice, practice, practice!* As policy analysts seeking to achieve excellence in our everyday lives, we can learn a great deal from reflecting on what it takes to give effective presentations.

THE ELEMENTS OF COMMUNICATION

Because we are always communicating with others in one way or another, it is easy to take for granted the nature of the communication process. In taking the process for granted, however, we run the risk of overlooking the ways that our actions and the assumptions that underlie them serve to support or undermine our ability to connect with others. Figure 5-1 presents a simple model of the communication process. This model is so simple that it can be used to characterize even nonverbal communication. A sender generates a message. The message is received and interpreted by the perceiver who, in response, may take a variety of actions, some of which will produce feedback for the sender of the message. For example, you visit a friend and press the doorbell (sender emits message). If all goes well, your friend will hear the doorbell ring (message received) and will answer the door (feedback). If your friend does not respond, you try sending the message again. By focusing on the model presented in figure 5-1, and the elements of communication depicted within it, we can begin to build our understanding of presentations as a form of communication and the factors that influence the degree to which both the presenter and the audience deem a presentation successful.

As a presenter, you have an objective. What response do you want to invoke from your audience as a result of them hearing your talk? If you are giving a presentation as part of a formal job interview, your

Figure 5-1. The Communication Process

objective is to convince your audience that you are the candidate they want. Having clarified this objective, you can begin to sort out the nature of the message that you hope to send. The message, if it is to have the intended effect, will be planned in a manner that recognizes the concerns and interests of your audience. You will think of ways to capture the attention of your audience so that they focus on what it is that you have to say and how you say it. The message you will communicate cannot be separated from who you are. When you speak, the audience will make judgments of you based on many things other than the words you use. In view of this, you will need to think of ways that you can play down those aspects of who you are and how you present yourself that could create unnecessary barriers to the achievement of your objective. You will also need to think about ways of playing to your strengths as a communicator. The more consciously you consider these issues of why you are speaking, who you are speaking to, what you need to say, and how you need to say it, the greater the likelihood that you will achieve your objective.

I am next going to discuss in more detail the kind of actions that you should take when striving to give a successful formal presentation. In many ways, this discussion can be seen as an effort to make explicit and explore more carefully a variety of issues that are raised when we think about the model of the communication process depicted in figure 5-1. To return to the analogy of ringing the doorbell, think of all the possible ways that this simple means of communication can break down. You might not press the doorbell hard enough. You might press it hard enough but the bell is in need of repair. You might succeed in getting the bell to ring but your friend is distracted by other sounds and does not hear it. If communication failures can happen in such simple, straightforward situations like this, it is clear that the possibilities for things to go wrong, even in subtle ways, can be quite high in a complicated situation such as when you are giving a formal presentation to an audience of people whom you have never met before. To increase the likelihood that your message will be perceived and understood in the ways that you intend, it is important that you pay attention to the nature of the communication process that you are initiating. What you most want is to have the whole situation wired for success ahead of time. There is a lot you can do to move things in that direction.

THE FORMAL PRESENTATION

Consider the following scenario. Word has got around about the project work that you are currently engaged in. As a result, you have been invited to give a presentation on your policy topic at an evening meeting of a local association whose members include a wide variety of professionals working in the corporate, government, and nonprofit sectors, as well as the media. You will appear on a panel along with two other speakers who represent groups having somewhat different—but not necessarily conflicting—interests in this policy area. You have been asked to talk for about twenty minutes and to also participate in a chaired, after-dinner question-and-answer session with your copresenters and the audience. Assume that your superiors at your place of work have agreed to your participation. They do not mind how you approach the talk, but naturally they care that, whether you like it or not, you will be perceived as representing the organization. How should you prepare?

Learn about the Audience and the Venue

When an invited speaker and an organizer are working together to set up an event, they typically communicate back and forth by telephone or e-mail several times. During these initial interactions, you should try to learn as much as possible about the audience and the venue. Here are some key questions that you should ask:

- How formal is the event?
- What is the organizer's expectation about what you will contribute?
- How much specific detail is the audience likely to want?
- Might there be a problem of overlap between your approach to the topic and the approach taken by the other invited speakers?
- Will you be expected to talk while seated at a head table, or will there be a podium?
- Will the room have equipment for the presentation of visual aids? If so, will you be expected to make use of it?
- Are the other speakers planning to use visual aids?

Answers to these questions will provide you with a sense of the parameters that you will be working with. Thus, before you even begin to think about the content of your talk and how you will organize it, you will know how long you will be expected to talk for, what people will want you to talk about, and how detailed you should get in the talk. You will also have a good sense of how formally you should dress for the occasion, how you will physically position yourself with respect to the audience, and how you might make use of technology to support your presentation. As trivial as some of these details might seem (for example, whether you will be seated or standing when delivering your talk), knowledge of them can give you a real advantage as you prepare your presentation.

Determine Your Objective

Whenever you are scheduled to give a presentation, it is likely that you will devote a reasonable amount of your time to preparing and giving it. This is time that you could otherwise spend on a variety of alternative activities. To minimize the opportunity costs of taking on this task, you need to make sure that the time you set aside for preparing and delivering it is well spent. And, because doing a poor job of giving a presentation can do damage to your reputation, you should make every effort to reduce the risk that this moment of public exposure will be counterproductive to your work as a policy analyst. Thinking carefully about what is at stake in this presentation and how you could benefit from doing the best possible job with it will put you on track toward making the most of the opportunity before you.

What do you want to achieve through this presentation? Naturally, you want to convey information to your audience, but you should be able to say more than this. Consider another question. What would you most like to have members of the audience do as a result of hearing your talk? Make a list of potential answers to this question. Then think about which of these possible outcomes matter most to you. Your objective in giving this presentation should be to maximize the likelihood that these outcomes will occur.

Having determined your objective for your presentation, you can begin to think about the primary message that you will seek to convey. What do you want to say in this presentation? (How will you use words to achieve your desired objective?) It might sound silly or redundant to say that a speaker must determine his or her message before speaking, but this is critical. Focusing on the message you want to convey is a great way to begin prioritizing the material that you could potentially intro-duce to your audience. Try to identify what material is critical to make your presentation convincing and what sort of material—while rele-vant—could be left out in the interests of avoiding bombarding the au-dience with too much information. With your objective defined, you should work toward ensuring that everything about the presentation you give is "on message."

Play to the Interests of Your Audience

Remember the doorbell analogy. Your efforts at communication fail com-pletely if the people you want to reach do not perceive your message cor-rectly and do not respond as you would like. As a speaker, you must strive to make sure that your audience receives the message you want it to receive. You want it to open the door, but if this is to happen, you must think carefully about the interests of your audience and how you might play to, or awaken, those interests. Surprisingly, many speakers often forget about the interests of their audience. Consider the absurdity of this. Forgetting about the interests of your audience is like forgetting to ring the doorbell when you arrive at the home of a friend, or believ-ing that there is no need to ring the doorbell because your friend will in-tuitively understand that you have arrived and that you are standing out-side the door. Is your friend at fault when you are left standing awkwardly in the cold?

I have occasionally heard professors complain that their students do not seem to understand or even be particularly interested in what they have to say in their lectures. Hearing this, I used to assume this meant the brilliant professor deserved sympathy. Then I began visiting schools and talking to school principals as part of my research. And one day a principal said to me, "You know, you have to meet the students at their level. If the students aren't learning, then you have to rethink you own strategy as a teacher. When it comes down to it, if the students aren't learning, you're not teaching." Whether we are giving lectures to students, teaching in small groups, or giving formal presentations at spe-cial events or at conferences, there is a vital lesson to be learned from this statement. Usually, we do not get to select the people who we are going to speak with. This means that we will rarely have what we might consider to be an "ideal" audience. Because of this, we need to work hard at the process of communication. The challenge is to find ways to connect with your audience so that those you are addressing will get excited about the topic, even if they have thought little about it in the past. (Remember, there was a time when you, too, knew little about the topic. What got you excited about it?)

Before you give a presentation, think very carefully about the members of your audience, their knowledge level, their expectations, and their needs as listeners. Usually, you will want to give a presentation that somehow serves to change the way your audience thinks about your topic and, perhaps, about you. You want to persuade these people that you have something important to say and worth remembering. To have any hope of doing this, you will need to pitch your message in a way that captures their interest. You can lose people by talking down to them (assuming they are more ignorant than they are) and by talking above their heads (assuming they have knowledge that they might not have). In either case, you run the risk of coming across as arrogant or self-important. Strive to build bridges to your audience. Because every audience is likely to be somewhat unique, think carefully about ways to customize your presentational style every time that you work with a different audience.

Think Carefully about Content and Structure

You have taken the time to learn as much as possible about the parameters of your presentation and the venue. You have thought carefully about what you would most like to achieve through giving this presentation. You have considered the likely backgrounds and interests of your audience and the level at which you should present what you have to say. These efforts to gather relevant information about the presentation and the audience will give you a lot more ability than you would otherwise have had to make the most of this opportunity to give a formal talk. Now what?

Next you need to think carefully about the content of your talk and how you will structure it. When you give your presentation, the content and structure will be difficult to discern from each other. But in the planning stages, that need not be the case, and I suggest that you think of the two as separable. From your day-to-day work on your specialist policy subject, you will have built up a considerable store of knowledge and understanding of the topic that you have been invited to speak about.

As you plan your talk, begin by listing some of the things that you feel you definitely want to address. You might think of this as a kind of brainstorming activity. Try to get as many thoughts on paper as possible. Once you have done this, look at your list and think about the kind of argument that you want to make in your talk. In beginning to develop your argument, ask yourself these questions:

- How have I been thinking about this policy topic?
- Why is that a useful way to think about it?
- What are some other approaches that people have taken in thinking about this topic?
- What distinguishes my approach from those others?
- Why should people find my approach persuasive?
- What aspects of my approach could generate controversy?
- How could I get the audience to engage with my argument?

Having determined the basic content and the argument that you wish to make, you can begin to think seriously about the structure of your presentation. Structured presentations that flow logically from point to point are easier to follow and, thus, are more persuasive. By thinking about structure, you force yourself to think more strategically about the content of your presentation and how to introduce it most effectively. To begin considering structure, think of your presentation as having three key parts: the beginning, the middle, and the end. You want to start strong, letting your audience know who you are, why you are there, and what you are going to do. Likewise, you want to end strong. You might even think of the end as being like the chorus of a song. You end with the chorus; emphasizing your message, so your audience leaves "whistling your tune."

One way to structure a presentation effectively is to build it around key questions. In the introduction, list them. (Keep the list to no more than four or five questions.) Then go through the presentation, raising and answering each question in turn. You can try to show how one answer leads logically to the next question. At the end of your presentation, summarize your points and the implications of what you have said.

Another effective aid to developing the structure of your presentation is to think in terms of patterns. For example, if you introduce an example or a puzzle near the start of your talk, think about how you might return to that same example or puzzle in the end section. As well as thinking about the larger structural elements of your presentation, it is also useful to think about how to structure each section. Often, people suggest that you should find ways to work with sets of three points. Thus, if you make a particular claim, you might then say, "There are three reasons why this is important to consider. First . . . second . . . third. . . ." Aside from giving your presentation more structure, working in threes like this can be helpful as you practice and seek to memorize parts of what you want to say. And, of course, because working with sets of points like this aids in your recall, inevitably, it is good for building the recall of your audience.

Keep Things Simple

You should pitch your message so that it is well understood and interesting to the majority of the people in your audience. Because policy analysts often deal with quite technical subjects and in technical ways, it is tempting to want to show off your technical abilities in a presentation. It is also a temptation to provide enough details that the technically most sophisticated members of your audience will not dismiss what you have to say as simplistic. When we present ourselves orally, we have to keep things simple. Suppose that you have written several reports on your speaking topic in the past. Undoubtedly, those reports will be great resources for you to refer to as you develop your presentation, but you cannot get too complicated in a presentation. The key is to engage and interest as many members of your audience as possible. If you can win people over during your presentation, they will be eager to read your written work later. So think of the presentation as a way to excite people and get them interested. Presentations are not the place to introduce every wrinkle of an issue or problem. If people want additional details, they can ask for them in the question-and-answer session.

Break Things Up

People have short attention spans, even people who are interested in policy issues and people who hold doctoral degrees. You need to factor this into the design of your presentation. Studies show that people are most likely to recall the start and the finish of something. Attention slumps in

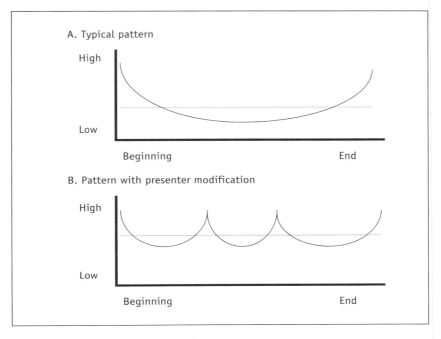

A. Typical pattern

B. Pattern with presenter modification

Figure 5-2. Audience Attention

the middle part of presentations (see figure 5-2A). To the extent that attention slumps in the middle part of a presentation, the average level of
attention for the whole talk will be quite low (see the horizontal line in
figure 5-2A). Knowing this, you can use a few "interventions" to keep up
the audience attention. One way is to break your presentation into parts.
If you have three parts to your presentation, then you will have four periods where audience attention is heightened (see figure 5-2B). By breaking things up, you can significantly raise the average level of attention
that you will receive from the audience over the span of the whole talk
(note that the horizontal line in figure 5-2B is higher than the same line
in figure 5-2A).

　　How can you break things up? Asking questions is a good way to
do this. You might think about introducing a new part of your presentation by asking a question. Even asking the question with the intention
of going on to answer it yourself (as opposed to seeking responses from
the audience) can be a good way to capture audience attention. In formal presentations, the typical expectation is that you will not switch to

a question time or other kinds of discussion-creating activities in the midst of things. By knowing that asking a rhetorical question will raise the attention of your audience, however, you can begin to think creatively about subtly breaking up your talk with the purpose of recapturing sagging attention. Stopping momentarily to have a handout distributed through the audience would be a low-key way to build a break into your talk. Stepping out from behind the podium and walking out into the audience area might be another way to simulate a break. For example, I have occasionally simulated a break by placing a short quote on a slide and then walking out into the audience space and reading the quote out loud from within the audience. The overall presentation remains formal and fairly seamless, but an action like this can nonetheless serve as a transition that helps to keep the audience engaged.

Strive to Build Audience Recall

Breaking up a presentation is a good way to increase average levels of audience attention. If people are paying attention during your presentation, they will be better able to recall afterward what you had to say. There are, however, additional ways to increase the likelihood that what you have to say in your talk with be remembered later. One way is to begin your presentation by making a statement that will capture your audience's imagination, that will spark their interest and get them engaged. This will be an easier task if you have already thought carefully about your audience and the sort of backgrounds and interests that members of the audience share. Presenters often find it useful to use the opening part of their talk to say something about how they became captivated by their topic and how they have come to think about it. Showing your personal interest in your topic and your enthusiasm for it can be very good for helping members of the audience imagine their way into the world of ideas and issues that you are seeking to introduce. Taking this approach, you give your audience reasons to listen closely to what you have to say.

You can also build audience recall by, at the outset, giving an overview of what you are going to do in the presentation. For example, you could do this near the end of your introductory statement. During the presentation, it might make sense for you to refer back to this overview now and then. This is a way of keeping the audience informed of exactly how each part of your talk relates to the broader story that you are seeking to tell.

Finally, in the body of the presentation, make sure that you repeat key points regularly. Think also of unusual, captivating ways to emphasize points. Anecdotes, carefully chosen examples, and so on can help here. For example, in their book on human cognition, Nisbett and Ross (1980) argue that people are often more persuaded and captivated by presentations when the speaker works with images and examples with which audience members can easily identify. Thus, when they have presented their work to specific audiences, they have changed their examples so that they use anecdotes from the world of computing when talking to computer scientists, and so on. Even though a formal presentation often leaves little room for you to engage in dialogue or questioning and answering with your audience, you still need to think of ways to increase audience involvement.

Use Notes

When you are preparing a presentation, I suggest that you write the entire script of what you plan to say. Think of yourself as a playwright, writing the script for a one-act play with just one character, you. Writing out everything that you want to say helps you to gain a sense of mastery over your material. As you write, you can play around with structure, add new examples, and take things away. Writing your script word for word gives you a good starting point from which to determine whether your presentation will be too long or too short, whether there are lapses of logic or gaps in your argument, and whether you have made enough effort to increase audience engagement and build recall of key points.

Should you work with a word-for-word script when you give your presentation? Here, a lot will depend on the level of formality of the venue. Having observed a large number of formal presentations, I remain somewhat ambivalent about how tethered one should remain to a script during a presentation. The key benefit of word-for-word scripts is that a speaker can build a greater degree of complexity into his or her ideas and arguments than would be possible if speaking from abbreviated notes or flash cards containing key points. In addition, in highly formal situations, the word-for-word approach will ensure that, even if you are nervous, you will not forget what you have to say. The major downside of working with a word-for-word script is that you might use it as a substitute for practicing and attempting to memorize key aspects of what you have to say. People in audiences most dislike situations where they feel that a speaker is reading to them. If you have a word-for-word script, it will be harder for you to make sustained eye contact with your audience, and that can be a problem.

Some of the best formal presentations I have seen have been delivered from word-for-word notes, but it was clear that the speaker knew the subject very well. Thus, although the speakers had word-for-word scripts in front of them, they were familiar enough with the material and at ease enough with their presentational style that they could depart from the script and talk completely naturally at various points before then coming back to their prepared statement.

There is a range of steps between having a fully written-out talk followed word for word and speaking entirely without notes. No matter how you approach your presentation, it is critical that you have a very clear sense of its structure and that this structure is visible to you as you speak. The more that you practice your talk, the more at ease you will feel with your notes and how you use them.

If you support your presentation with visual aids, such as overhead slides or a PowerPoint presentation, you can ease back on your reliance on word-for-word notes. Well-developed overhead slides and Power-Point slides will serve as excellent prompts for you. If you have carefully prepared what you wish to say, these prompts will be all that you need to begin speaking naturally and without word-for-word notes on your topic. Nonetheless, in some cases you probably will still want to keep note cards with you to ensure that you cover all key points when you take this more free-form approach.

Speak Naturally

A full script for your presentation is an excellent way to ensure that you will cover all the material that you want to, build your argument effectively, and follow a tight structure. Even so, how we write and how we talk are different. Once you have written out what you want to say, I suggest that you break the script into a series of one-sentence paragraphs (broken up, of course, with headings). Taking this approach, you will quickly find if you are using too many long, complicated sentences. When giving a talk, even more so than when writing, you must think carefully about varying the length of your sentences. With your words written out sentence by sentence, try reading out what you have to say. When you come across long sentences, think of ways to break them down or to reorganize the phrasing so that the key points are emphasized. When we talk, our sentence structures are different from when we write. Your written words on the page should reflect as much as possible your natural speech patterns. When you take this approach, no matter if on the day you talk word-for-word from your script or if you work from prompts and note cards, you will come across to your audience as being polished and prepared without appearing stiff or too much like a novelist at a bookstore reading.

You must strive to speak naturally. Of course, this is difficult because for an excellent formal presentation everything should be wired; and that is the very antithesis of *natural*. Working to use word patterns and phrasing that follow your conversational speech patterns is a starting point. You should also think of ways to vary the speed of your talk. Find ways to vary the pitch of your voice. Audiences soon tire when the speaker lectures in a monotone, word-for-word, from notes that are obviously being read. You want to give a presentation that is exciting and engaging for your audience. This requires a lot of effort and forethought, but the more effort you put in, the more comfortable you will feel with your material. That will give you space to feel confident before your audience, and that confidence will allow you to speak naturally, neither too fast nor too slow. It will also allow you to maintain good eye contact with your audience and, through your body language, to convey a sense of being both passionate about your topic and at ease introducing it to others.

Always Practice

Practice your presentation. The more you practice, the better you will be at the podium. Start practicing early. Knowing that the event is coming up, you should think about potential opportunities that you could use to practice your talk in front of a "friendly" audience. For example, you might present a version of your talk, or maybe just a portion of it, to some of your colleagues during a routine meeting. You might find ways to run some of your key arguments past colleagues or friends during informal conversations, but, to the extent that your performance on this presentation really means a lot to you, you should also make sure that you can run through the whole thing at least once with friends who you know will feel comfortable giving you straight, but constructive, criticism. It is all right to "bomb" in front of a friendly, mock audience. It is not all right to do so at the real thing.

When preparing for your presentation, try to have everything set so that you know exactly what you are going to do and when you are going to do it. You do not want to go into the presentation and give yourself a surprise. Worry about everything. Being a bit nervous before a presentation is much better than being overconfident.

Make sure that you time your practice presentations. You might find that you are spending too long on points that could be cut. Shorter presentations are always better than longer ones. Most important, you should never go over time when you present. If you are asked to talk for twenty minutes, plan to cover everything in fifteen.

Dress for Success

In his study of the diffusion of innovations, Rogers (1995) documented how people tend to copy the behaviors of others with whom they feel familiar. Thus, even when bombarded with advertising about a new consumer product, members of a family are more likely to buy such a product only when someone else in the family or a close friend has bought the item first. Why is this? People are most influenced by those with whom they identify. As presenters, we can learn from this.

When I suggest that you dress for success, I do not mean that you should always dress up when giving a formal presentation. Rather, you should dress in a way that seems appropriate, given the audience you will be addressing. You want to be persuasive. With that in mind, you do not want to seem underdressed or overdressed. Actually, what you would most like is to be dressed so appropriately that audience members—if asked—would have to think quite hard to recall exactly what you wore. In the end, how you dress must not be as important as what you say. You want people to go away remembering what you said, not what you looked like. That is why I urge you to dress appropriately, given the audience you will be with. That is what I mean by dressing for success.

Think Carefully about Using Microsoft PowerPoint or Other Visual Aids

PowerPoint is a very useful tool for helping you to liven up your presentations. The color and added structure that you can achieve by using PowerPoint can greatly improve the impact of your presentations. I do, however, want to sound a note of caution. Using PowerPoint is not a substitute for thinking carefully about the kind of points raised above. PowerPoint can add considerably to a presentation that has already been well thought out. PowerPoint can quickly lose its effectiveness, and a presentation featuring it can become quite boring if you have not mastered some key general points about giving presentations. When using PowerPoint, remember to keep things simple. Use the slides sparingly, and use them to support what you have to say, as opposed to trying to have the slides convey your message for you. Providing a handout for your audience still makes sense when you are using PowerPoint. My recommendation is that you work to perfect your skills as a presenter before incorporating PowerPoint into your presentations. Taking this approach, you will be better able to utilize this software to maximum effect.

Even in cases where PowerPoint is available, it is not always advisable to use it. If you are on a panel with two other presenters and they do not use PowerPoint, it is possible that your presentational approach will seem somewhat out of place. As with dressing for success, when thinking about using visual aids, focus on what would be most appropriate in light of your audience.

Whenever you decide to make use of technology during your presentations, make sure that you arrive early to the venue and check that everything is set up correctly. It can be hugely distracting for your audience and upsetting for you, as a speaker, if the technology you planned to work with does not function correctly. Problems of this sort can be anticipated and avoided. In general, regardless of whether you are planning to use technology, I would suggest that it could be helpful to visit the room a few minutes before the event is planned to start. This is a way of helping you to visualize the spatial characteristics of your presentation, how you will appear within the room, your relationship to the audience, and so on. It will improve your ability to give an excellent presentation.

Think Carefully about Using Handouts

Distributing a handout at your presentation can serve several purposes. First, it can allow you to convey complex information, perhaps through the use of tables, that would be virtually impossible for you to convey effectively by any other means. Second, by placing an outline of your presentation in the handout, it will serve as a road map that people can refer to as you talk. Third, the handout can be helpful as a prompt for the audience during the question-and-answer time. Finally, because people often take their handouts home with them, if you have given a great presentation, the handout will evoke a positive response from the audience members when they look at it afterward.

Be Prepared to Answer Questions

If you give a presentation that is interesting to your audience and in which you have worked to build audience engagement, people will want to ask you questions about your topic and the material you have presented. Question-and-answer times provide excellent opportunities for you to elaborate on your topic and develop ideas and arguments beyond what you were able to do during your talk. Because this is a more unstructured part of presenting, it is also a time when you can demonstrate your erudition and breadth of understanding by providing responses that connect your basic argument to issues and concerns raised by others. There is nothing more flattering and affirming of your presentation than to have the question-and-answer time filled with interesting ideas and approaches that emerge from discussion of what you have said. To make the most of the question-and-answer time, try to anticipate some of the questions and potential criticisms that people might raise regarding your work. Obviously, you cannot predict all questions or criticisms ahead of time; however, even giving a partial response to a difficult question, or showing evidence of how you have previously thought about the concern being raised, will win you a measure of respect.

When a question is asked, make sure that everyone in the room heard it. Sometimes, this might mean that you will have to repeat the question and ask the questioner if this is what was asked. Often people ask questions in somewhat incoherent ways. Because of this, it is fine to seek clarification from a questioner. It is entirely reasonable to make responses such as, "I'm not sure I understood your question," or "Let me see if I can rephrase your question in my own words. . . ." It is better to do this than to react immediately to the question and, perhaps, address issues that were not the primary concern of the person who asked the question. There are times when people will ask hostile questions, for whatever reason. When this happens, the most important thing for you to do is rapidly find a strategy to defuse the situation. You definitely should not respond to hostile questions in a hostile manner. It is possible that the question being asked is actually quite a reasonable one, even if the person asking it does not know how to act appropriately in the situation. A potentially useful strategy in a situation like this is to respond by being as analytical as possible about the question. For example, you might respond in this way: "Thanks. That's an important question. If I understood you correctly, I think there are two issues here. First, you're asking me to clarify a specific point that I made in the presentation. Second, you're asking me to think in another way about the implications of that point. So let me deal with these two issues one by one. . . ." Something vital to remember here is that the audience is much more likely to judge you for what you say in situations like this than what the person asking the question said. For that reason, it is important to respond to a hostile question in a cool, reasonable way. Doing so also opens room for other people to ask new questions, hopefully doing so in a less threatening manner.

Afterward

When the session that you have presented at comes to a close, take the time to talk informally with others who are in the room. Inevitably, you will find that people who did not speak during the question-and-answer time will introduce themselves to you and ask a question or share an anecdote with you. Taking the time to talk with others at the end of the presentation is good for several reasons. It will provide an opportunity for you to gain some feedback on how you presented. It will allow you to make connections with people you have not met before, and, for this reason, it is a good way to build your network of professional contacts.

It is also a very pleasant way to decompress after having been in a formal situation and under a high degree of pressure to perform well. Sometimes you will find at the end of a session that certain people want to monopolize time spent with you. Try to avoid this. If you are talking with someone and you see out of the corner of your eye another person wanting to talk, politely end your conversation and switch to the next person. Opportunities can come to you through this informal end-of-session time. You have done well and you will have earned the respect of many people in the audience. Moments like this are rare in our day-to-day lives. When they arise, make the most of them.

TEAM PRESENTATIONS

Often people have opportunities to give team presentations. For example, two people who have worked together on a project might be asked to discuss some of their findings at a formal presentation. Likewise, members of a team might be scheduled to give a conference presentation, and more than one member of the team desires to be involved in the presentation. My view of team presentations is that they should only be given when it makes good sense for people to divide up the tasks involved. The mere fact of people having worked together as a team on a policy project does not justify the presence of them all at an event where aspects of the project are being discussed. For formal presentations of the sort I have focused on here, my sense is that it will often work out better if just one person does it. When two people are involved, the success of the presentation will depend heavily on how much the presenters have worked together and sought to coordinate with each other beforehand. The key to deciding how many people should be involved in the presentation is to ask, How will this look to the audience?

Team presentations can work well when the presentation itself is designed to last for more than ten minutes and when the presentation has a number of distinct components to it. For example, two people might present their work so that the first person provides an overview to the topic and the second person provides details of the analytical work and findings of the project. Similarly, if a presentation is to involve an overview, a PowerPoint presentation on a particular issue, and a question-and-answer time with the audience, having a different group member take the lead on each component can work well. Again, the success of such presentational approaches will depend greatly on the level of coordinated planning that has been undertaken by team members.

There are some basic rules that teams can follow to make their presentations more effective. First, they should agree to the roles that each will perform, and they should stick to these roles. Second, they should find ways to make the transitions from one presenter to another as smooth as possible. Ideally, these transitions will work as a form of "break" that raises the audience's attention. Third, team members should find ways to ensure that they look like a team. For example, they should all dress at about the same level of formality and, if possible, find other ways to coordinate their clothing. Over the years, I have frequently required students to give team presentations in the courses I teach. Students who have paid close attention to the coordination of their presentations have occasionally also made an effort to coordinate their clothing (e.g., all wear white shirts and dark trousers). It might seem a minor detail, but when two members dress well and the other makes no effort, the lack of coordination is clear. The message sent in such instances is that maybe the team has not coordinated on other more central aspects of the presentation. Finally, during team presentations, considerable effort should be made to ensure that everyone on the team looks like a full participant. If roles are divided up, no single member of the team should dominate the proceedings. I once saw two people give a conference presentation. For the first part, a graduate student with English as a second language talked about the project. The student did a good job. In the second part, the professor launched into an unstructured, strident repetition of pretty much everything the student had said. From the audience's perspective, the presentation appeared unprofessional and poorly coordinated.

Overall, team presentations should be approached with caution. Everything that I have said for individuals giving formal presentations holds true for teams making such presentations. In the case of team presentations, though, considerably more effort must go into the planning and the coordination of the event. When done well, team presentations can come across as highly professional. They can be a great way to bring variation to the presentation and, therefore, maintain high levels of audience interest. Finally, they provide an excellent means through which experienced members of the team can provide quality mentoring to more junior members.

PRESENTING IN SMALL GROUP SETTINGS

Aside from giving formal presentations such as public lectures or conference presentations, there are many times when policy analysts are called upon to give formal presentations in small group settings. For example, you might be asked to participate in a ten-person workshop on a specific policy issue. During that workshop, you might be expected to lead some of the discussions or give overviews of how you have been thinking about some aspects of the policy issue. Similarly, you might be asked to give a short presentation to several staff members from an agency or a foundation that is interested in funding your work. Of course, there are many other venues where policy analysts might be required to give formal presentations to just a handful of other people.

How should one present in a small group setting? Typically, you should see the formality of your presentations as corresponding directly to the size of your audience. For a large audience, you should plan to be very formal. For a small audience, you should probably be less formal. But, in all cases, you should still put the same amount of effort into preparing what you will do. In many ways, planning to come across as somewhat less formal is even harder than preparing carefully for a formal presentation. This is because in a small group setting, you need to come across as both highly prepared but also as comfortable with spontaneity. You are much more likely to be interrupted and break into short conversations during your presentation in small group settings than in larger, lecture-type settings.

There are two key details that I suggest you think carefully about when preparing for a presentation in a small group setting. First, you should definitely avoid reading word-for-word from a script in such a setting. You might have developed a word-for-word script, but you should use this as the basis for making yourself a clear set of headings and abbreviated notes that you can then refer to as you give a more conversationally oriented presentation. Second, you should limit your use of visual aids, like overhead projectors or PowerPoint in small group settings. In such venues, you should make use of handouts, distributing them to people in the room at a strategically appropriate time in the meeting.

The likelihood is that, as a policy analyst, you will give many more formal presentations in small group settings than you will in large, public-lecture type settings; however, many of the same issues for presenters exist in both large and small group settings. Always, you need to think about the interests of your audience, your objective for the presentation, and how best to communicate your message. Because they are slightly less formal, small group settings can offer you opportunities for experimenting and innovating with your presentational style. They can be excellent venues in which to train yourself as an effective presenter.

LEARNING FROM EXPERIENCE

As a presenter, you can learn both from the times that you give presentations and from the times when you are a member of the audience, observing the presentations of others. The more conscious you become of your own presentational style and how best to prepare for talking in public, the more aware you will become of the ways that others present themselves. For example, my decision to write a full script and practice it almost to the point of memorization before giving a formal public lecture was based on observing public lectures given by a number of influential scholars whose work I greatly admired. While it might seem counterintuitive, I observed that these scholars, through having carefully scripted what they had to say, were more at ease with their subject matter and with the audience. They came across as both in control of what they were saying and highly engaged with the audience. No doubt, this is a big part of why they had developed their reputations as important, influential scholars. Similarly, you can learn a lot from observing the presentational style of more senior policy analysts in small group settings.

Just as we learn from experience when engaging in our day-to-day project work as policy analysts, so we can learn from our experience as presenters. The more presentations we give, and the more consciously we think about what works and what does not work, the better we can become at presenting, in both small group and large audience settings.

Aside from learning through reflection on the actions of others and on what we feel has worked or not worked for us, we can also learn a great deal from listening to feedback from others, especially mentors and managers. Whenever possible, you should seek out feedback on your presentations. Ask an observer with whom you feel comfortable to give you suggestions for improving on what you have been doing. A low-key way to manage this process is for you to work with one or two other colleagues and agree among yourselves to give each other feedback and tips on your presentations as a way that, together, you can all improve how you come across in formal settings.

Another useful way to gain invaluable feedback is to watch a videotape of yourself giving a presentation. This can be especially helpful if you watch it along with tapes of presentations by other people. A comparative review of how you and others come across is an important way to help you diagnose your performances and devise new strategies to make your presentations appear more powerful at future events. It is true that the thought of watching a videotape of yourself presenting might be quite daunting, but if you can overcome this fear, this expectation of feeling utterly mortified, you will learn a lot. What's more, in having the courage to confront yourself on video and treat the moment as an opportunity to learn, you will give yourself a huge advantage over those who think little about their presentation styles, let alone take the time to engage in critical self-examination with the objective of developing presentational excellence.

THE EVERYDAY PRESENTER

Learning to present yourself in formal settings can be hugely beneficial to your self-development as a policy analyst. I have suggested that, when developing presentations, you should think seriously about your objective. What do you want your audience to do as a result of having heard what you have to say? It is impossible for you to answer this question without thinking carefully about the backgrounds and interests of those you will be addressing. A good presentation should be designed to build bridges of understanding from the speaker to the audience. This means that you should always think carefully about the appropriate content of the talk and how you can structure it most effectively, in considering the audience you seek to communicate with. Once your message has been determined, you should consider ways to enhance your presentation. What visual aids will help you communicate your main points? How could a handout raise audience involvement and recall? How could you talk and act so as to achieve the appropriate presence in the room?

The discipline that goes into preparing for a formal presentation is also helpful for guiding your everyday forms of presentation. Even in activities that are as simple and routine as impromptu conversations with your colleagues, you can become more effective as a communicator if you remember to think in terms of the interests of others, limit what you have to say, and strive for clarity. Remember the constraints imposed by the venues you have to work in.

In thinking about giving presentations, we are forced to recognize that every audience is somewhat different and that we should take this into account if we want our ideas to have impact. We are also forced to consciously confront and adjust how we represent ourselves to others. As policy analysts, few of us work for ourselves. Thus, when we give presentations, we are actually serving as ambassadors for our organizations. For this reason, we should think carefully about the image we wish to project, keeping in mind what others in our organization would desire to be conveyed. All of this serves to reinforce a vital point of this book. That is, as policy analysts, we are embedded social actors. When we speak and act in the world, we should do so fully conscious of the ways that our ideas, our analyses, and our proposals for change can have material consequences for ourselves and for others around us. We have broader social responsibilities, responsibilities to others. When giving presentations, working with an audience, listening to questions, and engaging in intellectually intense conversation, that sense of broader responsibility should be uppermost in our minds.

Skill-Building Checklist

- Giving formal presentations requires time and energy. You should give a formal presentation only when the possible benefits from doing so are high and when you know you can give it your best.
- Before developing a presentation, find out as much as you can about the audience members and their interests. Then ask, what would be the best possible outcome of this presentation? You should set out to maximize the chances that this outcome will occur.
- When working with the content of your presentation, think of yourself as making an argument. Consider what evidence you will need to support it. Try to structure your presentation so that you will engage and persuade your audience.

- Develop a script for your presentation, just as playwrights develop scripts for one-actor plays. Once you have the basic script developed, think of ways to develop your notes and your visual aids so that in the actual performance you will appear both accomplished and natural.
- Practice your presentation. Ask friends to attend a practice session and give you feedback on how to streamline and strengthen your delivery. Good practice sessions provide structured opportunities for exploring creative ways to improve your performance.
- In your work as a policy analyst, you routinely present yourself to others in more or less formal ways. As an everyday presenter, strive to develop your presentational skills. In this way, you will raise your ability to prepare and give excellent formal presentations when opportunities arise for doing so.

Discussion Ideas

- Everyone should take a few minutes alone to think about one of the best presentations you have ever seen and one of the worst. You should write down why you thought these presentations were either good or bad. Then, divide into groups of three and tell each other about these presentations. On the basis of these experiences, as a group write a "Do and Don't" list for presenters. Next, consider this question: in what ways do the suggestions on your list correspond to or deviate from the suggestions made in this chapter?
- Think about your everyday life. Make a list of four to seven common situations where you interact with others. Then answer this question: in each of these situations, how might you be said to be "presenting yourself"? In a small group, discuss the situations that each of you has come up with. In so doing, think about ways that you could use these situations to build skills that will improve your ability to become an excellent presenter in more formal situations.
- Watching several groups give presentations on the same topic can provide useful insights into how we can each develop polished presentations while allowing our individual personalities to shine through. Break into several small groups. Using the ideas contained in this chapter and, perhaps, elsewhere concerning how to give presentations, develop a ten-minute group presentation called

"Giving Presentations." Think carefully about ways that you can use role playing and visual aids to enhance the persuasiveness of your presentation and capture the imagination of your audience.

FURTHER READING

Arredondo, Lani. 2000. *Communicating Effectively.* New York: McGraw-Hill.

Axelrod, Robert. 1985. "Tips for An Academic Job Talk," *PS: Political Science and Society* 28:612–13.

Gelb, Michael. 1988. *Present Yourself! The Simple Way to Give Powerful and Effective Presentations.* London: Aurum Press.

Jolles, Robert L. 1993. *How to Run Seminars and Workshops: Presentation Skills for Consultants, Trainers, and Teachers.* New York: Wiley.

Tierney, Elizabeth. 1999. *101 Ways to Better Presentations.* Dover, N.H.: Kogan Page.

6
...

Working in Teams

When a team works towards a set of common goals, the end product is truly greater than the sum of the individual parts. While this may be the case in a multitude of arenas from sports to business, it is equally applicable in the world of policy analysis. At the National Center for State Courts, projects are often staffed by employees with doctorates, by lawyers, former court employees and by consultants who may be substantive experts in the courts, methodologists, or experts in visual design. So the work is very collaborative and cross-disciplinary. The members of the team work on areas of strength while also learning from the expertise of the other members. Working in teams allows a group of individuals each with their own experiences and perceptual lenses to work in concert to identify questions, alternatives, solutions, and answers that may not have been obtainable had they each been working alone. The union of these diverse sets of actors leads to the creation of products that ultimately benefit the courts and the public.

—Dr. Matthew Kleiman, *Court Research Associate, National Center for State Courts, Williamsburg, Virginia*

People often express reluctance toward working in teams. The basic problem we face is that working with others requires cooperation and coordination. Now and then, the time it takes to figure out how to work as a team seems like time that could be better spent working on individually assigned tasks. In some instances, that judgment might be correct, but most complex activities—be they in the public sector, the private sector, or the nonprofit sector—require team effort. Teamwork is essential to the successful completion of policy-related activities such as conducting analyses to resolve strategic or operational issues, coordinating organizational budgets, reforming management structures, and designing and monitoring new programs. As Rasiel (1999, 57) has observed of consulting work, "In the face of complexity, many hands don't just make light work; they make for a better result." Further, finding productive ways to work with others can be enormously enriching and empowering. Yet even as we recognize the merits of teamwork, it must be acknowledged that working in teams can often prove difficult.

What is a team? Katzenbach and Smith (1993, 45) provide a useful definition: "A team is a small number of people with complementary skills who are committed to a common purpose, performance goals, and approach for which they hold themselves mutually accountable." Teams produce collective work products, products that could not have been generated simply through the one-to-one assignment of tasks to individuals. As a policy analyst, you will typically move from project to project, and you might find yourself serving on several teams at once, reporting simultaneously to multiple managers and team leaders. With this in mind, you need to learn how to create conditions rapidly under which you and others can cooperate to achieve goals that none of you could achieve alone. In this chapter, I discuss the nature of teamwork and identify ways that you—as a team member or as a team leader—can raise the chances of your teams achieving success.

THE LOGIC OF TEAMWORK

Contributors to the literature on teams have typically gained their training in disciplines such as psychology and sociology. Much of what I have to say in this chapter is based on such contributions, but a number of economists have also offered insights into teamwork through their studies of collective action and how incentives shape individual behavior. The work of economists is useful for identifying the efficiency implications of different organizational forms, including teams. Olson (1965) emphasized the importance of group size in determining how much individuals will contribute to a collectively desired outcome. His work contains important insights on the logic of teamwork. Likewise, a contribution to the economic theory of the firm offered by Alchian and Demsetz (1972) provides guidance on when to use teams and how to structure them.

According to Olson, the size of a group is critical to its effectiveness. As the size of a group expands, three factors reduce the chances that each member will contribute to the central goal. First, the larger the group, the smaller the fraction of the total group benefits each contributor will receive and the smaller the reward for group-oriented actions. Second, because the likely benefits of contributing will rarely outweigh the costs, the chance that members will choose to "free ride" on the efforts of others also increases as the size of a group increases. Third, larger groups have greater organizing costs than do smaller groups. Large organizing costs make it all the harder for collective goods to be obtained from group action. For these reasons, Olson concluded that large groups must give "selective incentives" to each member, incentives that generate collective goods as a "by-product" of the individualized transactions associated with group membership. In contrast to large groups, Olson suggested that small groups are more readily able to evoke group-oriented actions. This is because it is easier in small groups to monitor each member's contributions. Further, Olson argued that some small groups can be thought of as "privileged" because there are times when the desired outcome is of such value to at least one member that he or she will make sure that the collective good is provided, even when that means individually shouldering the full burden of providing it.

According to Achian and Demsetz, firms—and the various forms that firms take—reflect the efforts of entrepreneurs to answer a fundamental question: "How can the members of a team be rewarded and induced to work efficiently?" These authors argue that teamwork makes sense only when it yields an output that is larger than the separable outputs of each member. Because organizing teamwork requires use of scarce resources, a team *should not* be established if its total output is simply the sum of each team member's individual output.

Alchian and Demsetz claim that firms are most efficient when they embody an incentive structure that appropriately disciplines team members and reduces free riding, or "shirking." Differences in the kinds of goods being produced, and differences in the information available to managers, result in different forms of economic organization. For our purposes, the partnership—commonly found in firms that rely on the artistic or professional intellectual skills of the people involved—is of most interest. The partnership is a form of profit-sharing enterprise. Partnerships are more viable when they contain a small number of partners, because incentives to shirk increase with firm size. Profit-sharing partnerships make most sense when the monitoring of individual work effort can be done accurately only by the individuals themselves. As anyone who does intellectual work knows, it is virtually impossible for others to know how hard we work on a day-to-day basis, or how much of our thinking is fully devoted to our jobs. Alchian and Demsetz note, "If the management of inputs is relatively costly, or inefficient, . . . but, nonetheless, if team effort is more productive than separable production . . . then there will develop a tendency to use profit-sharing schemes to provide incentives to avoid shirking" (786).

Several design principles for teamwork emerge from these two contributions by economists. First, form should follow function. The organization of the team should be primarily guided by the nature of the task at hand. Second, teams should not be used when the same product could be generated through one or more individuals working on separate tasks. In fact, the anticipated gains from teamwork should significantly outweigh what could be produced through individualized activities, because the costs associated with coordinating teamwork can be high. Third, teams should be kept small enough that the final product can be achieved only if each member makes a significant contribution to the work. This reduces the costs of monitoring each person's effort and makes it easier for team members to hold themselves mutually accountable for the work produced. Fourth, when a team is being established, careful thought and effort must go into establishing a set of incentives that discourage shirking and promote quality contributions to the collective task. Favorable appraisal of the contributions of each member should be closely tied to the success of the effort as a whole.

In highlighting these basic design principles, I do not want to suggest that other things, like interpersonal relations in the team or team spirit, are unimportant. These are matters to which careful attention is given throughout the chapter. Rather, efforts to build team spirit and create good relations among team members are much more likely to generate big payoffs when prior attention has been given to clarifying the work to be done and establishing the right incentives for team members. Even economists, who have paid limited attention to the "people" aspects of teamwork, recognize their value (at least in a limited sense). As Alchian and Demsetz observe, "The team is better, with team spirit and loyalty, because of the reduced shirking" (790).

TEAMWORK IN A "ME-ORIENTED" CULTURE

Not long ago, the United States Army changed its marketing practices for luring recruits. "Be all you can be," a slogan used for two decades, was replaced by "I am an army of one." This change reflected the military's effort to appeal to a younger generation presumed to be highly individualistic and resistant to authority. The irony here is that armies have traditionally been built around such notions as strength through numbers, teamwork, and service to others. Thus, a broader question emerges: how can we reconcile our need to use teamwork to tackle complex tasks with a culture where the dominant message is "Look out for number one"? Various scholars who have studied and written about teams have confronted this question. In their view, teamwork is extremely difficult to implement effectively in organizations unless there is commitment at the highest levels to supporting it (Holpp 1999; Goleman 1998; Katzenbach and Smith 1993; Miller 1992). If the overall culture of the organization is individualistic, it is difficult to imagine how teamwork could ever be effective. Knowing that they will be judged on the quality of their individual performances, people in such organizational environments will soon learn the dominant strategy: make yourself look great, and make it hard for others to do likewise. If, however, the organizational culture is strongly supportive of teamwork, the prospects are good that people will become effective team players. Given the right incentives and training, even people who think of themselves as "an army of one" will go all out to support team goals.

Like other professionals who engage in creative, intellectual work, your career prospects as a policy analyst will be closely tied to your reputation. You need others to hold you in high regard for your analytical abilities. Likewise, you need others to know that you are a good, pleasant person to work with. The longer you engage in policy analysis, and the more experience you gain working on a variety of projects, the greater the number of people in your immediate policy community who will learn who you are and what qualities you can bring to working on policy issues. If you understand that, it becomes clear that working in teams can be a very good way to build your reputation with colleagues both inside and outside your current workplace. Teamwork represents a forum in which you can thrive. The key is to recognize that teamwork consists both of the team process and the team product.

You can perform well on teams through your contributions as an excellent analyst and as an excellent "people" person. A starting point to all of this is to acknowledge that, as Avery (2001) points out, teamwork is an individual skill. No matter what your position within a team (leader, member, junior member), you can do a great deal to help the team achieve success. For outside observers, who see the end product of the teamwork, the success of the team will reflect on you indirectly. For those on the team itself, however, your day-to-day contributions will be closely monitored and, through their eyes, the quality of your work and the quality of your interactions with them will reflect on you directly. Over the long term, your cumulative experience working in a series of highly successful teams will serve as excellent advertising, and it will undoubtedly open new opportunities for you. In view of the project- and teamwork-oriented nature of our profession, as a policy analyst mastering the skills needed to be an excellent team player is worthwhile. Of course, on those occasions when you are alone and working late, you might now and then draw comfort from the fanciful thought, "army of one."

MEMBERSHIP SELECTION CRITERIA

Who should be in the team? Two somewhat opposing answers are commonly given to this question. The first answer is that you should select team members based on necessary skills, given the task at hand. Thus, it is often said that a team should consist of members with the right "skill mix." The second answer commonly given is that you should select team members based on how likely they are to get along with each other. The argument here is that, if the interpersonal chemistry in the team is right, skill development will follow. In many ways, these two answers exemplify differences in how much we value technical skills and people skills. Because I believe that policy analysts need both excellent technical skills and excellent people skills, I contend that we should strive to build teams bearing both criteria in mind. Further, if we acknowledge that well-structured team activities can provide rich opportunities for people to develop new skills, striking a balance between the skill mix and personality criteria need not be viewed as a lowest-common-denominator approach to membership selection.

Several criteria should guide membership selection. First, you should select for the team only people who really want to be there and who show genuine excitement at the prospect of completing the team's mission. A technically proficient but disaffected, cynical, or lazy person can be a major liability for a team, because negative thinking can be both destructive and infectious. In contrast, a person who works hard, is eager to do well and willing to acquire new knowledge and skills, and gets along with others can be a major asset to a team.

Second, you should strive to ensure that, viewed collectively, the members of the team are likely to possess sufficient substantive knowledge, experience, and technical know-how to at least minimally achieve the team's purpose. It is clear that the purpose of the team should inform who is to be on it. In addition, it is obvious that no team will be able to achieve its purpose without developing all the knowledge and skills that will be required of it. Bringing people together as if they are items on a recipe list, though, should never be the sole organizing principle.

Third, you should seek to have a team that is diverse in as many ways as possible. Multidimensional diversity will ensure that the team members will bring different perspectives to the collective task. That raises the chances that orthodox thinking will not dominate group discussions and actions. As a result, weaknesses in any proposed approaches are likely to be identified and addressed within the group, and, through team dialogue, new opportunities are more likely to be discovered. As Avery (2001, 19) has observed, "From this utilitarian viewpoint, diversity is not about morality. It's not even about equal opportunity. . . . Diversity is about productivity, breakthrough, and synergy." Adopting a similar perspective, Goleman (1998) emphasizes the importance of striving to "leverage diversity."

Fourth, every effort should be made to build a significant learning component into the team's activities. When teams are required to achieve stretching targets, such learning will be unavoidable. Team diversity also promotes learning, as people come to understand differences in the approaches that they bring to their work. By treating teams from the outset as opportunities for every member to learn and to experience personal development, you acknowledge that the team members will require time to get up to speed and build the momentum that is necessary for producing a winning performance. Making this expectation explicit at the outset is a good way to reduce the chances that team members will later question the time that is going into learning on the job. Team tasks, by definition, should not be simple, routine, or easily achieved. Those are the attributes of work that can be parceled up and assigned to individuals.

Finally, teams should never be set up to fail. Membership selection should be informed by sensitivity to how likely it is that team members will get along with each other. People do not have to like each other from the outset. In fact, one of the merits of teams is that they provide venues in which people can come to appreciate others, discover what motivates them, and learn how others view things. Having said that, you should nonetheless avoid situations in which people with long-standing mutual enmity are likely to treat the team as a new opportunity to square off with one another.

It is something of a tall order to expect that people establishing a team will have all the necessary information on potential members to make truly inspired choices. In recognizing this, however, we see a potential solution. There is much to be gained from taking an appropriate amount of time to figure out who's who among potential candidates before the final selection is made. Team builders can also benefit from creating structured situations where potential team members face opportunities to work with each other in brief, face-to-face encounters, and where all concerned can achieve a sense of the kind of strengths that different people might bring to the team. Workshops, seminars, university courses, and training sessions provide ideal settings for facilitating these low-stakes engagements. When team members are drawn from permanent staff in an organization, there is typically a great deal of information available that can guide membership selection. In fact, organizations with a stable membership probably have a significant advantage over any other entity when it comes to having low-cost, high-quality information about people and their potential fit on a given team.

I have said nothing here about who gets to choose team members. Sometimes teams will be formed on the initiative of members themselves. Sometimes managers or supervisors will take the initiative and do the choosing. Neither approach is inherently superior. The most important thing is to ensure that all of the criteria mentioned above are taken into account during the selection process. When I have required students in my classes to form teams, I have typically given them some lead time to figure out with whom they would like to work. I have also pointed out the importance of striving to achieve diversity across a range of dimensions. On the few occasions when these teams have failed to perform up to expectations, or they have become mired in internal disputes, I have discovered that the people involved made little effort to think wisely about who they would like to be working with in their teams. In terms of performance and team process, they paid dearly for that negligence.

CLARIFYING TEAM GOALS

Every team member should have a clear sense of what the team is to achieve. From the outset, members should be able to answer two key questions: What is the central purpose of this team? What will be its lasting contribution? Team members should also be able to answer a third question: What is in this for me? When team members can readily answer these questions, it shows that the goals of the team have been clearly established. If you are a member of a team, you should strive to ensure that you know the answers to these questions by the time you leave the first team meeting. If you are unsure about your answers, seek clarification at the outset. By doing so, you will make an important contribution to the team process.

If you are the instigator or leader of a team, you can do a great deal to clarify its purpose, what you hope it will achieve, and the benefits of team membership. In some organizations where teamwork is commonplace, efforts have been made to create templates requiring team leaders to document items, the team's mission, the impetus for the team, when the team product must be delivered, and the list of team members. There will always be a fine line between micromanagement (to be avoided) and jump-starting the team by setting out your expectations and specifying some of the process steps you would like to see taken. Avoid having everything so nailed down from the start that team members feel they are being treated as functionaries who lack autonomy and are undervalued for the ideas and insights that they might bring to the task. At the same time, avoid situations in which people are uncertain about what is expected of them. As with micromanagement, this can cause low motivation, distrust, and resentment.

INCENTIVES ALIGNMENT

The ideal for a team is that every member be fully committed to doing an excellent job and to seeing that the final team product is of the highest quality possible. Screening during the membership selection process can help here, but having appropriate incentives in place is also vital. You should avoid instances where people who are not especially interested in the work of the team come to set the tone and dominate team discourse. There are at least two ways to increase the likelihood that everyone will do their best in the team. First, every member should know how excellent work for the team affects his or her own performance evaluation. In other words, people need to know that the team product matters. For example, if team members know that all eyes will be on the work of their team and that influential people will judge them individually on the basis of how well the team performs, members face strong incentives to perform well. Second, effort should be made to ensure that people derive a sense of purpose and belonging from being part of the team. Through their personal style, team leaders can do a great deal to give people a feeling of investment in the team. No matter what place anyone has on a team, he or she can contribute to everyone's sense of purpose and belonging. You can contribute to a team by setting a good example for others to follow. When you show goodwill toward others, it can create a demonstration effect, bringing out the best in the people around you.

University classrooms provide unique opportunities for structuring incentives so that people will care about both the product and the process associated with their teamwork. In the appendix to this book, I present a method that I have used to grade student teams. The most important aspect of this method is that everyone is judged according to the group product *and* how other members of the team perceived his or her individual behavior. Everyone knows this before the teamwork begins. Similar approaches could be used to assess people's contributions in teams of professionals. An even better situation would be one in which team members acted *as though* they were to be graded by their colleagues, even when such formal grading was absent. Is this idealistic? In fact, we should never underestimate the informal judgments that others will make of us. Those judgments will eventually feed into the collective evaluations that serve to establish our reputations within the policy community. Structuring team incentives is important, but a big part of that might simply involve bringing team members to understand that the stakes are high, even if that fact is not reflected in formal evaluation procedures.

TASK ASSIGNMENT

At initial team meetings, two items must be addressed. First, the team's primary task must be broken down into the major component parts. Second, an inventory should be made of the knowledge and skills that each member is bringing to the team. Where possible, this inventory should be developed using the component parts of the team's task as a prompt for people to state, in turn, what they have to offer the team.

Knowing what each member of the team could potentially contribute is a good preliminary step to brainstorming about task assignments, what the team's final product might look like, and so on. Once you have some ideas on the table about the task, you can begin to think of ways to break it down into smaller parts. Think about developing a critical path of steps that must be taken in logical sequence for you to eventually complete the task assignment. Once you have done this, you can discuss equitable and efficient ways to divide the subtasks among yourselves.

Consider a simple scenario. Suppose that Ashley, Hongying, and Chris have been asked to take four days to prepare an hour-long seminar for staff at the Family Independence Agency. The seminar is intended to give field officers an overview of new research on how changes in welfare support have affected children. Together, the team members decide that the major component parts of their work will include identification of current research efforts in their own jurisdiction and elsewhere, determination of questions and issues that are most likely to be of interest to the audience, review of research products and interviewing researchers with work in progress, development of a summary of research to be discussed at the seminar, and the structure of the seminar. Next, Ashley, Hongying, and Chris discuss these components of the project, identifying skills and knowledge needed to complete each of them. Following this discussion, task assignment can begin. Ultimately, the

Team purpose: Prepare hour-long seminar Time allocation: Four days Members: Ashley, Hongying, Chris Reporting to: Carol Phillips, Director of Policy				
Tasks	Identify research efforts	Audience assessment	Reviews and interviews	Research summary	Seminar development
Subtasks	Document searches, write-ups	Interviews, write-ups	Interviews, document searches, writing	Synthesis, writing	Design program, produce handouts, develop presentation
People	Ashley will lead	Hongying will lead	Chris will lead	Hongying will lead	Ashley will lead

Figure 6-1. Task Assignment Matrix

team should end up with a matrix of the type presented in figure 6-1. This matrix is designed to connect people to tasks.

The task assignment matrix provides a visual summary of the team's work. It allows everyone on the team to quickly grasp where his or her work fits into the whole. The matrix should be treated as a planning document, subject to change, as opposed to a binding contract. By taking this approach, it is possible for the team to respond rapidly to new information. Further, such flexibility reduces the likelihood that people will have serious grounds for complaints that the task assignments are unfair. If concerns like this are raised, flexibility means that quick, appropriate responses can be made. In this example, the team has a limited amount of time to prepare the seminar. This makes it all the more important that everyone rapidly focuses on the task at hand. The task assignments presented in figure 6-1 show different people taking leading roles on different components of the work. Such an approach provides opportunities for everyone to distinguish him- or herself through individual contributions to the team. When people have a sense of ownership over their tasks, they are more likely to give their all. Nevertheless, although it makes sense to match talents with tasks, task assignment should also be made in a way that builds learning and redundancy into the system. So there should be an expectation that each member of the team will contribute, in greater or lesser amounts, to completing all tasks. What would happen if, on the night before the seminar,

Hongying became ill? If the team process had redundancy in it, Chris and Ashley, in Hongying's absence, would be able to carry on and complete the seminar.

It is essential that all team members understand the nature of the tasks being assigned to them and what they are expected to deliver. With this in mind, before concluding the meeting on task assignments, it is a good idea to have the team members state, in their own words, what they understand their tasks to be. This is a way to ensure that no surprises arise when you meet to review what everyone has done and where you are in the process of task completion.

CLARIFYING PROCESS STEPS

Beyond getting initial agreement on task assignment, teams in their early stages also must pay careful attention to clarifying the process steps that they will take on the way to developing the team product. Devoting a team meeting to creating a project time line is a useful way to prompt discussion of these issues. One way to develop a time line is to begin with the desired end product and the team's delivery deadline and then work back to the present. With a basic time line in place, completion dates for particular components and subtasks can be determined. Planning to have team meetings on or near completion dates is a good way to ensure that everyone will be kept in the loop of how the work is proceeding, and early warnings of potential problems can be delivered and heeded. As with task assignment, there is merit in building flexibility into the scheduling of future meetings and completion dates. Giving people tight schedules to work within is a way to achieve focus, but care needs to be taken to ensure that people do not get overworked and feel demoralized because they face a daunting task. Tight scheduling is good, but it should be realistic as well. At each step in the process, it is also important that people know exactly what is expected of them and when that work is due. In short, it is critical that people leave every team meeting with a clear sense of what they will be doing next. Wherever possible at team meetings, have people draw linkages between their work and the big picture of the team.

At the initial planning meeting, it is important that everyone be reminded that all teams typically go through an initial slow period where everyone is trying to make sense of the primary task and how their particular pieces of work relate to it. This period can seem frustrating. If members of the team keep the broader goal in mind through this period, however, breakthroughs will start to occur and the team's performance will begin to take off. Inevitably, it might seem that there is more talk than action at the start of the teamwork. Yet, if that talk is clarifying and helps everyone achieve a greater sense of what they have to do and how it will fit with the work of others, it is extremely valuable. The better prepared people are for the work to be done, the better they will perform.

KEEPING LINES OF COMMUNICATION OPEN

A key to managing teamwork is to ensure that everyone remains on track with his or her tasks and knows what progress others have made with their work. Talking about progress with reference to a time line can help here. The level of formality involved will increase the odds that everyone will take a turn to speak. This is one way to avoid unpleasant surprises. Thinking about these matters from your own perspective as a team member, two key points emerge. First, you must do the work that was assigned to you. Second, you must keep the lines of communication open. If you are having problems with your work, let people know sooner rather than later. Aside from these formal efforts to maintain open communication, a well-performing team will develop a team culture where frequent, informal discussion among team members is encouraged. Often, important matters can be clarified through low-key, informal, one-to-one communication among team members. So long as these types of communication are not exclusionary or do not reinforce "good old boy" practices, they can prove invaluable for keeping the teamwork moving forward.

If a team member appears to be having difficulty with his or her subtask, try to avoid being critical. Rather than being severe with the person and thinking of ways to complete the task without his or her input, consider how you might be a good helper. Sometimes, people just want a bit of encouragement or reassurance. Give it to them. A structured report-back time at the start of team meetings is a good way to institutionalize opportunities for people to seek advice, feedback, or support regarding their work. No matter your position in the team, you can do things to make others in the team feel good about their work. When people feel good about what they are doing, they work more productively, and that is what you want.

Suppose we return to the example of preparing a presentation. As the team approaches the day of the presentation, time should be set aside for a practice run. Every member of the team should plan to be ready by the practice, so any final adjustments can be made to the end product. It is easy to think about what it means to do a practice run when the final product is a presentation, but every team should take the time to consider what might constitute a practice run, in light of the product to be delivered. A formal practice run provides a vital moment in the life of the team for everyone to see what has been produced. More importantly, it provides an opportunity to discuss and determine what must still be done to achieve an excellent team product.

ACCENTUATING THE POSITIVE

Teams working on policy issues often consist of people with different disciplinary training and professional perspectives. For example, a team charged with devising a pilot program to better rehabilitate prisoners might include prison staff, criminologists, social workers, educators, and economists. Such diversity on the team can be a major asset. At the same time, each of these professionals will be more familiar with talking to others who share their particular professional norms and vocabulary than with talking to outsiders. Another way to put this is that each member of the team will bring a distinctive "frame" to the task at hand. Sometimes, differences in the frames through which we view and make sense of the world can hinder communication. This is why Schön and Rein (1994) have appealed to policy professionals to engage in "frame reflection"—the use of dialogue to develop common ground when approaching difficult policy problems.

Several observers of teams have noted how the presence of one or two individuals with highly developed social skills can greatly improve the internal dynamics of teams. Goleman (1998, 221) calls such individuals "glue people." Aside from fulfilling their formal obligations to the team, such individuals make important informal contributions by setting a positive, friendly tone and helping others get along. One way to do this is by making a concerted effort to show interest in your fellow team members and adopt a caring attitude toward them. This does not simply mean that teams work better when someone serves in a parent role. The challenge is to find ways to reduce the language and status barriers that sometimes arise between professionals. Although this is often done informally, if it is done at all, this type of activity can be promoted through design decisions concerning the membership and activities of the team. For example, in her work with teams of chemists and engineers, Hara—a social scientist—and her colleagues (2001) have sought to map out the patterns and levels of communication between team members. Through these efforts, Hara and her colleagues have identified instances where team members were overlooking opportunities for working together, perhaps because they did not understand each other's jargon or were afraid to ask one another what might seem like stupid questions.

With the knowledge of potential barriers to effective communication in teams, we can take steps to increase the likelihood that our work with others will ultimately produce excellent results. One simple step is to increase opportunities for members of the group to interact informally. Often, it is when we are relaxing during breaks from a task that we have our most productive breakthrough insights or ideas about how to proceed. In light of this, finding ways to structure short, informal interactions among team members can be a starting point for improving relations and allowing people to get beyond their language differences or fears of appearing silly because of the questions they ask. Another more formal step might involve explicitly acknowledging the ways that our professional differences can create barriers to communication and inviting team members to think of themselves as cultural go-betweens, developing jargon-free ways to talk with each other.

When Things Fall Apart

Despite good intentions, there are times when teamwork runs into difficulties. Problems most often manifest themselves as clashes of personalities among team members, but these clashes might also be precipitated by the nature of the tasks that the teams are working on. When a task is difficult to accomplish and a team seems to be making little progress, it is easy for individuals to rationalize what is happening by blaming others and finding fault with what others have produced or with their style of work. At times, this might be justified, but at other times it might be quite unfair. For example, there may be instances where changes in the broader environment negatively affect the work of the team. If this is the case, there might have been nothing any team member could have done to avert the problem. When things fall apart, it is as if we are living out our worst fears about teams and the trouble that can accompany teamwork. There are several concrete steps that a team can take to get back on path and to limit the potential for things to fall apart again.

Cooperation is the heart of teamwork, but, as Axelrod (1984) has pointed out, cooperation is fragile. Thus, Axelrod suggests that people who want others to cooperate with them should find ways to extend the "shadow of the future." You can do this by giving people credible evidence that how well they behave in the present will have implications for how they are treated in the future. Because of the importance of reputation to our long-term career prospects as policy analysts, we should be constantly alert to how the actions we take today might affect us in the long run.

Individually and collectively, team members always bear a high, ongoing cost for team failure and for failure to deliver the team product. Most directly, the costs will come in the form of penalties from superiors or clients for late, or unacceptable, work. Everyone in the team will bear those costs. In addition, the costs of an interpersonal breakdown can be considerable. This is true even if, in the face of team troubles, the final product is delivered. Team failures, no matter their cause, make it difficult for team members to work together again, which can mean lost future opportunities. It also can mean special and ongoing difficulties if those people happen to be colleagues. Just as importantly, a breakdown can spell bad news for the reputations of team members. When tensions go unresolved and the result is project failure, it is inevitable that every team member will engage in "blame management." Stories will be told as to why the team failed to deliver as intended. Whether you see yourself as at the center of the trouble or an innocent bystander, some of those stories will reflect badly on you. In the face of these negative possibilities, it is critical to make a concerted effort to avoid team failure. You can do this by responding appropriately as soon as problems or concerns begin surfacing in the team. Quick responses are always better than carrying on as if matters will resolve themselves. Quick responses are justified and, even if it turns out that you were responding to a false alarm, the remedial actions you could take are unlikely to cause harm.

A useful starting point involves isolating the source of a problem. Regardless of whether you are the team leader, one helpful way to do so is to hold discrete private conversations with the other members of the team. During these conversations, try to ascertain from each person whether he or she perceives a problem with the team or the work being done. After these conversations, assess whether the comments people have made appear to point to a common source of difficulty. If you are the member of a team that has a designated leader, follow up on these conversations by alerting the leader to what you have discovered. If you are the leader of the team, plan to call a team meeting on the issue of concern. If a regularly scheduled meeting has already been planned, you might want to simply use some or all of that meeting time to attend to the problem. Before you raise the matter for discussion, you can make a positive contribution by briefly reviewing aspects of the team's interactions and output to date that appear to be going well. This is a way to underscore that there are good things happening with the team. Furthermore, focusing on what is going right is sometimes a useful way to promote thoughtful diagnoses of the problem that has arisen and prompt others to offer ideas for how the problem might be resolved.

When one or two people appear to be the source of trouble for the team, there is merit in turning the situation back to them and asking them to suggest remedies. For example, you might say, "I get the sense that you are unhappy with how things are going with our work. How could we change things in the team so that what we are doing would work better for you?" Then listen closely to what is said. By taking this approach, you give those who are unhappy an opportunity to voice their concerns. More importantly, you invite them to accept responsibility for helping to get the team beyond the present situation. The stakes can be high in such meetings, so it is essential that everyone listens closely and allows those who are unhappy to have their full say. Uncomfortable as this might seem, it can be the starting point for getting the team back on track, which is where you want to be.

Beyond asking those who are unhappy to present their views when things have become difficult in the team, it can also be helpful to solicit the views of all team members. Reminding team members of the shadow of the future and the importance of achieving a positive outcome to the team's work is an excellent way to prompt people to take sessions like this seriously. You can begin to defuse interpersonal tensions in a team by having every member take responsibility for addressing the problem at hand. You are also more likely to hear ideas that could help to remedy current troubles when everyone is asked to contribute. Sometimes, it can also be useful to invite people from outside the team (especially people with a lot of experience with policy projects and teamwork) to come to a team meeting and talk about the problems. This can help members of the team make smart choices about how to get back on track.

Other authors who have written about teamwork have made useful suggestions concerning how to deal with team problems. Avery (2001) suggests that it is useful for teams to engage in a "reorientation process." Among other requirements, this process calls for a team meeting in which each member is asked to contribute to answering several basic questions concerning the team: What has the team been formed to do? Why are we here, and, more importantly, why are you (the individual team member) here? What is in it for you to be on this team? How are we supposed to do the work we were formed to do? What are our team rules and agreements? Who is doing what? What does each of us bring to the team in terms of skills and responsibilities? Depending on the problem at hand, some of these questions might be more relevant than others, but the point of raising and answering questions of this sort is that they can bring everyone back to the basics of why we work together as teams.

Rees (2001) has suggested a set of four questions that a team might work through to regain its direction and sense of purpose. The questions are based on two categories: how well things are going (not well/well) and whether the team can affect the causal factors associated with these outcomes (flexible/firm). The questions are as follows. First, what is not going well and is flexible? Answers to this question can indicate opportunities for positive change. Second, what is not going well and is firm? The answers here can identify aspects of the team's work and context that are not likely to change or that the team is not well placed to change. The answers produced here, though, need not be viewed as indications that there is nothing the team can do in the face of obstacles. Discussions of those obstacles might bring forth ideas for working around them. Third, what is going well and is flexible? These are factors that the team should strive hard to maintain. Finally, what is going well and is firm? The team should count these factors as assets.

Like Avery and Rees, Katzenbach and Smith (1993) emphasize the importance of revisiting the basics of the team and the task it was established to complete. Beyond that, Katzenbach and Smith propose that the team members strive to achieve some "small wins" with the project. The logic here is that, although a team might be currently experiencing difficulties, it is unlikely that everything is going badly. By taking a short-term perspective and pouring energies into readily achievable aspects of the broader task, a team can regain the focus and momentum needed to tackle what has not been going well. They also suggest that new information about the task and new ideas about completing it can be helpful for teams that have run into difficulties. This suggestion is consistent with the proposal that teams consult with experienced outsiders as a way to gain perspective on what is happening. Finally, Katzenbach and Smith suggest that there are times when teams might have to consider taking drastic internal action. This would involve changing the team's membership. In some instances, that might mean changing the team leader. This is action that clearly should be taken only as a final resort, after good faith efforts have been made to take other remedial steps.

In thinking about ways to overcome troubles in your team, it is useful to remember the following line: "If you want to gather honey, don't kick over the beehive." This is the title Dale Carnegie gave to the first chapter of *How to Win Friends and Influence People* (1937). An implication of this saying is that patience is a very good thing when we are working with others. In the face of team troubles, there will always be a temptation to demonize one or two people and to pretend that firing them will make the troubles cease. The harder, but more laudable, response is to talk things through, doing so in a way that allows everyone to focus once more on why the team was established. The shadow of the future provides a powerful incentive for us to put aside our pride and find mutually agreeable ways to move forward.

ENDINGS MATTER

Because teams are assembled to address particular tasks, the natural lives of teams end when those tasks are completed. But when the team is no longer to meet formally, it is important that you find some low-key way to congratulate yourselves for what you have achieved. This can be as simple as taking a few minutes at the end of the final meeting to tell each other "well done" and "nice job." Another possibility involves doing things slightly more formally and having everyone in the team take turns to say something about the project and the team process. These are ways to achieve closure as a team. Making an effort to end projects formally ensures that the interpersonal ties created during the life of the team are respected. This also leaves open opportunities for members of the team to interact on good terms in the future. When the team process has been difficult and people have at times clashed, striving for a good ending is even more important. When a team disbands, you should work to ensure that nobody burns bridges and that everyone's reputation is stronger—or at least no worse—than it was before the teamwork started. Remember, no matter your position in the team, you can do a great deal to help shape the stories that subsequently will be told about what it was like to be in this team and how things were at the end.

SUMMARY

Teamwork is an important aspect of being a policy analyst. The complexity of the policy issues and tasks we often confront make it impossible for individuals to single-handedly address them. In this chapter, I have provided an overview and some guidance on working in teams. Throughout, I have sought to show how anyone can contribute to a positive team process, no matter what his or her formal position within the team. It is also clear that steps taken when a team is being planned and formed can crucially affect the chances that the work undertaken within the team will lead to success. Excellent teamwork requires people to get along well with each other, but even if people get along well, this will not be enough to overcome more fundamental problems, such as teams lacking a clear focus or a sense of each member's responsibilities.

Working in teams requires a range of people skills. For that reason, what I have said here might in itself seem somewhat inadequate. For example, everyone belonging to a team will be required to attend team meetings. Thus, it is essential that people on the team have a good understanding of how to facilitate meetings and brainstorming sessions. I have not discussed those skills here, but they are treated at length in the chapter to follow. In addition, when people are well organized, have good presentational skills, and are good at professional networking, they can bring an enormous amount of added value to any team. Thus, many of the people skills discussed elsewhere in this book could be put to very good use within the team context.

SKILL-BUILDING CHECKLIST

- Treat teamwork in a task-oriented fashion. Begin with the task and then assemble the team.
- Selection of team members must be done carefully. Choose people who are enthusiastic about the work, who—in combination—have enough knowledge and skills to tackle the task, and who will bring diversity to the team, in terms of background, training, and interests.
- Recognize that your fate is tied to the fate of the team. Go out of your way to help the team produce excellent work. This will bring you benefits through your association with a high-performance team and through what your teammates think of you and say about you to others in your workplace and the policy community.
- Allow plenty of time for team members to discuss their primary task, how it can be broken into subtasks, and the sort of knowledge and skills that they can draw on to ensure the work gets done.
- Build a team time line, starting with the date when the task must be completed and working back to the present. This should be used to decide target dates for subtask completion and for setting meetings to assess progress and discuss next steps.
- Strive to set a good example in the team—to be a model team member—by adopting a positive, friendly tone and helping others get along. By showing genuine interest in your teammates, you can create the conditions for strong working relationships, synergy, and conceptual breakthroughs.

DISCUSSION IDEAS

- People often express reluctance to working in teams. Take a few minutes to make a list of the "negatives" that you associate with teamwork. Next, with one other person, compare your lists and build one composite list. With the composite list of negatives in place, work together to suggest four design elements of a team and the team process that could serve to minimize those negatives.

How easy would it be to implement these design elements? At the conclusion of your discussion, choose one design element to report to the larger group. Make sure that both of you are prepared to discuss this design element and how it might interact with other aspects of the teamwork.

- In *Working with Emotional Intelligence,* Goleman (1998, 229–30) reports the efforts of a professor at Rensselaer Polytechnic Institute to promote skills for effective teamwork among students in an engineering design course. The professor suggested that rapport, empathy, cooperation, persuasion, and consensus building are crucial ingredients of teamwork. He then proposed activities to underscore each concept. Here is a variation of that approach. For each concept, ask members of the full group to offer descriptions. Record these so that everyone can see them. After the descriptions for a concept have been recorded, randomly assign people into pairs. For rapport, ask the pairs to take three minutes to establish understanding. For empathy, have one person tell his or her partner about something in their lives they feel they need support for. The task of the other partner is to identify with the first. For cooperation, have members of each pair develop a plan whereby together they could make the best use of each other's skills to analyze a policy problem. For persuasion, think about a controversial policy topic. If possible, assign people into pairs where there is a difference of opinion. Have one member of each pair try to persuade the other that his or her position is reasonable. Working with the same pairs, for consensus building, have both members work together to develop a policy position with which both of them could agree.
- In the appendix to this book I present an approach that I have frequently used for evaluating student teamwork. This approach is designed to force students to focus on delivering an excellent end product while paying close attention to how they contribute to the group process. Think about an instance of teamwork that you have engaged in (or are about to engage in) at your workplace or in a course setting. In small groups, provide brief descriptions to each other of these teamwork situations. Then, using the evaluation method presented in the appendix as a starting point, think more carefully about one of the teamwork situations you have shared. Work together to devise an evaluation method that would promote

excellent work and bring out the best in people in that specific situation. Prepare comments so that you can report back to the full group, explaining your approach, comparing and contrasting it with others—such as the approach I have presented.

Further Reading

Alchian, Armen A., and Harold Demsetz. 1972. "Production, Information Costs, and Economic Organization." *American Economic Review* 62:777–95.

Avery, Christopher M. 2001. *Teamwork Is an Individual Skill: Getting Your Work Done When Sharing Responsibility.* San Francisco: Berrett-Koehler.

Axelrod, Robert. 1984. "How to Promote Cooperation." In *The Evolution of Cooperation.* New York: Basic Books, pp. 124–41.

Goleman, Daniel. 1998. "Social Radar" and "Collaboration, Teams, and the Group IQ." In *Working with Emotional Intelligence.* New York: Bantam Books, pp. 133–62 and 198–231.

Katzenbach, Jon R., and Douglas K. Smith. 1993. "Team Basics: A Working Definition and Discipline." In *The Wisdom of Teams: Creating the High-Performance Organization.* New York: HarperCollins, pp. 43–64.

7

...

Facilitating Meetings

While some people might complain about them, meetings allow us to build our relations with others. As such, they often lead to more effective communication and decision making. Meetings are held for many different reasons and with a variety of different objectives. It is important to know what your objective is for a meeting. Perhaps more importantly, it helps that you know what expectations other people in attendance will be bringing to the meeting. Many meetings are held with colleagues from within your own organization, for a mutual exchange of information, usually with the objective of reaching a consensus on an issue. Given the complexity of many issues, just reaching internal agreement can be very time consuming. Other meetings are held with members of the community, where lobbyists or experts in a given field come to provide information and discuss the possible impacts of the actions you are contemplating. A third type of meeting falls under the category of negotiation. Here, your interactions with other parties at the meeting are for higher stakes. Your strategy—including your choice of language, approach, and level of exchange of information—is critical to achieving your objective. Equally important is the deadline you may have set for reaching agreement. Oftentimes all the pieces of the puzzle must fall into place at once. Finalizing one objective too soon may leave you without leverage for accomplishing your other objectives.

—Jocelyn Dax, *Deputy Director of Budget*
Studies, Ways and Means Committee,
New York State Assembly, Albany, New York

Meetings are integral to organizational life. At the workplace and in our social activities outside of work, all of us participate with differing frequency in structured or semistructured meetings. Although we rarely talk of them as such, these meetings serve as policy forums in which we transform problems, ideas, information, and motivation into mandates for considered action. Seen as policy forums, it is clear that high-quality meetings are essential for producing high-quality decisions. And, of course, high-quality decisions are the lifeblood of excellent organizations.

From our experience in meetings, we know that some go much better than others. Actually, it is fair to say that the prospect of attending meetings often leaves us decidedly underwhelmed. Meetings can be dreadful, but this need not be the case. In this chapter, I present steps you can take to ensure that the meetings you arrange can be engaging for everyone in attendance and highly productive. Like the other people skills discussed in this book, the ability to facilitate meetings effectively is a valuable skill for many people, not just policy analysts. As a policy analyst, however, you can improve your contributions to public policy formulation and policy debate by striving to be a great meeting facilitator. In terms of your reputation, you stand to gain a lot in this way. People will want to work with you, they will want to attend meetings that you call, and they will respect your leadership abilities.

Throughout this discussion I assume that you are the person responsible for setting up and facilitating meetings; however, chances are that, although you might attend many meetings, it is less often the case that you are responsible for calling them and ensuring that they run well. No matter. By reflecting on what makes for effective meetings, you will increase your ability to contribute to the success of all the meetings you attend. The approaches presented here might be thought of as providing benchmarks against which you can judge your own performance as a meeting facilitator as well as the performances of others. Having a clear sense of what factors determine the success of a meeting, you can seek to lead by example, making the meetings you facilitate stand out as quality events. In addition, by knowing what makes for successful meetings, even as a meeting participant you can change your behavior in ways that might well have a demonstration effect, leading others—again by your example—to also contribute to successful meetings. Equipped with an understanding of why some meetings are better than others, you might find low-key ways to suggest improvements to those responsible for running the meetings you attend. Because everyone prefers great meetings to mediocre ones, your suggestions for improvements, if given in positive, nonthreatening ways, will most likely be welcome.

WHY HAVE A MEETING?

Among the many complaints we hear about meetings, "the meeting was pointless," "I didn't need to be there," or "nothing happened" are the most common. There is a reason for this. People often call meetings because, to them, calling meetings is part of the managerial or leadership ritual. Yet, if we can get beyond thinking of meetings as rituals and consider them as opportunities for information sharing, discussion, and decision making, we can begin finding ways to make meetings into meaningful events. Reminding ourselves of the costs associated with calling a meeting can also help us maintain focus. As self-respecting policy analysts, we should always weigh the costs and benefits of our meetings. We should strive to ensure that everyone present at the meetings we call consider their attendance to be the best use of their time.

Meetings can take a variety of forms, from brief one-to-one meetings to longer meetings involving a large number of people. In this chapter, I focus on meetings involving somewhere between three and twenty people. Regardless of the number of people in attendance, the fundamental aspect of meetings remains constant. That is, there are only three actions you can perform in meetings: announce things, discuss things, and decide things (Tropman 1996, 5). Of course, meetings are not the only medium through which we can make announcements or come to decisions. Often, e-mail exchanges can suffice. And quite a few discussions can also take place through e-mail or telephone conference calls. Thus, we face a range of choices concerning how we should go about making announcements, holding discussions, and reaching decisions. Meetings represent effective venues for all three, which is why they are so commonly held. Compared with other choices, however, meetings can be slow (because they take time to set up) and costly (because they take us away from other things we could be doing).

Devise an Outcome Statement

Why hold a meeting? You should always ask this question. In doing so, you open yourself to considering several other matters to do with the nature of the meeting and who needs to be there. As a starting point, it is useful to develop an outcome statement. This statement should specify what you hope to achieve in the meeting. It should be written in such a way that you would be able to readily tell at the end of a meeting whether the outcome was achieved. In working on an outcome statement, you might realize that, in fact, you could achieve your outcome just as easily without calling a meeting. Alternately, you might find ways to sharpen the focus of the meeting so that everyone will come prepared and chances are better that you will make progress by working through matters together. Either way, time spent thinking about why you initially contemplated calling a meeting will be time well spent.

Consider this example. Suppose that you are working on a team project and several members have expressed concern about the team's relations with the client and with other players external to the team. This would appear to be a serious issue that could have major implications for the success of the project and, hence, that of the team. One approach would be to call the team together, stating simply that the meeting is about external relations. That statement, however, is too vague. It is better to take the approach that the team needs to accomplish two goals. First, through discussion, you need to find out the nature of people's concerns about external relations and why those concerns have arisen. The outcome you desire here is clarification of the problem and what might be done about it. Second, as a team, you might need to decide on new procedures to use in working with the client and other external players. Because right now there is some uncertainty about the nature of the problem, it would be premature to talk in terms of changing team behavior. Therefore, you should plan to hold an initial meeting with an outcome statement like this: "List ways to improve our relations with the client and other external players." The statement says nothing about decisions. The initial team meeting will be a discussion. Of course, that discussion will need to be broken up into a series of logically sequenced steps leading up to the listing and sifting of suggestions for change. Thinking in terms of an outcome statement forces you to focus on the purpose of the meeting and how you might arrange it to achieve what you set out to do.

CHARACTERISTICS OF GOOD MEETINGS

Instinctively, we know when a meeting has gone well, just as we instinctively know when one has gone badly, but what underlies these instinctive reactions? People who have observed a variety of meetings and written about the conduct of meetings tend to agree on four points.

First, good meetings have a lot of participation. When we attend meetings and have nothing to say or nobody asks us for our views, it is hard not to conclude that the meeting was a waste of time. It might not have been a waste of time for everyone there, but it felt like a waste of time for *us*. This is never good. When you set up a meeting, you should strive to ensure that people know why they will be attending. At the meeting itself, you should use your role as facilitator to ensure that everyone gets to speak and participate fully in the proceedings. When people participate, they often think of what they are doing as fun. Odd as it might seem at first, good meetings are typically fun to attend.

Second, good meetings are places where work gets done. This means that we should avoid situations where people simply sit for a long time hearing a series of announcements or listening to a few others give reports on their activities. Of course, there is a place in meetings for announcements and for reports, but these points can be conveyed effectively through other media. In the case of reports, it is likely that the content could be better absorbed by individuals reading relevant material alone. If we think of meetings as involving announcements, discussions, and decisions, it becomes clearer how we can make meetings places where work gets done. In good meetings, the bulk of the time should be spent on having discussions and reaching decisions. These are activities that call for plenty of input from those in attendance. When planning your meetings, make conscious decisions about how best to turn them into working sessions.

Third, good meetings make people feel energized. Most of us feel energized when we have a sense that what we are doing is important and that other people are cheering us on to do the best we can. How can meetings do this for people? At the outset, you should make it clear why the meeting has been called and why each person has been invited to attend. Initiating discussions with a clear statement of a problem or issue to be addressed is good for achieving focus. Taking a few minutes to go around the room having people briefly state what they can contribute to thinking about the problem or issue can be very helpful as well. This pulls people into the discussion, allowing them to draw linkages for themselves between their knowledge and skills and the matters to be addressed. How you act as a facilitator can do much to energize others.

Even small things, like genuinely complimenting people on their contributions, can do a lot to make people feel good about being at the meeting and sharing their ideas and views. This is what you want.

Fourth, good meetings spark action. At the conclusion of a good meeting, those in attendance know what will happen as a consequence of the discussions that occurred and the decisions that were made. People know what next steps, if any, they should take. One of the dissatisfying things about many meetings we attend is that they seem inconclusive. A question many people hear in the hallway days or even weeks after a meeting is "Whatever came of that discussion?" Busy people crave a sense of closure in their lives. With meetings, closure can come simply from knowing that your contributions were heard and appreciated. Closure can also come by knowing exactly what is now expected of you. Of course, leaving a meeting with a set of new tasks to undertake might not feel like closure. But compare the reassurance of knowing what you have to do next with that vague disquiet associated with not knowing for sure if you are meant to be doing something or if you should be waiting for additional instructions. Having a clear sense of what is expected of you is always preferable.

As these comments suggest, when it comes to setting up and facilitating meetings, you can do a lot to determine just how good they will be. If you want high levels of participation, much accomplished, and people to leave feeling energized and ready to take action, you must be prepared to put in serious effort before, during, and after your meetings. Treating meetings as just the most public, observable parts of a more involved process is one way to better understand what you must do to make meetings successful events. Parallels can be drawn between what goes into making a successful meeting and what goes into making a triumphant performance by a chamber orchestra or a successful dinner party. Members of a chamber orchestra know well in advance of every performance what instruments they will play and when they will be called on to play them. They know what piece will be played as an encore, and they will have rehearsed it several times. And, of course, a good host would never dream of waiting until the guests turned up before deciding what food to serve at a dinner party. Things might look natural or spontaneous; that is the effect that the consummate planner strives to achieve. If you want successful meetings, you must be prepared to put in a great deal of behind-the-scenes effort.

The next three sections of this chapter cover meeting preparation, aspects of the meeting itself, and what to do after a meeting. Having gone over what might be thought of as the mechanics associated with productive meetings, I devote the four sections that follow to facilitating, brainstorming, guiding analytical discussions, and decision making. These sections deal more closely with the "what" and the "how" of meetings. Good meetings must be set up and run in ways that give equal emphasis to process, people, and content. In practice, it is virtually impossible to separate these elements of meetings. Yet, for the purpose of this discussion and to raise our consciousness of what makes meetings work, here I have deliberately sought to treat these elements more or less separately.

Preparation

Meetings might take place on a regular basis—perhaps weekly or monthly—or they might take place in an ad hoc fashion. Regular meetings tend to cover multiple topics. In contrast, ad hoc meetings typically cover one specific topic. Differences between the broader contexts within which regular meetings and ad hoc meetings occur mean that preparations for each kind of meeting will differ. In spite of these differences, many aspects of meeting preparation should be followed no matter whether the meeting is part of a series or one of a kind. Here I discuss various steps you can take to prepare for your meetings. The proposed approach may well be too formal for some circumstances, but I have erred on the side of formality because I have unhappily sat through many meetings where minimal preparations were made and, as a result, little was achieved. In the end, we should strive to adopt approaches that are appropriate to the nature of the work at hand. A good way to do that is to start with a formal ideal in mind and then relax that ideal as you see fit.

Decide the Meeting Content

A first step in preparing for a meeting is to think carefully about content. Developing an outcome statement can help with this. Such an approach is particularly helpful when planning a meeting that will revolve around one particular issue. Team meetings or regular group meetings, however, often serve as forums for addressing multiple issues. In the lead up to meetings of this sort, you might ask people to tell you in advance if there are any matters they would like to have covered in the next meeting. When you take this approach, you should allow yourself plenty of time before the meeting to sift through possible items for consideration. If you have meetings every month, you should ensure that you have received word of all matters to be covered in the next meeting at least two weeks ahead of time. Likewise, if you have meetings every week, you should make sure that you can begin finalizing the content about two and a half to three days in advance of the meeting itself. Cutting off opportunities to add new items for discussion at the last minute is important to the management of meetings. When items for consideration are added late or, worse still, at the meeting, the odds are greatly reduced that they will receive careful consideration. You also must avoid having new items crowd out time to work on matters that everyone has previously had time to think about and has come to the meeting prepared to address.

Once you have a sense of the content of the meeting, sort the various items into one of the three categories: announcements, discussions, and decisions. Some items might not fall neatly into just one of these categories. In those cases, think carefully about how to break them up. At the same time, though, to ensure the smooth flow of business, it is important that like activities are bundled together in your meetings.

Decide Who Should Be There

Knowing the basic content of your meeting well in advance gives you the time to think carefully about who should be invited to attend. For example, suppose you are in a team that is currently working on one component of a large project. Other teams are working on other components. An issue has come up that involves the compatibility of some of the policy recommendations that members of your team plan to make and the recommendations of another team. Although your team could probably make some headway in addressing the issue of compatibility through internal discussions, at some point, it would make sense for your discussions to include one or more members of the other team involved. As you prepare for your approaching meeting, if you have given yourself sufficient time, you will be able to request that people from the other team attend, if not for all the meeting then at least for some part of it. You might find that a subsequent meeting involving representatives of other teams and the client might also be fruitful for keeping everyone on track and producing recommendations that are consistent and useful to the client.

Should all members of a team or group attend all meetings? The simple answer is *no*. People should be invited to attend meetings only when the business of the meeting is directly relevant to them and their presence would allow them to make useful contributions. Having said that, it is also important to observe that meetings provide invaluable opportunities for building team spirit and helping members of groups to get to know one another. From this perspective, we can see that there is merit in seeking to have all the members of a team or a group attend all major meetings, if at all possible. The onus is then on you to ensure that everyone knows why they are at each meeting and that as many opportunities as possible are provided for everyone to contribute to the business.

Solicit Background Information or Reports

So far, I have noted how your decisions about the content of a meeting will affect your decisions about who should attend. Typically, your decisions about people to invite will be driven by your sense of who has ideas or information that will be of value to the planned discussions, or who should be involved in making specific decisions. At times, you will want vital information to be circulated among all attendees prior to the meeting. Thus, it is important that you allow time before your meeting to ask for and receive background information or reports that will have a bearing on the discussions to be held and the decisions to be made.

Many meetings quickly become boring because they involve people giving a series of reports, many of which seem quite unrelated. In many ways, the giving of reports in meetings is a waste of time. This is neither the most efficient use of people's time nor the most efficient way to convey important information. Soliciting and circulating reports in advance is a way to increase the likelihood that your meeting will be focused and remain engaging for everyone.

Written reports need not be long. In fact, short reports are best. If reports cannot be kept to just a few pages, though, it is vital that the authors provide an executive summary. That summary should capture the essence of the report's content. Any recommendations made in the report should also be highlighted immediately following the summary. The whole point of receiving reports ahead of time and circulating them is to allow people to come to the meeting having read all relevant background material and ready to engage in informed discussions or to make informed decisions.

Establish a Time Line

Most meetings take place for a set amount of time. The longer meetings run, the more people's energy levels will flag. To some degree, this problem can be overcome by breaking up the activities that will take place in the meeting. Once you have a clear sense of the content of your meeting, you should establish a basic time line. Begin by allocating time to announcements, discussions, and decisions. Among these items, announcements should be dealt with reasonably quickly at the beginning of the meeting. These should be followed by discussion time, which should take up the bulk of the meeting. Decisions should be made near the meeting's end. On the basis of your judgment about how much time to allocate to different activities, you can determine how much time you think the meeting as a whole should take. Think about ways to provide logical breaks every forty-five minutes or so. They will help to keep people alert and engaged. Also, think about how you might work to finish the meeting on a high note. Placing something light at the end of the meeting can be a good way to allow people to decompress from the more intense work associated with holding discussions and making decisions.

Construct an Agenda

At the most basic level, the agenda for a meeting simply sets out the items to be covered. People often develop meeting agendas in a highly cursory fashion: only the most basic information is given about items to be covered. You can, however, make your meetings more productive by taking time to think about the sequencing of items and by providing enough details on each item that everyone can come well prepared. Agendas can follow a variety of formats.

In figure 7-1, I present one approach to setting out a meeting agenda. Several details deserve mention. First, note that each item has a time allotment. As you develop your meeting agendas, try to pad the time devoted to each item. This way, if discussions do run over, the entire meeting will still conclude by the stipulated hour. Second, note that

```
Meeting Agenda

1:05–1:15  Announcements

1:15–2:00  External relations—John (Discussion)
           Explore concerns about external relations and why they have arisen.
                 Outcome: List ways to improve our relations with the client and
                          other external players.

2:00–2:05  Break

2:05–2:20  Developing relations with Public Sector Consultants, Ltd. (PSC)—
           Meredith (Decision)
                 It is recommended that we hold lunch seminars with
                 PSC every six weeks on techniques for program evaluation.
                 Please see Meredith's report (attached).

2:20–3:00  Topics for future meetings (Discussion)

3:00       End
```

Figure 7-1. Sample Meeting Agenda

the agenda follows the announcements-discussions-decisions sequence. Further, most of the time in the meeting is allocated to discussion. This means that everyone at the meeting should be engaged in the meeting's business for most of the time. Third, agenda items are marked so that people know whether they will involve adding to discussions or making decisions. In addition, the people who are most central to each item are named. Fourth, an outcome statement is given for the discussion item. This limits the possibility of the discussion wandering off track. Fifth, each of the main agenda items is explained with a brief sentence. This way, people know what to expect and can prepare accordingly. Finally, time is made for a short break. Time is also reserved at the end for people to discuss topics for future meetings. This way, people who might have raised important, but somewhat extraneous, points in the body of the meeting will get a hearing. Further, any new issues that arose as a consequence of the earlier discussions can be considered here as candidates for in-depth discussion at a later date.

Assign Meeting Roles

Meetings become much more productive when several key tasks are undertaken. First, someone must facilitate the meeting. The facilitator works to make the meeting run smoothly. He or she opens and closes the meeting and guides the discussion. I will discuss this role in more detail below. Second, someone should keep time. If one person can keep an eye on the time and alert the group to how much time is left to spend on various parts of the meeting, everyone else is free to focus closely on the actual business at hand. This might seem a trivial role, but it is actually quite important for keeping the meeting on track. Third, someone should serve as a scribe. The scribe records ideas and elements of the discussion on a board. It is a way to help everyone to visually keep track of the discussion and, hence, remain focused. Finally, somebody should serve as the note taker, sometimes known as the rapporteur. This person helps by building the record of what occurred at the meeting.

Potentially, one person could play all four of these roles. It is almost always better, though, when different people fill the roles. To reduce the risk of a person becoming typecast in particular roles (for example, Quiet John, who always takes the notes, or Police Officer Kelly, who calls the time), rotating roles from meeting to meeting ensures that responsibilities are spread throughout the group. Further, rotation gives everyone insights into what it is like to play each role, what the business of the meeting looks like from different perspectives, and how they might each contribute—regardless of their role—to making the meetings work well. Dominating these roles yourself and worrying that assigning them to others will take you out of the limelight is petty-minded and puts your ego's needs ahead of organizational effectiveness. Although it is true that you might be able to claim credit when things go well, you will also be in the hot seat when things go wrong. You can do better than that.

Conduct "Rehearsals"

It might sound strange to suggest rehearsing prior to your meeting, but I have some quite specific matters in mind. By rehearsing, I mean doing all that you can to increase the chances that the meeting will go smoothly. Make sure that the meeting room is booked and that refreshments, if they are to be served, have been ordered. When you are assigning roles to people, make sure that each of them knows in advance what his or her role will entail and how he or she can shine in it. If you have requested that some people provide reports for circulation before the meeting, make sure that you touch base with each of them well in advance so that they understand what you want from them, what the report should be like, and when you need to have it. If you have invited someone from outside the team or group to attend a meeting, make sure to supply information about the meeting time and place. You should also clarify what you expect from the person and what he or she can expect from the group. Taking care of small details such as driving directions and parking permits is not only courteous, but is important for ensuring things run smoothly.

As someone with full information about the content of the meeting, you can anticipate possible points of disagreement among those who will be attending. With this insight, you can reduce the risk of surprises or unpleasantness in the meeting. If you have a sense that somebody is going to be upset by what someone else has written in a report, try to talk with that person one-on-one before the full meeting. When people have been forewarned about possible problems, they can ruminate on how to deal with them. This is not to say that conflict is a bad thing. The airing of differences of opinion is often an important part of coming to good decisions. Your task is to try to reduce the emotional heat that might otherwise accompany such differences.

Circulate All Written Materials in Advance

A meeting announcement, with the agenda and any relevant reports, should be circulated in advance of the meeting. In figure 7-2, I provide an example of a meeting announcement. It could readily be sent by e-mail or circulated in other ways. Circulating all written materials in advance gives people time to prepare mentally for the meeting and to set aside time for it. For regular monthly meetings, you should plan to circulate these materials a week in advance. For regular weekly meetings, circulation at least a day before the meeting would suffice. Wherever possible, avoid overwhelming people with paper. The fewer the pages that people have to deal with, the better. When a large stack of papers arrives on a busy person's desk, the natural tendency is to set it aside and, if possible, keep it aside. One of your tasks as a meeting planner, however, is to avoid that scenario, and by reducing the volume of paper you contribute, you are doing just that.

Meeting Announcement

Main purpose: _____

To: [List of attendees]

Date: _____

Time: ___ to ___

Location: _____

Roles:

Timekeeper   _____
Facilitator   _____
Scribe   _____
Note taker   _____

Please review the attached agenda and reports before the meeting.

Figure 7-2. Sample Meeting Announcement

THE MEETING

Discussion and decision making lie at the heart of most meetings. Good meetings proceed in ways that allow these activities to be coordinated, cordial, and productive. Below I will focus more closely on what you can do as a facilitator to guide discussions and decision making, but for now I will deal with four basic steps to improve the flow and the productivity of meetings.

Establish Ground Rules

Meetings of any sort run more smoothly when those present adhere to a set of ground rules concerning participation. For many of us, these simple rules are the good manners we learned in our early years of school. Yet it is surprising how many people behave as though they never learned them. Arredondo (2000, 156) suggests the following ground rules for meetings:

1. Show up on time.
2. Come prepared.

3. Stick to the agenda.
4. One person to speak at a time. No interrupting.
5. Don't dominate the floor. Address one point, and then give someone else a chance.
6. Don't be a distraction: no cross-talk, sidebar conversations, or cell phone calls while the meeting is underway.
7. Show courtesy and respect to others.
8. Return from breaks promptly.

To my mind, we need to be sensitive about how we introduce rules like this. After all, it would be counterproductive if stating these rules at the outset of a meeting made those in attendance feel as if they were being infantilized. To avoid such problems, I offer two suggestions. First, preface the circulation of ground rules by stating your concern that your meetings run as productively as possible. If you are working with a new group of people and plan to have a series of meetings, the ground rules should be circulated at the first meeting. Unless problems arise later that clearly demonstrate that one or more rules are being violated, there should be no further need to discuss them. Second, you could present a list of rules as some ideas that you have about how to conduct ourselves in our meetings. You could then ask participants to review your suggestions in pairs and come up with any other rules that they think would be helpful. After that, a short discussion involving the whole group could be held where the group's meeting ground rules are finalized. This collaborative approach to setting ground rules offers the benefit of ensuring that everyone feels they had a chance to contribute to them. The ground rules become "our rules," which can increase the chances that everyone will agree to follow them.

Stay on Task

Inevitably during the process of good discussions, people will raise topics, ideas, or questions that, though related to the main point, are somewhat peripheral. This is often fine. The danger, however, is that too much time devoted to such matters will draw the meeting's focus off task. Keeping to the agenda is vital for ensuring that the important business of the meeting is addressed as intended. People often come away from meetings deeply dissatisfied when issues that they had hoped to discuss were crowded out by unwieldy discussion of items higher up the agenda. To keep this from happening, avoid letting new issues crowd out those that people have come to the meeting prepared to address. Not only do such impromptu changes to the agenda do a disservice to people who have conscientiously prepared for the meeting at hand, but it is likely that any discussion of these additional issues would be better informed by the presence of certain other people who know the issues well or by some fact checking and individual reflection prior to the meeting.

To allow discussions to stay focused, but to acknowledge the value of giving consideration to additional issues, Micale (1999) suggests that groups make use of a space in the meeting room that she calls the "parking lot." This space is used for writing down any topics that, while seemingly important, are not directly related to the main topic of discussion. The idea here is not simply to note such topics and then forget them. Micale suggests that we "make sure that all parking lot issues are addressed at some point, or that there is group agreement on how those issues will be addressed" (46).

Keep Time

Meetings can quickly turn messy when participants lose track of time. Every effort should be made to start and finish meetings on time. Because most people have little spare time, when meetings run beyond the planned finish point, some people will find themselves having to leave while discussion is still occurring. This can disrupt the flow of conversation and be frustrating for all participants, including those who leave wondering whether the points they wanted to make will be considered. In a way, then, we might say that keeping to time is democratic. Discussions and decisions should never be dominated simply by those who have the time and energy to remain to the bitter end.

To keep time in meetings, two things are necessary. First, you must plan the meetings so that the number of items to be addressed and the time devoted to the meeting are compatible. There are limits to the number of issues people can address in one sitting, so plan your meetings accordingly. Second, during the meetings, one person should keep close track of time and inform the rest of the group when the time devoted to specific topics is starting to run out. This role need not be performed in an officious way, but gentle reminders during the course of the meeting can be helpful for keeping the flow of business on task and on time.

Record Ideas

Meeting productivity will be affected by the effort put into recording ideas. Discussion and decision making during the meeting itself can be usefully supported by efforts to capture ideas as they are expressed. The scribe who jots things down for the group to see should try to distill the key points of discussions as they arise. Jotting down a phrase or a question as someone is speaking can be an excellent way to jog the memories or spark the imaginations of others. Good scribe work, while apparently mechanical in nature, can promote the flow of ideas and, thus, enhance the quality of a meeting.

The work of the note taker should parallel that of the scribe. Unlike the scribe, the note taker's role is to record the main points of discussion and the major decisions emerging from the meeting. These notes should not be written as a blow-by-blow account of meeting business. We leave that style of note taking to court reporters. The key to writing good notes is to continually ask, "What elements of this meeting will we need to record for afterward?" Recording decisions is clearly important. Recording any agreements about tasks to be done and who will take care of them is also important. But, in addition, the note taker should seek to capture the essence of major discussions.

Tropman (1996) suggests that each heading in the meeting notes or "minutes" should correspond to the headings on the agenda. The note taker should write "a summative reflection" of no more than two paragraphs on the item under discussion. According to Tropman, "a summative reflection involves listening to the discussion and then providing a summary in which the main points are covered. The tilt and spin of the discussion is reflected but names are not mentioned" (31). Tropman suggests that dropping names is important because, if particular people are identified with a position that turns out to be unfavorable, they will spend energy trying to save face by defending their views. Elimination of names creates a space for such people to begin working with others after the meeting to craft proposals that all could eventually agree with. Tropman also suggests that the note taker can do a service to the group during the meeting. When a discussion is drawing to a close, he or she can provide a brief oral summary before writing it down. Although this might appear to be done primarily to check with others about how to characterize what has been said, the approach serves to remind people within the meeting of what has been achieved through the discussion. An oral check of this kind can be a prelude to achieving closure to a discussion.

AFTER THE MEETING

The hardest work associated with good meetings occurs during the preparation stage and the meeting itself, but there are several steps worth taking routinely after your meetings have come to a close. These steps will help you to maximize the value of your meetings and will also help you to lay the foundations for equally good or even better future meetings.

Evaluate the Process

How did it go? After facilitating a meeting, we typically have some general sense of how well it went. In addition to our own impressions, however, hearing the impressions that others have of the meeting can be a valuable way to help us reflect on what took place. Such reflection can give us clues about follow-up actions we should take. It can also help us learn about our facilitation skills and discover ways to improve the quality of the meetings we hold.

In the cut and thrust of meetings, there are times when people get quite emotionally involved with the positions they take. As a facilitator, you can attempt to reduce tensions in meetings, but, no matter what, when the meeting has come to a close you should try to view events from the perspective of those who did get emotionally involved in the discussion. It can be helpful to touch base quietly with these people after the meeting. The last thing you want is for people to feel alienated as a consequence of what happened in the meeting. Taking the time to listen to people who were at the center of differences of opinion can be an effective way to defuse tensions and clear the way for more productive engagements in the future.

Although it might seem overly self-conscious, I have found that there is considerable value in requesting written feedback on meetings as the last thing that people do before they leave the room. The evaluation forms I have used are quite simple, often asking only two questions:

What did you most like about this meeting? and What could I have done to make the meeting better? When people know that you take their comments to heart and that you often act on them, they will continue to give you valuable feedback. Over time, incremental adjustments from meeting to meeting can add up in impressive ways and improve the overall quality of the experience for everyone.

Several authors have suggested questions that you might ask of yourself and of others in order to diagnose your meetings and determine how to improve them. Arredondo (2000, 164) suggests using an evaluation form of the kind presented in figure 7-3. My preference is to work with open-ended questions, but a form of this sort is a useful way to help you and others to discover ways to improve your meetings.

Circulate Meeting Notes

It is a good practice, within a few days of the meeting, to circulate among all the participants the notes that were recorded there. Clear, concise notes can ensure that meeting participants know what is expected of them

Evaluation Form *(For each item, please circle the applicable response.)*			
Item	**Response**		
Our meetings start on time.	Usually	Sometimes	Rarely
Our meetings follow the agenda.	Usually	Sometimes	Rarely
Everyone observes the ground rules.	Usually	Sometimes	Rarely
Everyone comes prepared.	Usually	Sometimes	Rarely
Everyone participates.	Usually	Sometimes	Rarely
Communication is courteous and constructive.	Usually	Sometimes	Rarely
Our meetings follow a process for solving problems.	Usually	Sometimes	Rarely
Our meetings accomplish the purpose.	Usually	Sometimes	Rarely
Follow-up actions are done and reported on time.	Usually	Sometimes	Rarely
Leadership is effective.	Usually	Sometimes	Rarely
Our meetings end on time.	Usually	Sometimes	Rarely

Figure 7-3. Sample Meeting Evaluation Form

as a result of decisions that were made. In addition, these notes can be particularly important when a discussion was held but no decision about action was taken. The notes on the discussion can prompt new thoughts about the issues at stake and how they might be resolved. Circulating the notes in a timely fashion is a low-key way to remind people that the work of a meeting does not conclude when they walk out the door.

Solicit Additional Input

People often call meetings to gain ideas and insights from others concerning a pressing problem. Recording suggestions made at the meeting can be helpful, and many might think that such a record is all they need—that is, the ideas and insights gained at the meeting are sufficient to guide next steps. As we all know, however, there are many times after we leave meetings, perhaps in the car driving home or the following night or day, when we are struck by new thoughts or ideas that are relevant to what was discussed. As a meeting facilitator, you can capitalize on this postmeeting inspiration. For example, try circulating your meeting notes, or a brief summary of them, as part of your effort to thank people for attending. Then, within your message, include a statement such as "As you can see from this list, we received several excellent ideas for ways to proceed. If, while looking over this list, you think of other ideas that we should also consider, please let me know. I am eager to receive any additional insights you might have." If invited to provide additional input, some people will respond. It is worth asking.

Monitor Task Completion

Earlier I noted that good meetings spark action. They produce decisions about tasks to be performed and who will perform them. This does not mean, though, that you should take it on faith that people will automatically follow-up and do the tasks assigned to them in your meetings. People are rushed, have much on their minds, and often they forget things. There are, however, steps you can take to make sure that your meetings prompt action. In the days after every meeting, find low-key ways to contact people who had tasks assigned to them. During brief conversations with these people or within e-mail messages to them, make sure that you check on how the work is proceeding. For example, you can prompt action by asking a question about the work or whether clarification is needed following the discussion in the meeting.

Determine Next Steps

Good meetings spark action for you. At the end of a productive meeting, you are likely to have a lot of material to work with concerning tasks others are to perform, follow-up items for you, and additional information or reports to pursue. Thus, it is important to take time soon after the meeting to develop a task list. With all tasks listed, you can begin to work through them systematically. In doing so, you can keep up the momentum of a good meeting and ensure that it really does add to team or organizational productivity. The quality of your follow-up work will have a significant bearing on how you and others judge the value added to your meetings.

A Focus on Facilitating

Holpp (1999, 128) has observed, "When meetings fail, it's usually from a lack of planning, rather than a lack of control during the meeting." Nonetheless, there is much that you can do as a facilitator to elevate the quality of your meetings. More than anything else, the task of meeting facilitator requires you to coordinate the actions of others. This is a bit like an air traffic controller at a busy airport. By keeping your wits about you, it is possible to cut through a lot of business in a calm, systematic way, but letting your concentration wander, or spending too much time on one issue while ignoring others, could quickly lead to a crisis. As a meeting facilitator, it is vital that you maintain a certain distance from the actions taking place. If you step out of your role to become just another participant, you risk being like an air traffic controller who abandons his or her post to pilot a plane. In the heat of the moment, perhaps that makes sense, but from the broader perspective of keeping everything on track, such an action can be disastrous. This suggests that it is always easier to facilitate a meeting if you do not have any strong opinions about the specific issues under discussion, or if you are able to keep your personal views to yourself. When this is impossible, you should turn over the role of facilitator to someone else who can be more neutral regarding the discussion topic.

When you facilitate a meeting, your role is to help everyone work through the agenda items in a manner that ensures engaging discussions and good decisions. At the outset, you should make sure that everyone knows everyone else and that everybody understands why he or she is at the meeting. If necessary, you should also cover the issue of ground rules. Beyond that, your task is to manage the interactions of the group.

One of the most important tasks of the facilitator is to encourage balanced participation. This can be achieved by inviting input from quiet members and by limiting the contributions of those who would otherwise dominate discussion. Calling people by name is a vital way to connect with them and to convey that you really care about what they have to say. You should also work to promote the sharing of differences of opinion and perspective. Meetings become especially valuable to groups and organizations when they serve as forums for the airing and reconciling of differences. A good facilitator should be able to encourage disagreement, but it is essential to work with participants in such a way that those disagreements lead to positive, not negative, outcomes. Finally, as facilitator, you should seek to guide the flow of talk by choosing the right moments to pause and summarize what others have said, by drawing out similarities and differences of perspective, and by moving conversations toward resolution and decision making.

Ask Questions

Good facilitators ask open-ended questions that require people to respond using more than simple "yes" or "no" answers. When responses are given to those questions, facilitators should listen attentively, making good eye contact, nodding, and asking follow-up questions where appropriate. In meetings, questions can be used for many useful purposes. Here are some examples:

- Suppose somebody has been talking a lot, making it difficult for others to make contributions. You might say, "John has made his point of view fairly clear. But what do others of you think? Rhonda, I don't think we've heard from you yet. What are your views on this issue?"
- Suppose the group appears to be going over the same ground and getting nowhere. You might say, "I get the sense that we are ready to move on. Rebecca, how would you summarize the discussion to this point?"

- Suppose most members of the group appear to ignore ideas put forward by one or two members. You might say, "Josh's idea gives us another option. Graham, how does Josh's idea square with yours?"

Manage the Group Process

When disagreements arise in a meeting, the facilitator must find ways to manage them. The most difficult situations arise when people show a high degree of emotional attachment to the views they are expressing. In moments of conflict, one way for you to move things forward is to separate the emotion from the idea that is being expressed. For example, rephrasing what various speakers have said can take the heat out of the exchange. This requires practice, and there will be times when your efforts will not work. Having a good sense of timing can help. Knowing how long to leave an interaction going before you intervene can be just as important as the nature of your intervention. Calling impromptu breaks can also be a way to reduce emotions. It is surprising how a five-minute break can help people to achieve some perspective on a discussion and find ways to reconcile their differences with others. As a facilitator, you have a lot of room to move here and to guide people toward seeing how best to handle themselves and each other.

At the conclusion of a meeting, as facilitator you should take a few minutes to review what has been accomplished. Also use this time to note any commitments made in the meeting by group members. Another important task you should always do at the end of a meeting is praise or thank the group for what has been accomplished. You need not gush compliments, but finding sincere, low-key ways to acknowledge the efforts of others will make people feel that the meeting was worthwhile and that their presence was appreciated.

BRAINSTORMING

Brainstorming sessions are designed to generate lists of possible solutions to problems. Something approximating brainstorming occurs during many discussions in meetings. Proper brainstorming sessions are distinct kinds of meetings, however, and they call for distinctive behaviors on the part of participants and the facilitator. A good brainstorming session can occur in the space of thirty minutes. Because they call for energy and creativity, rarely should these sessions run for more than an hour. Outcome statements for brainstorming sessions typically begin "List ways to. . . ." Kelley (2001), who uses brainstorming sessions—he calls them "brainstormers"—as an integral part of his highly successful product design company IDEO, has observed:

> Hot brainstormers may generate a hundred or more ideas, ten of which may be solid leads. They can help put a team on course, and the rush of adrenaline can keep team members buzzing for days. There's a ripple effect. People talk after brainstormers, sharing wild or practical ideas that may have come out of a particularly vibrant session. A great brainstormer gives you a fantastic feeling of possibility, and an hour later you walk out of the room a little richer for the experience (62).

As the facilitator, you can do several things ahead of time, or at the start of a brainstorming session, to improve the chances that it will be productive. First, you should work to develop a clear description of the problem to be tackled. The better articulated the problem, the easier it is for others to propose ideas for appropriate solutions. Kelley has suggested that, if a session seems to lack direction, you should stop and spend a few minutes working on the problem statement. The idea is to express the problem in a manner that makes it tangible, while not limiting the possible solutions. Second, strive to invite a diverse range of participants who can bring distinctive points of view to thinking about the problem. Third, when you circulate invitations to the brainstorming session, you might also propose a homework exercise for participants. This might involve talking with informants, making a site visit, or reading over material related to similar problems or issues. Fourth, you should get the right equipment into the room where the session will occur. Having lots of boards and paper to write and draw on is essential. The boards should be set up so that you can move from one to another, keeping each listed idea visible to participants.

Brainstorming sessions should be lively, and they should be enjoyable for the participants. Balancing this liveliness with a degree of orderliness can be hard. One way to do so involves having well-understood ground rules. Going over them at the beginning of the meeting can be a good way to establish norms of appropriate behavior. Again, this need not be done as a grim task. Just pointing them out and explaining why they matter should suffice. An early popularizer of brainstorming sessions, Osborn (1963, 156), suggested four rules for brainstorming:

- Criticism is ruled out.
- "Freewheeling" is welcomed.
- Quantity is wanted.
- Combination and improvement are sought.

Osborn went on to suggest that the only strictly formal feature of these sessions should be the written record of all ideas suggested. The onus is on the facilitator to work with participants to encourage the generation of ideas and efforts to build or "hitchhike" one idea on another. At IDEO, the company's version of the brainstorming rules are displayed in large letters in several locations in the conference rooms before each session, so that every participant can continually see them (Sutton and Hargadon 1996). These rules, similar to those proposed by Osborn, are as follows:

- Defer judgment.
- Build on the ideas of others.
- One conversation at a time.
- Stay focused on the topic.
- Encourage wild ideas.

As the facilitator, during the meeting you should write ideas down, numbering them as you do so. Numbering motivates the participants to generate more and more ideas. It is also a great way to allow you and the participants to jump quickly between ideas—hitchhike—without losing track of where you are. To do so, promote dialogue and idea generation while at the same time lightly enforcing the ground rules. In the rapid-fire interactions of brainstorming sessions, the most effective way to enforce the rules might be simply to point to a rule on the board when you detect that it is being frequently violated. This way, you keep things on track, but maintain the general levity that is required of such sessions. At the end of the session, you should look for ways to provide feedback to the group members concerning their performance, how well they kept to the ground rules, and how they might work to consolidate or improve on their group performance next time.

At IDEO, many brainstorming sessions are videotaped. At the end of the sessions, all notes taken by the facilitator and by the participants are recorded and a formal report on the meeting is prepared to guide subsequent work. According to Sutton and Hargadon (1996, 698), "Brain-storms are among the main ways that design solutions are added to, stored in, and retrieved from IDEO's memory."

There are also several missteps to avoid during a brainstorming session. First, do not let organizational hierarchies be reflected in the meeting. Having "the boss" speak first and tell people what kind of ideas are being looked for can inhibit the creative flow. Second, avoid formalities. Going around the room, letting each person speak in turn, will also inhibit the creative flow. Finally, avoid earnestness. Having food at the brainstorming session and encouraging humor on the part of participants is fine. Good ideas are more likely to emerge when people are having fun.

The actions taken after a brainstorming session, like the actions taken after a regular meeting, can do much to contribute to its overall productivity. Thus, make sure that ideas generated in the meeting are recorded, solicit additional input, and take the time to follow up on good ideas rapidly.

ANALYTICAL DISCUSSIONS

Productive brainstorming requires us to hold our judgment in abeyance. This is how we can generate many ideas rapidly. Analytical thinking represents something close to the reverse of that process. Typically, in analytical discussions we begin with a variety of ideas or options and then proceed to scrutinize them with the goal of identifying a handful worthy of further pursuit. Our outcome statements for such discussions might begin in these ways: "Isolate possible causes of . . . ," "Plan a study of . . . ," "Create a flow chart of . . . ," "Propose a model of . . . ," "Define criteria for judging . . . ," "Evaluate the merits of . . . ," "Recommend options for achieving . . . ," and so on. Because they can be intense—and that is what you want them to be—meetings devoted to analytical discussions should run no longer than an hour. When appropriate meeting preparation has taken place, a great deal can be achieved in this time.

As policy analysts, much of our training involves being introduced to analytical frameworks and learning how to make productive use of them. Guided by such tools as cost-benefit analysis, we work to break policy issues into manageable parts and to focus intently on each of those parts, seeking to gain new insights. It is through such activity that we come to develop reasoned, fact-based advice for our clients. Although much of the work we do as policy analysts involves working individually on particular parts of larger projects, there are many times when we can benefit from engaging in group-level analytical discussions. Through such discussions, we can gain clearer understandings of policy problems and come to see which approaches to studying them might be most fruitful. Our discussions provide opportunities to share knowledge and ideas. Having people at the table who approach the problem from several distinct perspectives can increase the chances that each different option will be given a fair hearing.

Myriad possibilities exist for using frameworks to guide analytical discussions. The most useful frameworks are often quite simple. For example, we might take the time to share causal stories. "How might we account for this increase in teenage pregnancies?" The answers we provide can serve as the starting point for undertaking more detailed studies of a social or economic phenomenon and its causes. As another example, we might construct "What if" scenarios. "What if we could identify teenagers at risk and give them special counseling?" "What if we place whole families, rather than just individuals, in the risk set?" Answers to questions of this sort can help us to identify policy options worth exploring in more depth. More complicated variants on these approaches can also be used. For example, once a number of policy options have been developed, it can be helpful to have an analytical discussion with the goal of identifying appropriate criteria against which to judge every option. Identifying appropriate items to include in cost-benefit analyses can also be done in this way.

I have often found that SWOT analysis works well in analytical discussions. As originally conceived by business analysts, the goal of working with this framework is to identify a company or business unit's *strengths, weaknesses, opportunities,* and *threats* (Wright, Pringle, and Kroll 1992). Although this form of analysis was originally designed for business applications, its framework is useful to help us think through a variety of scenarios in which individual or collective capacities are likely to interact in positive or negative ways with external conditions. Another business framework, the structure-conduct-performance (SCP) paradigm found in the industrial organization literature, asks that we think about the ways that institutional *structure* affects organizational or individual *conduct* and how that conduct is in turn likely to influence

performance. Economists and political scientists have applied this framework to explore the effects of institutional arrangements in a variety of
settings (Eisner and Meier 1990; Myerson 1995; Porter 1979).

When brainstorming, having a good definition of the problem at
hand is critical for ensuring the flow of productive ideas. In analytical
discussions, the key to productivity lies in finding an appropriate match
between the issue at hand and the framework being applied to thinking
about it. This is something that can be considered well before the meeting. Still, serendipity has its place here, too. Just as Weick (1995, 54)
noted that "any old map will do" as a sense-making device and a prompt
to discussions when you are lost, we might say that even an apparently
inappropriate framework can be a good starting point for moving analytical discussions in productive directions. The most important thing to
strive for is a focused, engaging discussion. Applying simple frameworks
will often be sufficient to get you to that point. Our analytical discussions can do much to sharpen our thinking and thus improve the quality of the work we do as individual policy analysts.

DECISION MAKING

Earlier I suggested that high-quality meetings produce high-quality decisions. As policy analysts, we know that a large amount of scholarship has
gone into developing analytical tools and models that are designed to
support decision making. From the analytical perspective, we often take
the view that a specific choice is superior to all others, yet we are surprised to find that other people do not see matters in such cut-and-dried
ways. The psychology of decision making can be complicated. For those
of us seeking to guide decision making in meetings, Tropman (1996, 94)
has suggested that we think in terms of "decision crystallization." In
meetings, decisions can be thought of as emerging through a three-stage
process. First, the foregoing discussion is summarized. ("Well, based on
what everyone has said, it seems to me that we have arrived at two basic
options.") Second, a suggestion for action is vocalized and justified. ("I
suggest that we go with the first option because . . . .") Third, people engage in "decision sculpting." This is where you stand back from the decision or set of decisions that have been made and decide whether the entire package is coherent and acceptable. Depending on responses to that,
efforts can be made to adjust the decision to make it work for everyone.

Rule	Name	Description
1.	Majority rule	One person, one vote.
2.	Preference intensity	Consider how strongly people feel on the issue.
3.	Involvement	Pay closest attention to those most affected.
4.	Expertise	Ask if expert advice is needed. When it is, seek it.
5.	Power	Do what the boss or most powerful person wants.
6.	Negativity	If there is no good reason to change, do nothing.

Figure 7-4. Common Decision Rules

How do we make decisions? Tropman (1996) contends that people in meetings tend to invoke six different decision rules. I have summarized these rules in figure 7-4. Often in combination, these rules are used to justify the choices people make. Some of these rules will be more familiar than others, but there is nothing inherently superior about any one of them as a device for producing good decisions, and each might be more or less applicable given the topics under discussion. By familiarizing ourselves with these decision rules, we can become savvier at figuring out the rhetorical strategies people employ to gain influence in meetings. Forearmed, we can improve our ability to guide discussions in ways that lead to the making of good, reasoned decisions.

Looking over the decision rules listed in figure 7-4, we can begin to see why decision making in meetings is often accompanied by emotive language, fear, or resignation. We can also start to appreciate why people so often put off making decisions until absolutely necessary. Even in light of these tendencies, as a facilitator you can take actions to increase the odds that good decisions will be made. One useful strategy involves separating the discussion of options from the making of a decision. Creating a separation of this kind reduces the possibility that decisions will be made in the heat of the moment. It also opens space for individual rumination by meeting participants in the period between the discussion and the making of the final decision. Although some people might consider this separation approach as a cause of unnecessary delay, sometimes this approach has the opposite effect. The separation of discussions from decisions eliminates the high-stakes aspect of talking about a subject. Thus, work toward a decision can begin in a timely fashion. Achieving closure might still be difficult, but setting up a sequence of events in advance gives everyone a sense of when you expect decision crystallization to occur. Rather than feed into procrastination, then, separating of discussions and decisions might actually serve to push the process forward, toward closure.

IMPROMPTU MEETINGS

Throughout this chapter I have deliberately suggested that a fairly formal approach should be taken to organizing and facilitating meetings. This is because I believe that the formal approach is likely to ensure that issues of structure, participation, and content are given appropriate consideration. That said, there are times when people are caught up in events and the need arises for an impromptu meeting. Such meetings can never be expected to be as productive as planned meetings simply because, by definition, people will not have had time to prepare for them. Nevertheless, impromptu meetings can still be helpful. For you, being able to hold your own in an impromptu setting is a way to demonstrate your leadership potential. Given enough time to prepare, even plodders can do a lot of things well. Being able to quickly organize and calmly facilitate a productive meeting at a moment's notice is a good test of someone's people skills.

Good facilitation, and the desire to follow a logical structure, can do wonders for an impromptu meeting. Thus, I suggest that, when an impromptu meeting is called, you should do as much as you can to make it parallel a planned meeting. Take a few minutes at the start to work with the other participants to devise and write down an agenda. As the agenda is developed, make sure that all the relevant people will be present to discuss items on it. Try to follow the sequence suggested earlier: first announcements, then discussion items, followed by decision items, and then some light business to bring things to a close. Again, as with planned meetings, make sure that the usual meeting roles are assigned. The impromptu meeting will be more productive if you have a facilitator, a timekeeper, a scribe, and a note taker. If you have a choice of spaces to meet in, try to use a room that is well equipped for meetings, so that you can use writing boards and presentational tools quickly and effectively to promote discussion and to move things along. In short, the more practice you have working in formal settings, the better you will be at working in impromptu settings. That point holds true for musicians, painters, dancers, and cooks. It holds true for meeting facilitators as well.

Summary

All of us frequently attend meetings of one sort or another. From our experiences in these meetings, we know that they represent occasions where people skills—or their lack—can make a dramatic difference to the quality of the proceedings. Here, I have suggested a variety of actions that you can take before, during, and after meetings to make them high-quality events. Good meetings are characterized by focused discussion, participation by all in attendance, and the generation of considered decisions. As a facilitator, the amount of effort you put into setting up and managing meetings will have a material bearing on their overall effectiveness. Because meetings are so commonplace, people have a tendency to assume that how well they work has much to do with chance or with the personalities of the people in attendance. What I have said here should put an end to that kind of thinking. There are a variety of levers that you can work to help your meetings run smoothly. None of this is easy. Managing people during meetings can often be difficult, but over time, as you become practiced at setting up and running meetings, you will develop the skills and intuitions that are the hallmarks of excellent facilitators. You also should not discount the power of leadership by example. The good behaviors that you model as a facilitator will rub off on other participants in your meetings. When this happens, you make it easier for everyone to work together to produce high-quality decisions. That is exactly what you want from meetings.

Skill-Building Checklist

- Meetings can be used to announce, to discuss, and to decide things, but tasks can be accomplished by other means, too, such as e-mail or telephone. Before calling a meeting, devise an outcome statement, specifying what you want to achieve. This will help you determine whether a meeting is necessary and who should attend.

- In good meetings, there is a great amount of participation, work gets done, people feel energized, and action is sparked. You should strive to ensure that these four goals are achieved.

- The more you work in advance to organize the content of your meetings and to develop an agenda that appropriately sequences business, the better. Before a meeting, you should assign roles (facilitator, timekeeper, scribe, and note taker). You should also work to ensure that everyone comes ready to participate. People should leave your meetings judging that their attendance was the best use of their time.

- Four things can make meetings more productive. First, the group should follow a set of ground rules. Second, you should avoid issues that are not on the agenda. Third, you should never run over time. Finally, you should record the main points of discussions, decisions taken, and commitments made to future action.

- As a facilitator, your role is to help everyone work through the agenda in a way that promotes engaging discussions and good decisions. You should invite participation, draw out similarities and differences, summarize progress, and move conversations toward resolution and closure. Maintaining a certain distance from the action is important. It is easier to facilitate when you do not have strong opinions about the issues under discussion, or you are at least able to withhold your own opinions and maintain a critical distance during the discussion.

- You should distinguish between times when it is appropriate to call brainstorming sessions and when analytical discussions are needed. You should also learn to recognize the rules people follow as they strive to reach decisions. Such knowledge can raise your ability to facilitate productive meetings.

DISCUSSION IDEAS

- Individually, reflect on some meetings that you have attended and then list five or more things that often serve as barriers to effective meetings. Share your list with two other people. In your group, discuss similarities and differences across your lists. From this discussion, build a composite list that captures the key elements of the three individual lists. Working with the composite list, discuss possible actions that could be taken to remove each of these barriers to effective meetings.

- Often, people participate as equals in teams or groups, and the notion of having a team leader does not really apply. In fact, in many instances, it is better if people who would like to dominate the proceedings are kept from doing so. Effective meetings, however, require someone to take the initiative, to ensure that everything is organized before the meeting begins, and to facilitate the proceedings. Hold a discussion about this issue in a group of three to four people. Specifically, work to develop an answer to the following question: Within a group of equals, how might the task of meeting planning and facilitation be appropriately handled? You might generate several responses to the question. Make sure that you discuss the merits of each alternative. Be prepared to report your responses to the full group.

- In many organizations, meetings are habitual events with their form, and to some extent their content, having long become part of the organization's "standard operating procedures." What are some good aspects to this situation? What are some bad ones? With respect to facilitating effective meetings, how might you work toward change, even where the organizational culture has led people to hold set ideas about how things should be done?

Further Reading

Kelley, Tom. 2001. "The Perfect Brainstorm." In *The Art of Innovation*. New York: Currency/Doubleday, pp. 53–66.

Micale, Frances A. 1999. *Not Another Meeting! A Practical Guide for Facilitating Effective Meetings*. Central Point, Ore.: Oasis.

Rees, Fran. 2001. *How to Lead Work Teams: Facilitation Skills*. 2d ed. San Francisco: Jossey-Bass/Pfeiffer. See especially the six chapters making up part 4: "Facilitating Team Meetings."

Sutton, Robert I., and Andrew Hargadon. 1996. "Brainstorming Groups in Context: Effectiveness in a Product Design Firm." *Administrative Science Quarterly* 41:685–718.

Tropman, John E. 1996. *Making Meetings Work: Achieving High Quality Group Decisions*. Thousand Oaks, Calif.: Sage.

8

∎∎∎

Writing for Multiple Audiences

A boss once told me, "You have the makings of an excellent writer but at this point you are a good writer." Advice like this from a respected mentor is something that most policy analysts dread. Yet, that would be the wrong reaction. Becoming an influential policy analyst requires becoming a first-rate writer. One of the most important things in fine writing is mastering the subject. But this is less than half the battle. The more important step is transferring that information into written words that both convey knowledge while emphasizing the importance of the material. Even when writing about non-sexy issues such as capital expenditure funds in a municipality or the effects of unionization of school bus drivers, it is essential that the analyst take the time to write graphically, succinctly and—most importantly—passionately. Otherwise, no one will be affected by what has been written. Writing is a lot of work. Sometimes we want to judge our contribution by counting words. Yet length of the written document is rarely a measure of the power of the words. So much of writing is in the presentation. Writing to meet the rigorous standards of academia while meeting the needs of policymakers is an art. Policy analysts must do both. Becoming an excellent writer hinges on continuously improving. Successful analysts will meet the challenge.

—Dr. Emily Van Dunk, *Senior Researcher,*
Public Policy Forum, Milwaukee, Wisconsin

Writing is a core activity for policy analysts, as it is for everyone connected with the production or distribution of knowledge, but why treat writing as a people skill? I do so because, fundamentally, policy analysis is undertaken to inform and persuade policymakers, and this informing and persuading is done through different kinds of writing. We can raise our chances of having influence by reflecting on how best to communicate with various members of our immediate policy community and the broader polity. Knowing the needs of our audiences, and playing to those needs, can help us promote a more informed policy dialogue. This requires that we be sensitive to how differently situated people think about specific issues and how they make use of available information.

Another reason to treat writing as a people skill is that others judge us on our writing. We get judged on many things, but our writing matters a great deal. Everything we write provides new opportunities for others to upgrade or downgrade their judgments of our professional worth. Viewed in this way, writing becomes an exercise in managing your reputation, an exercise presenting both risks and opportunities. The good news, of course, is that we can control both the substance and the style of everything we write. The more consciously we work at our writing, the better able we are to advance our professional standing.

Writing is both a private and a public activity. We write to think and to communicate our thoughts to others. In his statement, "On Intellectual Craftsmanship" (1959) Mills elaborated on these two purposes of writing.

> At first, you "present" your thought to yourself, which is often called "thinking clearly." Then when you feel that you have it straight, you present it to others—and often find that you have not made it clear. Now you are in the "context of presentation." Sometimes you will notice that as you try to present your thinking, you will modify it—not only in its form of statement but often in its content as well. You will get new ideas as you work on the context of presentation (222).

Mills's observation is important because of what it says about the connections between writing, whom we are writing for, and how we think about the issues we are seeking to understand. Mills suggests that our thinking on specific issues is shaped in substantive ways by who we see as our audience. Thus, a group of policy analysts asked to assess noise problems and recommend noise abatement strategies for a busy airport are likely to approach the task differently, depending on who they perceive to be their client or their target audience. It is not just that the pre-

sentation of the analysis might differ across different groups. More profoundly, perceptions of target audience are likely to inform the policy analysts' thinking and writing at every stage in the study, from the terms
of reference to the construction of the final policy report.

In this chapter, I focus on writing as a means for communicating
effectively with your target audience. Because your target audience often
changes as you move from one piece of writing to another, as a policy
analyst, you should think of yourself as someone who writes for multiple audiences. Because most of us do at least some writing each day, my
purpose here is to suggest how you might improve your current practices. Throughout, I emphasize the importance of thinking about your
writing from the perspective of the intended audience. I also define the
term "writing" broadly. Hence, as part of the chapter, I discuss the importance of using visual displays, such as diagrams, tables, and charts to
effectively convey information to your readers.

Everyday Writing

As a policy analyst, you do much more than produce policy reports.
Each day, you usually write many e-mail messages. Each week, you typically write a variety of letters, memos, and notes. Even if you do nothing but project work, you know that such work requires you to engage
in a variety of writing tasks, the production of the final policy report
being just one.

We could probably divide many people's work into three categories: "nonwriting tasks," "conscious writing tasks," and "unconscious
writing tasks." Conscious writing tasks are those where people know
that they must pay serious attention to how they write. When you work
on policy reports, conference papers, journal articles, or book chapters,
you need to engage in carefully structured, deliberate writing. In contrast, unconscious writing tasks are those that people do not typically
think of as acts of writing. The prospect of completing such tasks does
not create anxiety. The writers know their audience, and they write with
a high level of comfort. They write what they want to say and then dis-
patch their work. That is why I call it "unconscious writing." For many
people, e-mail messages, memos, notes, and many letters fall into this
category. But earlier I said that, whenever we write, we give other people new opportunities to judge us. For that reason, I believe no writing

should be "unconscious." My preference is to think of all those e-mail messages, memos, and so on as "everyday writing." How you approach your everyday writing is just as important for your reputation as how you approach more complex writing tasks.

Get to the Point

Clarity is important for all writing. Whether you are writing an e-mail, a memo, or a letter, you should strive to follow a logical structure and keep things as simple as possible. Writing of this sort differs from murder mysteries. You should get to the point as quickly as possible so that your readers do not have to guess continually where you are leading them. Placing the subject of the communication in a subject line or title is a good way to start. It is also important to avoid covering more than one main subject in each of these types of communication. Keeping to one subject also makes it easier for you to structure the points you want to make.

Treat People Respectfully

All of your everyday writing should be simple and short, but it should not be brusque. As others have observed, since politeness costs nothing, there is no point in being stingy with it. I am not advocating going to the other extreme and being obsequious or "greasy." Rather, observe a few pleasantries. Always begin faxes and e-mail messages with a greeting to the recipient, instead of simply starting in on what you have to say. (A simple "Hi _____" is all that is required.) Likewise, end your text with your name. In the body of your text, using "please" and "thank you" at appropriate times can help to keep your relationships on good terms. Avoid using words or concepts that your reader will not understand. People do not like to feel stupid. Another way to convey respect to your reader is to always use correct spelling, grammar, and punctuation. Arredondo (2000) has noted that many people are not just informal, but they are careless in their e-mail writing. Thus, she has warned: "If you write carelessly when you compose e-mail messages, before you know it you're writing less carefully in more formal documents" (199–200). It requires minimal effort to transform an otherwise terse or sloppy note into a respectful one. The effort is worth it.

Adopt a Positive Tone

There will be many occasions when you will hear things around the office or you will receive communication that you find provocative or annoying. At such times, it would be easy to react in self-righteous ways, or to "fight fire with fire." Either response would be misguided. When you adopt a negative tone in your writing, you risk harming your reputation and laying traps for yourself. In your communication with others, and especially in what you write, it is essential that you strive to sound collegial. This is possible even when you wish to express concerns or offer criticism. Among his suggestions for achieving career success, Fox (1998, 15) has advised, "Never write a memo that criticizes, belittles, degrades, or is hurtful to a colleague. Never write a memo that is cynical, condescending, or unkind." Fox notes that things said thoughtlessly in one context might come back to haunt you in another. Yet, as policy analysts, we should bring a critical edge to our work, and we should be prepared to raise pointed questions. The trick is to write in ways that persuade others of the merits of what we have to say. If you find it difficult to express yourself on a matter without being wholly negative, it is probably better that you write nothing at all. An easy way to check for the tone of your writing is to apply this test. Suppose everybody could see what you have written. Is there anyone who would find it offensive or upsetting? If even just one name comes up, change what you have said.

ASSESSING AUDIENCES AND THEIR NEEDS

Virginia Gray, a political scientist at the University of North Carolina, told me this anecdote. "A legislative committee is holding hearings, and the committee chairman asks the time. The lobbyist who is testifying responds, 'Well, Mr. Chairman, here's how you make a clock.'" The anecdote reminds us that, even with the best of intentions, we often fail to give people direct answers to their questions. As policy analysts, we want to be informative and persuasive. Sometimes, that leads us to offer information intended primarily to make us appear knowledgeable, but the best way to impress the users of your analytical work is to answer the questions that they ask. This requires finding straightforward ways to tell people what they need to know. If you do this well, it is highly likely that these people—your audience—will ask you to tell them more. The starting point for gaining the confidence and respect of audience members is to find out how they think and what information they require.

Define Your Audience

Who am I writing this for? When you are writing an e-mail message or a letter, the answer to that question is always clear. When you are working on a policy report or a research paper, this question often becomes harder to answer. That is because many people could potentially find your policy analysis helpful as they think through particular policy issues. Musso and her colleagues (2000, 637) have implored, "Do not write for God; write for your client." This is good advice, because it urges you to narrow down the focus of your study. When you write with a specific audience in mind, you are better able to make appropriate choices about what is worth investigating and reporting on and what matters can be ignored. In contrast, if you define your audience too broadly and strive for omnipotence, you run the risk of substituting breadth of coverage for depth of insight. At the start of any writing exercise, take the time to think very carefully about whom you are writing for. It is easier to do this when a specific client has commissioned the work.

Learn about Your Audience

Having defined whom you are writing for, you should learn as much as you can about that individual or group. Suppose you have been asked to summarize what is known about the relationship between funding for family crisis centers and local reports of violence within the family. With an understanding of social scientific research methods, right away you can see that to answer this question well you would have to pay close attention to the methodological sophistication of the investigations conducted on this topic. Further, with experience in producing literature reviews, you will know that many studies are likely to have some findings of relevance here, but far fewer are likely to address the matter directly. In view of these facts, you need to find out more about what is expected of you. The best way to do this is to spend time asking your client questions. The client stands as the mediator between you and your audience.

When you interact with your client about the project, try to obtain answers to questions such as these:

- Why is this relationship of interest to this audience?
- What do the audience members know right now about this relationship?
- What is the link between the audience's policy goals and a study of this sort?
- How much technical detail should be covered in the report?
- What information would be of most value to this audience right now?

In most cases, a client acting as an intermediary between you and your audience will be pleased to answer such questions. After all, people do not want to fund studies that tell them what they already know or what they do not need to know.

Seek Advice as You Write

As you work on a study, it is useful to keep in close touch with your client. This way, you can receive ongoing feedback concerning the fit between what you are doing—or plan to do—and what your audience expects. For most policy projects, I would suggest that you plan to share some of your work with your client three times before you deliver the final document. First, it is useful to give the client a copy of your proposed outline for the policy report. An early exchange about the content of the report can help you determine areas to emphasize, items that might be dropped, and items that should be added. Second, you should give a progress report when you are about midway through the project. Your progress report could take a variety of forms, depending on how busy your client is and how closely he or she wants to monitor your work. I think it is particularly helpful to develop a progress report in which the contents parallel the structure of the proposed final report. In this way, you can provide information on how each section is developing and what key points will be covered in each.

You should always deliver a *draft* final report. From your perspective, this document should represent exactly how the final report should look. The point in sharing it with your client prior to the project deadline is to give your client one last chance to propose ways for you to make improvements to the work. If you have kept in touch with the client throughout the project, the final report should not contain any surprises. In terms of seeking to lay the groundwork for productive future relationships, it is vital that you show a desire to produce work that is as useful as possible for your target audience. Listening closely to your client and making the changes that he or she calls for is the best way to ensure that your final report will be viewed favorably.

TELLING THE SAME STORY IN DIFFERENT WAYS

As policy analysts, we generate and synthesize knowledge that often has the potential to change the minds of people holding a variety of positions in the policymaking community and the broader polity. Although presenting that information in one way might make it persuasive to one particular group, to extend the influence of our work, we will usually have to find other ways to reach other audiences. Thus, we need to tell the same story in different ways. Doing so means emphasizing different points to different audiences while maintaining a consistent broader message. The mechanics of telling the same story in different ways are most readily seen when people present the results of a major policy project.

In a recent policy project, I set out to assess the consistency between the theory that underpinned the creation of charter schools in the United States and the actual practices of those schools. My particular interest lay in assessing the claim that greater school autonomy, the elimination of a guaranteed student base, and competition among schools would lead to higher educational innovation (Mintrom 2001). My motivation to conduct this study was primarily intellectual. I believed that through it I could advance my understanding of the development and diffusion of policy innovations; however, part of the funding for the project came from a university program funded by the state of Michigan. My immediate client for the project became my university's vice president for special projects. Although my primary goal involved conducting research that would lead to scholarly publications, I knew that the vice president wanted me to produce a policy report that could be circulated to many people in and around the state government. Once the policy report was delivered, the vice president also asked me to work with the university's media specialists, so that we could gain broad exposure for my research findings in the local and national press. Thus, I ultimately produced a variety of documents, for a variety of audiences, all based on the one project.

Develop the Basic Story

When you are producing work that could be of interest to multiple audiences, it is important that you nonetheless start out with a clear focus. In the case of my study of innovation in charter schools, I took the view that an audience of my academic peers would hold me to rigorous methodological standards. Thus, I developed a research design that would allow me to answer questions of the sort that other scholars might ask. For example, I choose to study innovation in not just charter schools but also in traditional public schools. I further refined the research design so that the group of traditional schools was divided into two groups: those that were exposed to competition from charter schools and those that were not. I could now compare the level of educational innovation across groups of schools that faced different levels of motivation and ability to innovate.

When I first drafted the results of my study of innovation in schools, I wrote it as a report that could be circulated among people in and around the state government. The policy report began with an executive summary followed by my policy recommendations. Although that report contained a careful description of my research methods, I placed all of that information in an appendix. Putting the discussion of methods at the end allowed me to emphasize my findings and their implications in the body of the report, while still providing the crucial information on the study design that would be of interest to just a handful of policy analysts and scholars (a secondary audience for the document).

In general, it is important to find a way to develop your basic story and to write it up as thoroughly as possible. This is sometimes difficult, because different aspects of the story will appeal to different readers. At times, you might find that some of the material you have produced is not appropriate for inclusion in the basic story. When that is the case, you should leave that material out, but store it for its potential relevance when you write a different version of the story for a different audience.

Think in Terms of Questions and Answers

All policy projects involve efforts to answer sets of questions. When you begin a project, you need to gather background on your policy topic. The motivating question here is "How did we get to this point?" As you sift through background material, you will also attempt to review as much relevant literature as possible. The motivating question then is "What have other people written about this topic?" The metaphor of the storyteller is useful here. When we tell stories, people often ask questions. People with different interests, concerns, and experiences ask different sorts of questions. As a policy analyst writing for multiple audiences, you need to be able to anticipate the questions that you will be asked.

Busy politicians are most concerned to know what you know, not how you know it. Verdier (1984, 429) has suggested that, when you present the results of your analyses to legislators, they will almost always want answers to the following questions: "What is the decision that has to be made and when?" "What is the underlying problem the decision will address?" and "What are the alternative solutions to the problem, and how much of the problem will each alternative address?"

When I was working on my project on innovation in Michigan's charter schools, I judged that policymakers would be most interested to know what charter schools were doing, and how they differed in their practices from traditional public schools. My policy report answered questions such as "What are charter schools?" "How many of them are there in this state?" "What are they doing?" and, "How different are they from traditional public schools?" Yet, even as I worked to answer these questions, I knew that my academic peers would tend to place more emphasis on different questions. Those questions would be designed to assess the relevance and the validity of my findings. Thus, in an article I published on this topic in an academic journal, I gave primary emphasis to answering questions like these: "Can states design policies to promote local innovation?" "Why should we care about this?" and, "How can you compare innovativeness across different local organizations in a rigorous manner?"

In general, thinking in terms of questions and answers helps you generate a full set of components, or blocks of writing, associated with your single project. While considering the needs of each audience you are writing for, pick and choose how much emphasis you will give to each of these components in any given document. When you have a sense of what people already know, then you need not waste their time by providing answers to questions they would never ask. When you are dealing with busy people and you know their greatest concerns, give them the information that will be most useful to them. With each of your audiences, strive to answer all the questions you expect to be raised. You should give additional information only to the extent that you believe it is of relevance to your audience. You should never swamp people with too much information. Most importantly, remember, different audiences care about different things. As long as you keep your basic story the same, it is both ethical and smart to emphasize different points to different people.

SUMMARIZING INFORMATION

Writing is a way of organizing and summarizing what we know in order to convey that knowledge to others. Although as writers we distinguish between substance and style, as *readers* we appreciate seamless work where all of our attention is drawn to the substance. Here, I want to highlight how different devices—both verbal and visual— can help you to present your work as clearly and appropriately as possible, in view of your target audience. You must first be familiar with the conventions of style (and, hence, the expectations) that are associated with particular audiences. It is essential that you follow those conventions. For example, most policy reports contain executive summaries. Similarly, most conference papers and nearly all publications in scholarly journals contain abstracts. Some conventions are less well established, and you need not rigidly conform to them. When you do violate a convention, however, you should definitely know what you are doing and why you are doing it. Although different verbal and visual devices can greatly improve your ability to convey your message to your audience, used inappropriately these devices can distract or disorient your readers.

Making Your Structure Visual

You can make the structure of a policy report visual in a number of ways. Here are some basic verbal devices that you can employ to help your readers quickly grasp the overall purpose and design of your report. First, when you include an executive summary, make sure that the key components of your argument are presented in parallel to the structure of the report itself. Second, you should state in the executive summary how the report is structured, even numbering the sections if doing so would make it easier for your readers to navigate the report. Third, the sequence of your recommendations should also follow the same sequence in which they are discussed in the report. Fourth, when your report is long, a table of contents at the beginning will help guide the reader. Finally, you should always make clear and consistent use of headings and subheadings throughout your text, to help your readers relate each element of the work to the overall story.

Diagrams can also add considerably to the structuring of your writing. As policy analysts, we often study and discuss complex systems. Thus, taking the time to represent those systems visually can enable your readers to comprehend them more readily. These diagrams need not be complex. In fact, simplicity is preferable. Writing on this general topic, Tufte (1983, 51) has observed, "Graphical excellence is that which gives the viewer the greatest number of ideas in the shortest time with the least ink in the smallest space."

A few years ago, a colleague and I wrote a proposal calling for better integration of the research, teaching, and outreach work of faculty at our university. We believed that this could best be achieved through the creation of a policy institute on campus. After some discussion, we decided that it would make sense to add a diagram to our proposal. We used this diagram both to convey our sense of the linkages between research and policymaking and to help us structure our argument. I have reproduced that diagram as figure 8-1. Though simple, the diagram offers a visual summary of a more complex argument. Often, simple diagrams placed near the beginning of a policy report can help familiarize your audience with the focus of your argument.

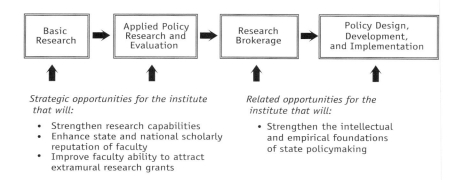

Strategic opportunities for the institute
that will:

Related opportunities for the
institute that will:

- Strengthen research capabilities
- Enhance state and national scholarly
  reputation of faculty
- Improve faculty ability to attract
  extramural research grants

- Strengthen the intellectual
  and empirical foundations
  of state policymaking

Figure 8-1. Portraying How Research Informs Public Policymaking

Using Matrices

Matrices are tables in which column and row items are systematically related. As such, they can be used to portray a vast variety of relationships.
For example, they can be used to summarize such things as the differences among agencies in meeting various performance criteria, who will
do what in a project team, and the differing interests and resources of
individuals and groups embroiled in a public dispute. In figure 8-2, I
show how a matrix can be used to summarize the sequencing of the data
collection and analysis portion of a policy project.

Task	Time period					
	Jan.–Feb.	March–April	May–June	July–August	Sept.–Oct.	Nov.–Dec.
1. Identify cases	▒					
2. Contact cases		▒				
3. Data collection, phase I			▒			
4. Data collection, phase II					▒	
5. Data analysis				▒	▒	▒
6. Meet advisors		•		•		•
7. Project management	← Continuous →					

Figure 8-2. Portraying a Project Time Line

Using Tables

As we conduct policy analyses, we frequently end up working with datasets and generating a variety of tables containing summary statistics, regression results, and simulations. When it comes to writing policy reports and research papers, we need to exercise judgment in deciding how to present our numerical findings. Because this work often takes a lot of time, it is easy to be tempted into sharing too much of it with our audience. This can be dangerous. Verdier (1984) has suggested that, in advising politicians, you should "emphasize a few crucial and striking numbers." He observes,

> Congressmen love numbers, but not in the same way economists do. Congressmen look for a single striking number that can encapsulate an issue and can be used to explain and justify their position. They have little use for endless columns and rows of unassimilated data. One good number can be worth pages of analysis. (432)

I believe that, in the course of their work, policy analysts should seek to extract all relevant insights from available information. I also believe that policy analysts should be willing and able to collect and analyze new information, when such an effort is called for and the project budget and time frame allow it. Yet as a reader, I have little tolerance for working through pages of tables, and I think many other readers share this disposition. It is fine to engage in sophisticated and complex analytical work, but when it comes to presenting that work to your audience, I urge minimalism—or, in Tufte's (1983, 191) words, "the clear portrayal of complexity."

Consider this example. Beginning in the 1960s, a number of economists in the United States began to conduct detailed investigations of the effects of fare and route regulation on the operation of the airline industry. These studies soon established that an airline cartel existed in the United States and, further, that this cartel was supported by the policies of the Civil Aeronautics Board. The Board regulated all routes that crossed state lines. In 1975, as public criticism of the Civil Aeronautics Board began to grow, a subcommittee of the U.S. Senate Committee on the Judiciary, chaired by Edward M. Kennedy, subjected the actions of the Board to close scrutiny. The work of this subcommittee paved the way for subsequent deregulation of the airlines. At the subcommittee hearings,

Table 8-1. Portraying the Effects of Airline Regulation on Fares

City-pairs	Miles	Fare ($)	No. of passengers
Los Angeles-San Francisco	338	18.75	7,483,419
Chicago-Minneapolis (CAB)	339	38.89	1,424,621
New York-Pittsburgh (CAB)	335	37.96	975,344
Houston-San Antonio	191	13.89	490,000
Boston-New York (CAB)	191	24.07	2,493,882
Reno-San Francisco (CAB)	192	25.93	312,811

Note: This table originally appeared in U.S. Congress (1975). I have reproduced it from McCraw (1984, 267). CAB denotes a flight regulated by the U.S. Civil Aeronautics Board.

Kennedy presented a simple table, which I have reproduced (table 8-1). According to McCraw (1984, 266), this table served as the "clincher" in Kennedy's case against the Board. It effectively portrayed the stark differences in fares on flights regulated by the Civil Aeronautics Board and flights of equivalent length operating within states, beyond the Board's reach.

The broader issues surrounding airline deregulation were complex, but the authors of this table were able to cut through that complexity. Here, relevant information was presented in a clear and compelling fashion. When using tables to summarize numbers, your primary goal should be to meet the needs of your audience as simply and clearly as possible.

Using Graphics

Good graphic displays can also help you to summarize important relationships quickly for your audience. In a series of books on the display of information, Tufte (1983, 1990, 1997) has provided many excellent ideas that policy analysts could apply in their work. Likewise, Miles and Huberman (1994) have introduced and discussed a variety of approaches to presenting qualitative data.

To underscore the potential value of such displays, here I provide a striking example. In her analysis of the decision-making process that led to the fatal launch in 1986 of the *Challenger* space shuttle, Vaughan (1996) portrays the relationship between the air temperature at the time of the shuttle launches and the incidence of thermal distress to the O-rings that sealed the rocket joints. In figure 8-3, I have reproduced the main elements of Vaughan's portrayal of that relationship. This figure

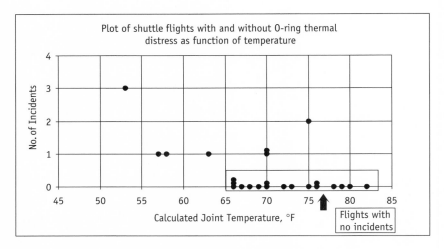

Figure 8-3. Portraying the Relationship Between Temperature and Thermal Distress

Note: Thermal distress defined as O-ring erosion, by-blow, or excessive heating. This chart is a simplified rendition of that presented in Vaughan (1996, 383).

indicates that when all shuttle missions prior to the fatal launch were considered, a strong correlation between O-ring anomalies and temperature appears. To quote Vaughan, "Of the flights launched above 65°F, three out of seventeen, or 17.6 percent had anomalies. Of the flights launched below 65°F, 100 percent had anomalies" (382).

Prior to the fatal *Challenger* launch, some engineers expressed concern about the effects of cold temperature on the O-rings. In spite of this concern, no effort was made to plot the relationship in a manner that included the flights with no incidents. Without including these data, no obvious relationship can be detected between temperature and O-ring damage. I mention this example because it represents an instance where relevant information was available to the people involved, yet nobody thought to summarize it in the way that it is presented in figure 8-3. Vaughan has argued that this analytical oversight occurred because of organizational conformity. "It can truly be said that the *Challenger* launch decision was a rule-based decision. But the cultural understandings, rules, procedures, and norms that always had worked in the past did not work this time" (386). Fortunately, policy analysts usually do not engage in work that has direct life and death consequences. Nonetheless, this example reinforces the importance of looking for data gaps, filling them, and presenting your results in ways that both inform and persuade your audience.

Inviting Discussion

Policy analysis should be done to promote discussion, not close it off. When we find effective ways to summarize information and present it to others, we can often provoke dialogue and debate that leads to fresh ways of thinking about policy problems and potential solutions. Here, I have discussed several ways that you can use verbal and visual devices to make it easier for your readers to appreciate the points you seek to make. For any given topic and audience, it is likely that you could use a variety of devices to arrange and augment your written work. Try to find ways to captivate your readers and keep them focused on the substance of what you have to say. As you do so, remember that it is best to keep things simple.

REVISING AND SEEKING CRITICAL FEEDBACK

If you want to write well, you have to be prepared to revise. It is through our efforts to revise our work that we move from writing as thinking to writing as an effort to communicate our thoughts to others. In their manual on writing, Strunk and White (1979, 72) have observed, "Revising is part of writing. Few writers are so expert that they can produce what they are after on the first try." Similarly, Mankiw (1996), an economist, has noted the importance of good writing as a means for conveying ideas. According to Mankiw, as a writer you should put effort into both getting your substance and your style right. "If you want to sell your substance, you have to worry about your style" (18). Mankiw recalls asking John Kenneth Galbraith how he had managed to be so successful as a popular writer on topics associated with economics and government policy. Galbraith's response? "He said that he revises everything many times. Around the fifth draft, he manages to work in the touch of spontaneity that everyone likes" (18).

We can make a lot of progress toward improving our work through self-directed revisions. Nevertheless, seeking critical feedback from others can be extremely valuable. Each new set of eyes brings a new set of experiences and insights to a piece of writing. The best people to seek feedback from are those who know the substance of the subject we are working on and who also have a good sense of the needs of our audience. This is why managers and other senior colleagues can be so useful as sources of feedback and mentoring. Most academics whose work is routinely subjected to the anonymous peer review process used by scholarly journals and publishers know the value of critical feedback. Of course, accepting the criticism of others can be difficult, even when those critiques are offered with the purpose of indicating how your work might be improved. But revising your work along the lines suggested by those who have cared enough to give it a close read will almost always make it better.

Sometimes, researchers and policy analysts who are designing new projects take the step of establishing an advisory board. Typically, such entities contain a small but diverse group of people who are asked to serve as "critical friends" over the life of the project. As such, these outsiders offer guidance, insights, and feedback to the project team. When it comes to obtaining suggestions on how to present project findings to different audiences, having an advisory board can be very helpful. It is a way to institutionalize—and hence normalize—the seeking and the giving of feedback on work coming out of the project. In general, the more you are able to call on people with appropriate knowledge of the subject matter and the concerns of your target audience, the better able you will be to produce work that is highly valued. Building up relationships of reciprocity with colleagues can be helpful here. After all, we often gain insights into how to avoid pitfalls and make our own work stronger by wrestling with other people's work and taking the time to explain to others how their work might be improved.

SUMMARY

Writing well requires effort. This is especially true for professionals who must find ways to communicate with those who do not share their specialist knowledge and language. As policy analysts, we draw on the concepts and techniques of economics, statistics, and the social sciences to interpret the world around us and to produce recommendations for public policymaking. On the one hand, we conduct conceptual and empirical investigations that should be of sufficient quality to survive the close scrutiny of our peers. On the other hand, we must present our conclusions to people whose interests, everyday concerns, and ways of thinking differ greatly from our own. These dual demands require that we find effective ways to present our work to multiple audiences. In reflecting on the difficult task of writing for people who do not share our training and vocabulary, Friedman (1995, 28) has observed, "If I think Congressmen, or bankers, or businessmen may be interested in the findings of the research I have been doing . . . I have to decide whether I want to convey my ideas to those audiences or not. And if I do, then I know I have to write an account of those ideas directed at the audience I want to reach." The more effort you make to write so you will be clearly understood by your target audiences, the more influence you will have on public policymaking.

Like any skill, the ability to write well comes with deliberate practice. In this chapter, I have emphasized the importance of adjusting both the substance and the style of your writing to meet the needs of your audience. Thinking of your writing from the perspective of your readers will help you to convey your message. Different audiences care about different things. Obvious as that point might seem, it is surprising how often policy analysts misjudge their readers. A colleague once said to me, "First, write what you want to say for yourself and for the other analysts around here. Then put it in cartoon form for the politicians." Although condescending toward politicians, this comment captures the audience problem policy analysts must wrestle with as they write.

SKILL-BUILDING CHECKLIST

- Everything you write presents new opportunities for others to judge your professional worth. Treat writing as an exercise in managing your reputation.
- At the start of any writing task, clarify whom you are writing for. When you write with a specific audience in mind, you are better able to make appropriate choices about what is worth investigating and reporting on and what matters can be ignored.
- The best way to impress your readers is to answer their questions. Try to anticipate the questions that your readers will ask. The starting point for gaining the confidence and respect of your readers is to find out how they think and what information they require.

- To extend the influence of your work, you must be prepared to write for multiple audiences. This requires you to tell your basic story in different ways, emphasizing different points to different readers. People with different interests, concerns, and experiences ask different sorts of questions. As long as you tell the same story, it is both ethical and smart to emphasize different points to different people.

- Always look for ways to captivate your readers and keep them focused on what you have to say. Potentially, you could use a variety of verbal and visual devices to arrange and augment your written work; however, you should first familiarize yourself with the conventions of style associated with each audience and tether your creativity accordingly.

- You can do a lot to improve your work through self-directed revision, but it is also important to seek critical feedback from others. The best people to give you feedback are those who are familiar with the general subject matter and who know the needs of your target audience.

DISCUSSION IDEAS

- In reflecting on what he learned as a consultant at McKinsey & Co., Rasiel (1999, 34) described "the elevator test": "Know your solution (or your product or business) so thoroughly that you can explain it clearly and precisely to your client (or customer or investor) in 30 seconds." Rasiel observed that many companies use the elevator test (or an equivalent, such as one-page memos) to ensure that their executives use their time efficiently. Consider a project that you are currently working on. Could you pass the elevator test with your primary audience? Using three bullet points, summarize the study's purpose, approach, and findings. Now consider an audience shift. What would your bullet points look like if you had to explain this project to high school students? What about if you had to explain it at an interview for a promotion from policy analyst to chief policy analyst?

- People seeking to influence policy debates need excellent communication skills. In a paper written for advocates of welfare reform, Greenberg and Laracy (2000, 18) noted the importance of "creating an 'echo chamber,' through which public policymakers repeatedly hear, understand, and retain messages educating them about policies." According to Greenberg and Laracy, the release of one or two reports, even when they represent very good work, is not sufficient to create an echo chamber. Rather, you change people's minds through "effective social marketing" and by "paying . . . attention to the details of message development" (18). Think about a policy issue that you are currently working on or that happens to be of particular interest to you. If you had as your goal the creation of an "echo chamber" of messages on this issue, what would you do? How would your efforts require you to write for multiple audiences?

- The economist Alfred Kahn was a central figure in the deregulation movement of the 1970s. As well as being a superb academic economist, he was also a brilliant communicator. McCraw, in his portrait of Kahn and his accomplishments, illustrates the importance Kahn placed on good writing. As chairman of the Civil Aeronautics Board from 1977 to 1978, Kahn acquired a reputation for holding his staff to high standards in their written work. McCraw (1984, 271) quotes three statements Kahn made to staff at the Board:

> "May I ask you, please, to try very hard to write Board orders and, even more so, drafts of letters for my signature, in straightforward, quasi-conversational, humane prose—as though you are talking to or communicating with real people."

> "If you can't explain what you are doing to people in simple English, you are probably doing something wrong."

> "I really have certain very profound not only esthetic but philosophical objections to people in Government hiding behind a cloud of pompous verbiage which creates a gulf between them and the people."

Working with a partner, write brief, clear explanations for average citizens of the following concepts: marginal-cost pricing, provider capture, contestability, and opportunity cost.

- Over a one-week period, have everyone in your group collect one or more examples of the use of graphics, tables, or diagrams to convey policy-related information. In groups of three, introduce your examples to each other, explaining what you like about them. In each case, who is the intended audience? How might the presentation of information need to be changed to make it accessible to a different audience? Together, think of one or two ways that you could modify the approaches found in each of these examples for use in your own policy projects.

FURTHER READING

Friedman, Benjamin M. 1995. "Decide who is the audience, and learn how to reach it." In "Principles of Economics." *American Economist* 39:28–36.

Krieger, Martin H. 1988. "The Inner Game of Writing." *Journal of Policy Analysis and Management* 7:408–16.

Majone, Giandomenico. 1989. "Analysis as Argument." In *Evidence, Argument, and Persuasion in the Policy Process*. New Haven, Conn.: Yale University Press, pp. 21–41.

Miles, Matthew B. and A. Michael Huberman. 1994. "Producing Reports." In *Qualitative Data Analysis: An Expanded Sourcebook*. Thousand Oaks, Calif.: Sage, pp. 298–306.

Musso, Juliet, Robert Biller, and Robert Myrtle. 2000. "Tradecraft: Professional Writing as Problem Solving." *Journal of Policy Analysis and Management* 19:635–46.

Strunk, William, Jr., and E. B. White. 1979. *The Elements of Style*. 3d ed. New York: MacMillan.

Tufte, Edward R. 1983. "Graphical Excellence." In *The Visual Display of Quantitative Information*. Cheshire, Conn.: Graphics Press, pp. 13–52.

Verdier, James M. 1984. "Advising Congressional Decision-Makers: Guidelines for Economists." *Journal of Policy Analysis and Management* 3:421–38.

9
...

Conflict Management

Before I became a policy analyst I worked as a police officer. That's when I realized that conflict lies at the heart of many people's lives. Now, while the conflicts I see are different, it is clear to me that, as policy analysts, we must be able to manage conflict. Conflicts between two sides of an issue, conflicts between objectivity and subjectivity, and conflicts in defining costs and benefits are obvious examples. A skillful police administrator once showed me the value of managing conflict by directly engaging a group of racially charged citizens at a public forum. He listened to them carefully, even through their anger. He asked broad clarifying questions to show that he understood their perspective. Then he enlisted their help in addressing and resolving their issues within the existing structure. He changed a very difficult, confrontational event into a first step toward community healing through successful conflict management. As policy analysts, our professional usefulness and value depend on the quality and relevance of our analysis. Often, this requires that we go right into the jaws of conflict, listen to and work with everyone involved, and move things toward achieving clear, comprehensive policy recommendations. Skillful management of various interactions between individuals and groups is essential. Well-handled and well-utilized communications with stakeholders help foster greater understanding of everyone's issues and concerns.

—Joe Meehan, *Management Analyst,*
City of Covina, California

The ability to manage and resolve conflict effectively is a valuable people skill. All of us now and then are drawn into conflict with others, in both our personal and professional lives. As policy analysts, we are more likely than many other professionals to encounter conflicts related to the substance of our work. The making of public policy need not be—but frequently becomes—a highly conflictual process. This is because much is at stake when policy is being made. Moe (1991) has suggested that policy controversies emanate principally from the winner-take-all aspect of democratic politics. Unlike the marketplace, where individuals and organizations enter into voluntary agreements, in politics those in power can compel others to abide by the rules they make. This has important implications for the making of public policy. According to Moe, the need for adversaries to reach compromises in the design of institutions and organizations typically produces weakly performing administrative structures. Viewed from an efficiency perspective, these structures make no sense. Yet, when we appreciate the processes through which they are created, the design logic of these structures becomes clearer. Conflicts among contending interests are played out within the politics of policy design. In theory, problems of policy design—and the organizational waste they engender—could be reduced, but doing so would require great effort on the part of policy analysts to manage and creatively channel policy disagreements.

In this chapter, I suggest ways that policy analysts might effectively manage conflict when they encounter it. To manage broader conflicts effectively, we must first know how to manage lower level, personal conflicts where we are central players. Moreover, discussions of the resolution of public disputes indicate that strategies appropriate to resolving one-to-one conflicts can be replicated to good effect for managing broader disputes (Carpenter and Kennedy 1988; Forester 1999). For these reasons, I begin here by considering how we might manage our own conflicts. I then suggest how we might mediate conflicts among other people around us. Only after that do I examine how policy analysts might assist in the management of public disputes. Ultimately, policy analysts are valued for their analytical incisiveness, not for their conflict management abilities. Thus, in presenting ideas for how policy analysts might manage conflict, I do not mean to suggest that we should also strive to wear the hat of the mediation specialist, but an awareness of strategies for effective conflict management can positively inform our everyday practices. Further, that awareness can allow us quickly to recognize situations where professional mediators are needed.

THE FUTURE ORIENTATION

Conflict can be found in many contexts. Once we become aware of a conflict situation, we face a choice: we can either take steps to address it or we can choose to do nothing. As a guiding principle, I suggest that we approach any conflict situation with a future orientation. Thus, we should ask, "Looking to the future, what is the best thing to do about this conflict?" The question invites us to consider the consequences of our actions. Those actions—which include deciding to do nothing—should be thought of as investments.

The time we give to any activity is always sunk, that is, we cannot get it back. Therefore, if we are going to take time to think about and address a conflict, we should take actions that could be objectively viewed as wise investments. The future orientation warns us against taking actions designed primarily to "get even" with an opponent, to be punitive or spiteful. The time spent on such actions is wasteful. Worse, efforts to get even can lead to the unnecessary, and more wasteful, escalation of conflict. Because we cannot change the past and our time is precious, trying to get even with others is the equivalent of throwing good money after bad. At any juncture in a project or endeavor, rational decision makers should determine how best to allocate their future time and energy, recognizing that what seemed sensible in the past may no longer appear so (Dawes 1988, chap. 2). Economists note the folly in honoring sunk costs, even though psychologically there is a strong temptation to do just that. When it comes to managing conflict, the future orientation can lead us out of temptation.

You can adopt the future orientation in every conflict situation. Here are three guidelines for action. First, *act with the goal of making your working environment more productive.* Conflicts sap energy, at both the individual and the organizational level. This is why it is worth searching for positive ways to resolve them. Second, *act as if you will meet people again.* In both your personal and professional life, you cannot afford to "write people off," having relationships end angrily or with bad feelings. If you find it easier to deal with a conflict by thinking, "Well, at least I'll never have to see those people again," matters have not been appropriately resolved. Conflicts should end in ways that minimize the risk of people feeling awkward when they next meet. Third, *assume everyone is watching and that your reputation is on the line.* Conflicts can be highly damaging to your reputation, but this need not be the case. If you genuinely strive to manage conflicts in productive ways, your actions will not harm your reputation, and they might even enhance it.

Managing Your Conflicts with Others

As individuals, we can improve the quality of our lives and the quality of our work by recognizing and appropriately responding to conflict situations where we represent one of the central protagonists. These conflicts can range from somewhat minor (such as disagreements about levels of noise in a household) to fairly major (such as disagreements with colleagues about the merits of work being produced for a team project). We potentially could choose to ignore a variety of matters that bring us into conflict with others, but this avoidance strategy can be self-defeating. We may feel aggrieved or angry and end up releasing our hostility in ways that create more conflict. Here, I suggest some basic steps that you can take toward managing your relations with others and constructively handling conflicts.

Identify and Manage Sources of Stress and Triggers

To become better at managing conflicts, it is vital that we recognize the linkage between our emotional state and our perceptions. Objectively similar events might evoke quite different responses from us, depending on our emotional state. For example, when you are near the beginning of the workday, you might welcome a colleague entering your office to seek advice on a problem she is tackling. You might think to yourself, "I'm really glad she felt I was a good person to approach on this topic." In contrast, after a day of rushing from meeting to meeting and frantically trying to keep your desk clear between appointments, you might feel somewhat peeved to have your colleague drop by to ask for your advice. This time, your might think to yourself, "Why can't she do her own work? Haven't I got enough on my plate without having to help others out as well?" Notice that nothing has changed about your colleague and her request. It is your situation and your level of stress that have changed.

The request from your colleague, coming at a time when you are feeling considerable stress, might serve to trigger angry thoughts. In turn, these thoughts might lead you to perceive a conflict with your colleague. For her part, she might interpret your responses to her as hostile and wonder why you are so disagreeable.

It is important that we avoid provoking unnecessary conflict. One way to do this is to recognize that getting angry is a choice. We find ourselves in particular situations and we choose our responses. We are most likely to choose an angry response when we are feeling stress and when we receive a trigger (McKay, Rogers, and McKay 1989). By reducing our level of stress, we pull ourselves back from the territory where a trigger is likely to lead us to feel and express anger. Similarly, when we acknowledge that we are experiencing stress, it is easier for us to find ways to avoid possible triggers.

How might we replay the scenario of a colleague requesting your advice when you are under stress? There are several ways to reduce the likelihood that you will have an angry response. For example, when you recognize your own stress level, seek to reduce it before placing yourself in situations where you are likely to receive triggers. Think about ways to structure your workdays so that you do not have to attend a series of meetings one after the other and catch up in between. Alternately, think of ways to intersperse your meetings with brief "time-out" sessions for yourself, where you might get away from the workplace for a few minutes to relax, reflect on recent events, and gather your thoughts for the time ahead. In addition, you might try to prepare in advance for stressful meeting days, doing everything you can beforehand to reduce the amount of work you will have to do between those meetings. Taking this approach, it would be perfectly reasonable for you to explain to your colleagues in advance that you are likely to be quite stressed on an upcoming day. You might then ask that they use e-mail or voice mail to reach you on those days, rather than come directly to your office.

By thinking in terms of stress and triggers, you can begin to negotiate with others and structure your work and home environment so that you do not receive triggers at moments when you are feeling highly stressed. It is a good idea to reflect on sources of stress in your life. These can include physical discomfort, health problems, family trouble, financial worries, too much work and too little recreation, and problems in your relationships with others. By identifying the factors in your life that produce stress, you can begin to find appropriate antidotes to them. What things trigger negative or angry thoughts? Again, by identifying triggers, you can start to explore ways to ensure that those triggers do not crop up when you are feeling stressed. This simple preventative strategy can help you to reduce the instances where you find yourself in petty conflicts with others. In general, any efforts that you can make to eliminate unnecessary conflict at work or at home will pay off in terms of better interactions with others and more energy to focus on making high-quality contributions to the things that really count.

Choose Your Battles

Many factors in our personal and professional lives might serve as sources of conflict for us. Yet, being continually embroiled in one conflict or another—no matter how petty—can seriously drain our energy levels. On some occasions, we might argue that we have been drawn into conflicts. At these times, we might think that our only choice is to engage with others over specific issues that they have raised, but typically we do face choices. We can choose how and when to respond if others raise issues that could be construed as sources of conflict between them and us. Further, we can choose when and how to raise potentially conflict-causing issues with others.

Before responding to a perceived provocation by another and before confronting others over matters of concern to us, it is useful to think in terms of priorities. How important is this issue compared with other things in my life right now? Does engaging with this other person to work out a conflict represent the best use of my time? For some people, stopping to ask questions of this sort might seem unrealistic. In the heat of the moment, can you really be expected to step back from a disagreement and ask rational questions like this? Developing the ability to stop, take a deep breath, and think about the situation somewhat dispassionately takes practice. It is difficult to break what might have become instinctual ways of responding to perceived conflicts, but breaking instinctual responses is crucial if you are to become effective at managing conflict. As a discipline, policy analysis serves to inhibit groups and communities from acting on hasty and inappropriate judgments regarding what to do in specific situations. Although we might often fall short of what might be expected of rational actors, as policy analysts, we should aspire to display exceptional levels of self-control and thoughtfulness regarding our individual actions in the world.

Gain Information and Perspective

When you find yourself in a situation of conflict with another person, it is important that you work directly with that person to resolve the issues at stake. Before engaging the other person directly, though, take time to think carefully about the situation. Wherever possible, it is also useful to talk with a trusted friend or colleague about the situation. Whom you choose to talk with is important. The best choice is someone who knows a lot about the context you are working in and who knows about the person who you perceive as your adversary. Somebody like this can help to give you perspective on the situation. Beyond seeking out an appropriate and trustworthy person to talk with, you should also seek to acquire any available information that will help you to gain a better sense of the conflict and the context.

Consider an example. Suppose that you are about to receive word of an increase in your salary. The increase will be based partly on your performance over the past twelve months and partly on general economic conditions. Over the past few weeks, you have done some mental calculations and you have come to expect an adjustment of at least 15 percent. You have figured this out based on your salary adjustment last year, what you have heard that some other people have received in the past, and your sense of your own performance on the job. To your mind, you have done excellent work over the past year and so you are in line for a good adjustment. When the letter of notification comes, you find that your salary increase is just 5 percent. Over the course of several minutes you go through a range of responses: disbelief, anger, sadness. You think about the future: maybe I will just leave; maybe I will ask to transfer to a new boss; maybe I am never going to make it in life. A few hours later, you hear a rumor that a colleague whom you consider less deserving than you has received a large adjustment. What should you do?

First, you should *learn as much as possible about the process* that managers in your organization use to determine pay increases. The more information that you have on the process, the better able you will be to assess the reasonableness of the increase that you have received. Some information might be difficult to discover. For example, it would be useful to have a sense of other people's salary levels and, even better, to have a sense of the range of the salary adjustments that have just been made. Learning that two-thirds of people in the organization received adjustments of less than five percent would no doubt change how you perceived your pay increase.

Second, try to *determine whether negotiation is possible and worthwhile*. Sometimes, procedures or constraints might prohibit others from being able to negotiate with you on the matters that you would like to have changed. At other times, power relations might be such that your perceived adversaries will believe that they have no interest in negotiating with you. Prior to negotiation, everyone has a best alternative to negotiated agreement (Fisher, Ury, and Patton 1991). This alternative is typically unstated, or implicit. In the case of salary increases, the managers of an organization might reasonably take the view that entering into negotiations with one individual might open the way for many others in similar circumstances to challenge their adjustments. It might, however, also be the case that you could change the balance of power and give the organization reason to negotiate. You could do this, for instance, by receiving an offer of employment elsewhere at a higher salary. In general, before raising an issue, you should think very carefully about your best alternative to negotiation and the other side's best alternative to negotiation. As Fisher, Ury, and Patton (1991, 105) observe, "If both sides have attractive best alternatives to a negotiated agreement, the best outcome of the negotiation—for both parties—may well be not to reach agreement. In such cases a successful negotiation is one in which you and they amicably and efficiently discover that the best way to advance your respective interests is for each of you to look elsewhere and not to try further to reach agreement."

Separate the People from the Problem

When we are upset or aggrieved about something, it is a typical human response to treat other people as the problem. For example, if you are unhappy about your salary increase, it is quite likely that you will say things like "My manager is to blame" or "Those people should show me more respect." In conflict situations, people have a tendency to assign blame to others or to judge other people's behavior, pointing out what others should or should not have done. Because none of us are saints, it is probably not a bad thing that now and then we give vent to our anger or annoyance. If you are going to do this, though, the trick is to do it in private. You must avoid venting in a forum where what you say could get back to the people you seek to demonize. Training yourself to be self-limiting is also important. Wherever possible—in both your professional and personal life—you should strive to keep control of your emotions and take time out from the immediate site of trouble when you feel yourself getting upset. Dale Carnegie's (1937, 3) old line applies: "If you want to gather honey, don't kick over the beehive."

To manage a conflict situation effectively, you must find ways to separate the people from the problem. You can begin to create such a separation by putting your energies into quietly gathering relevant information, something you will need to do anyway. Similarly, seeking out someone to talk with who is somewhat removed from the situation but who can provide perspective can also be calming. Explaining your situation to a trusted third party is an important way to begin viewing the conflict more objectively.

All conflicts take place within a broader context that is defined by past and present relationships. Good conflict management involves isolating a problem and then looking for appropriate ways to address it. Thus, the call to separate the people from the problem can be thought of as part of the broader prescription of using the positive aspects of your relations with others to gain leverage on the problem at hand. In a situation of conflict, you should aspire to act in ways that minimize the harm that could be done to your relationships with others and, hence, to your reputation.

To paraphrase Fisher, Ury, and Patton (1991, xviii), in negotiations it is important to be resolute in the way you tackle problems but soft on the people involved. The quality of forgiveness has significant merits. As challenging as it might be at times, whenever possible you should try to suspend negative judgments of people's motives and try to see how they might have innocently or unwittingly done something to upset you. The quality of forgiveness embodies a future orientation and urges that you choose your battles, place conflicts in perspective, and treat others with dignity and respect. To be forgiving does not mean that you always let others walk all over you. Rather, it means that when you raise an issue

you do so because it is serious and because you have thought it over suf-
ficiently to be sure that you have good reason to call a perceived adversary on his or her actions.

Role-Playing Scenarios

Role-playing scenarios in which you attempt to tackle the source of the
conflict can be highly effective as a means to prepare yourself for the moment in real life when you confront the matter directly. This can be done
with another person, or you might simply take the time to work through
the scenarios in your mind. Through role-playing, you can identify ways
to avoid doing harm and to keep positive relations with your adversary.
You can also gain a sense of what might go wrong and how you could
avoid eventualities of that sort. Role-playing takes time, but this time can
serve as an important emotional firebreak between the moment when
you perceive a conflict and the instance in which you raise the matter
with the other person involved. In this sense, role-playing helps you to
gain perspective and to choose your battles. Perhaps, during the course
of role-playing a meeting, you will come to realize that the issue at stake
is less important than you originally thought, or that what you perceived
as a conflict is not a conflict at all. The possibility of achieving such
perceptual breakthroughs is justification in itself for taking the time to
engage in role-playing.

Let us now return to the example where you are unhappy with
your salary increase. Being angry with your manager, firing off a nasty
memo, and sulking around the office are counterproductive responses.
Behavior of that sort would provide good reason for others in the organization to claim that you are something less than a star performer. It
is much better that you display behavior that is beyond reproach. Thus,
even when you feel that you have a conflict with others, you should act
in ways that signal your professional value. Begin by thinking about the
broader context of your workplace and considering what you value
about your work and your colleagues that extends beyond the size of
your paycheck. As you learn more about the way that salary increases
are determined in the organization and who you should meet with to
discuss your recent adjustment, make a concerted effort to weigh the
likely costs and benefits of requesting that the adjustment be revisited.

How might your actions affect your relationships with your immediate manager and with your other colleagues? What positive aspects of your work and your relations with those around you would you wish to emphasize, even as you raise concerns about your remuneration?

Clearly State the Problem

You receive a salary adjustment that is considerably lower than you had expected. What is the problem? A simple, face-saving response might be: "My boss has been mean to me." Yet we know from the public policy literature that problem definition is a complicated exercise. Situations or events are not inherently problematic or conflict-ridden. Rather, we make them so through the causal stories we choose to tell about them (Stone 1997). Each of those stories might offer quite distinctive definitions of the problem (Rochefort and Cobb 1994). This point holds true for our private troubles and conflicts, even though sophisticated discussions of problems and problem definition have tended to focus on public disputes and the emergence of policy choices. From here, we can draw a useful—and familiar—implication: *there is always more than one side to a story*. Given this, we must take care in how we talk about situations in which we perceive ourselves to be involved in personal or professional conflicts. If we choose the right words, our talk can point us in the direction of conflict resolution. If we choose the wrong words, a harmless misunderstanding can rapidly escalate into a major standoff. Language matters.

A useful way to confront a matter yet avoid fueling conflict involves describing the situation in relatively neutral terms, stating how it affects you, and then seeking change. This assertive approach to problem solving has three parts: I think . . . I feel . . . I want . . . (McKay, Rogers, and McKay 1989). Suppose that you decide to approach your manager to discuss your salary increase. You could do this either by dropping by your manager's office or sending an e-mail, whatever represents the least conflictual way to raise an issue like this within the culture of your workplace. The basic message might go something like this:

> I would like to meet with you sometime soon, at a time that is convenient for you. I am requesting this meeting because I would like

to talk about my recent salary increase. While I am pleased to have received the increase, I had been expecting a larger increase. For this reason, I would like to know more about how my increase was determined, what possibilities exist for the increase to be revised, and what I might do in the future to improve my chances of receiving higher salary adjustments.

Here, the problem—as you see it—is stated clearly as "I had been expecting a larger increase," but plenty of room is left for discussion and the pursuit of a mutually satisfying resolution. The problem is stated clearly, and you have not given an ultimatum. With the opening you have given her, your manager could choose a range of responses, from explaining why you did not receive the increase you expected to actually offering to make an adjustment. In general, when you request to meet with someone to discuss a source of conflict, you should state what you want to talk about. This is an important way to allow the other person to prepare for the meeting. When both parties are adequately prepared, the meeting is more likely to be productive.

Discuss the Problem

Creating space for discussion is an essential prerequisite for conflict resolution. The quality of that discussion can be materially affected by such factors as the timing of the meeting, how long it can proceed, what the participants have been doing prior to the meeting, the privacy of the meeting space, and whether the meeting is subject to interruptions. Because discussion of a disagreement or conflict is likely to be stressful, you need to establish a discussion space that is conducive to productive and personable engagement. As a starter, both you and your perceived adversary should be prepared in advance of the meeting. You should meet at a time when neither of you is experiencing pressure or stress relating to other issues. Private, quiet settings are best places to meet. It is also helpful if you can find a place where the furniture is comfortable, and where you can talk face to face without large obstacles—like an intimidating desk—between you. Setting aside sufficient time to allow for a reasonably long conversation is also helpful. I would suggest blocking out at least an hour for discussions on issues such as a disagreement over a salary adjustment. Even if the meeting does not run that long, it is good to have space at the end of the meeting for both of you to decompress alone before moving on to other activities.

In the discussion itself, you should make a conscious effort to ensure that both you and the other person are able to make your points without interruption. In cases where you have initiated the meeting, it makes sense that you begin by setting the scene, explaining why you have asked to meet. At this stage, it might also help if you propose a way to proceed. For example, you might say, "I would like to begin by talking about the matter from my point of view. But I would then like to hear your point of view, and, hopefully, we can engage in more of a dialogue after that." If it turns out that the meeting deteriorates so that there is a lot of interruption of what is being said, or both of you are speaking over each other, then you should pause, and listen until the other person has stopped speaking. Then, if it seems necessary, you might refocus the discussion by pointing out the nature of the interaction and suggesting that you each try to keep calm and hear each other out before responding.

Focus on Interests, Not Positions

In the example where you are unhappy about your salary adjustment, it is easy to imagine a scenario where both you and your manager focus on positions. Your position is that you were expecting an adjustment of at least 15 percent. Your manager's position is that the appropriate adjustment is just 5 percent. When you focus on positions, you end up haggling. You look for more and more reasons why you deserve the higher amount. Your manager looks for reasons to defend the smaller adjustment. In the end, it is hard to see how haggling can lead to an outcome that both of you consider acceptable. Another problem with focusing on positions is that the terms of the discussion are kept overly narrow. Rather than looking for areas of agreement, both of you fixate on what is, after all, a minor difference of degree. After all, both of you agree that an increase in your salary was warranted. The difference is simply in how large that increase should have been.

When discussing a source of conflict, you should strive to focus on interests, not positions. In the salary example, you need to think about and articulate your interests. Your concern about the size of your salary adjustment is not driven by fear that you will not be able to eat. Rather, you view the adjustment as indicative of the value your manager and others in the organization accord to you, relative to your other colleagues. You worry that the size of the adjustment signals something about how your superiors judge your future trajectory in the organization. With this in mind, it would be much better for you to move the discussion in directions that allow your manager to be candid with you about your work performance, how she views your performance relative to other colleagues, and what you might do in the future to improve your performance. For your manager's part, it is important that she also gets an opportunity to talk in terms of interests. You could prompt such a discussion by asking open-ended questions: "What was the range of salary adjustments this year?" "How was my adjustment determined?" "What could I have done to raise my chances of receiving a higher adjustment?" "How concerned should I be about the difference between the adjustment I received and the adjustment I expected?"

Leverage Shared Interests

Conflict resolution is most likely to occur when both sides are able to say, "If I were in their place, maybe I would see things the same way." Finding ways to place yourself in the other person's shoes is critical. This is how you will come to recognize the other person's constraints, problems, and key interests (Cohen 1980, 161). Of course, this means that you must be willing to listen carefully to what other people have to say and to ask questions that help them articulate their views. Moving the discussion away from positions and toward interests opens possibilities for you and the other person to identify areas of agreement, areas where your interests coincide. In most situations of conflict, you will find that you and your adversary have many more shared interests than conflicting ones. Given this, it will often make sense for you to work together in your meeting to list your points of agreement and your points of disagreement. Having made these lists, you might then begin to talk about your disagreements, working from the smallest to the greatest. The idea is to try to invent options for mutual gain, using shared interests as starting points for discussing ways to move forward. Every breakthrough that allows you to resolve minor disagreements can serve as a basis for building the trust and good relations that are necessary for tackling the more major aspects of the conflict.

Collaborate to Design a Solution

A meeting with another person to discuss a conflict between you will be productive only if you both leave with a clear sense of how the conflict can be effectively resolved and a joint commitment to make that happen. If either person leaves the meeting feeling annoyed, upset, cheated, or angry, conflict resolution has not occurred. In light of this, beyond ensuring that there is a full discussion of the issues at stake, as viewed from both sides, it is important that you find ways to work with the other person to design a solution.

Let us return one last time to the salary adjustment example. Suppose that through the discussion with your manager, several matters are clarified.

1. You expected a higher increase and interpreted the adjustment you received as an indicator that your superiors in the organization judged you to be performing below your potential.
2. The organization had lower-than-normal room for salary adjustments this year. The average adjustment was 3 percent. Your adjustment was among the highest. One person received a one-off bonus in addition to her adjustment, but the bonus was part of an earlier agreement to keep her from leaving to join a rival organization.
3. Increases cannot be revised once senior managers have signed off on them.
4. Superiors in the organization value your contributions and hope you will stay.

On the basis of this sharing of information, it appears that your original interpretation of your salary adjustment and the concerns you voiced were unfounded. With this in mind, perhaps the meeting could end without the need for you and your manager to develop a plan for where to go to from here. Nonetheless, it should be of some concern to both you and your manager that the lack of quality information accompanying the salary adjustment notifications led you to feel upset. Also, you want to continue to do well in the organization and receive above-average increases in your salary in the future. For these reasons, it makes sense that you and your manager end the meeting by exploring possibilities for changes in future behavior. The meeting might end with an agreement that your manager will take the following actions:

1. She will suggest to the senior managers that future letters of notification to staff contain more information about the context of salary adjustments, so people have a clear sense of their relative, merit-based rankings.

2. She will meet with you, at your initiation, two or three times per year to discuss your on-the-job performance and to give you guidance on areas for improvement. At these meetings, you will also discuss longer-term career development issues and what you can do to move toward your goal of being a manager yourself within the next five years.

In general, all meetings to resolve conflicts should end with a clear statement like this of agreed next steps. Usually, these statements should identify *behavioral changes* that are to occur. Authors who write on conflict and negotiation often emphasize the important role that a positive attitude can play during discussions and as part of the resolution of conflicts. It is, however, almost impossible to monitor changes in attitude. All of us know that it is possible to act pleasantly toward another person (the behavioral response) while privately loathing them (the attitudinal response). Yet, as McKay, Rogers, and McKay (1989, 187) have observed, "Even though you can't demand a change in attitude, when behavioral changes do occur, attitudes and feelings often change as well." Thus, in devising a solution to a conflict, place the emphasis on behavioral changes. Any cognitive dissonance between thought and action on the part of either person will—one hopes—eventually resolve itself in a positive manner as well.

Finally, behavioral changes that are agreed on during your discussions must be monitored. It is best that you strive to promote changes that can be monitored in a low-key fashion. The costs of compliance should be as low as possible for both you and the other person involved. If either party to the agreement fails to do what has been agreed on, you will have to engage in more discussion. In some instances, this might mean that you will have to turn to a third party, such as a superior or a professional mediator, to help both of you resolve your conflicts. Instances of that sort take us beyond the realm of the conflicts for which I have developed this advice on conflict management. That said, I believe that the steps suggested here could be readily used to help you resolve many conflicts as they arise. Further, adopting a future orientation and identifying sources of stress and triggers should help you to reduce the number of conflict situations in which you find yourself.

MEDIATING CONFLICTS BETWEEN OTHERS

Our conflicts with others can be emotionally draining. Left unresolved, or poorly handled, these conflicts can escalate. Not surprisingly, such conflicts can lead to productivity losses generated by such things as ill-considered personal or organizational decisions and an unpleasant working environment. In the midst of a conflict, we are likely to be upset and distracted. Try as we might, when we are embroiled in conflict it is difficult to conduct business as usual, or even keep up the pretense of it. Thus, our conflicts with others are likely to have adverse consequences for those around us. Having discussed ways that we might manage such conflicts, I now want to change perspective. What if we wear the shoes of a third party? As a third party, you stand outside of a conflict, but you are nonetheless affected by it. Suppose you observe a conflict between two people, let's say two of your colleagues. Should you get involved? How might you work to mediate, and help resolve, that conflict? In what follows, I offer some responses to these questions.

Avoid Doing Harm

There is much to be said for trying to keep the level of conflict around us as low as possible. With this in mind, there may be times when it seems appropriate for us to intervene in a conflict, with the goal of helping to resolve it. We must take care, however, to understand the social and political dynamics of a conflict fully before deciding whether intervention on our part would have the intended effects. There is an African proverb that states, "When elephants fight, it is the grass that suffers." Many people in a variety of organizational settings have come to learn the truth in this proverb. When powerful people are in conflict, often the people who work for them are the ones who suffer most, both immediately and in the longer term. When you are concerned about a conflict and are contemplating an intervention to help in its resolution, you must avoid placing yourself in harm's way. Nothing is gained if you end up embroiled in the controversy or if both sides to the conflict come to suspect your motives and to view you as meddlesome.

When thinking about intervening in conflicts between others, the suggestion that you do no harm holds two implications. First, you should avoid bringing harm to yourself. Second, you should avoid doing anything that might serve to escalate the conflict. One conclusion we could draw from these statements is that, if others are in conflict, the best thing you can do is just stand back and let it happen. Sometimes, that conclusion will be the right one. If you are unable to manage your own conflicts with others effectively, or if you have only limited experience with conflict and how to handle it, you really have no business seeking to intervene in other people's disputes. Further, if the other people are more senior to you in your organization, your direct intervention will almost always be considered inappropriate.

Our choices for action are rarely as stark as to intervene or not to intervene. Even if you lack experience in conflict management or the people involved are senior to you, it is still possible to do something positive. If a conflict is resulting in a significant drop in your own productivity, you might consider taking the following actions. To begin with, you could look for a low-key way to tell the disputant with whom you work most closely that the conflict is making it harder for you to do your job. If this course of action is not open, or if it has no effect, you might request a meeting with a senior person who is not involved in the conflict. In that meeting, you could explain how the situation is affecting you and suggest that some kind of intervention is called for. Handled carefully, these actions will do no harm, and perhaps they will prompt efforts by others to manage the conflicts.

My exhortation to "do no harm" is intended to prompt reflection on your part about the conflicts going on around you and the possible consequences of any efforts to intervene. I have focused on instances where intervention is likely to be inappropriate, but there will be many other situations in your workplace and elsewhere in your life when intervention makes sense.

Suppose you have been working for several years at a policy research organization that employs twenty-five policy analysts. Along with your other project duties, about six weeks ago you were assigned to a new in-house work team. This team of five people has been charged by senior managers to review current processes for undertaking internal evaluations of project work. The team must produce a report on the effectiveness of current processes and propose new guidelines for the internal evaluation of project work. The team has been given three months to produce the report and the new guidelines. In the brief to the team, the senior managers have noted that high-quality internal evaluation is critical if the organization is to maintain an excellent reputation among clients for the work it produces.

The senior managers' brief to your team does not mention any current problems with internal evaluation processes. Nevertheless, everyone in the organization knows about an event that happened shortly before the review team was established. Analysts in the state's legislative support office challenged the costs that members of the state teachers' union said would be associated with a new high school testing plan. Those cost figures had been produced by your organization, and the organization's name was prominent in discussions and media reports of the matter. After some debate, the cost figures were reanalyzed within your organization. It was found that the cost estimates had been too high, although the reanalysis suggested that the alternative estimates produced by the state's legislative support office were probably too low. All of this is material to your work because both Paul, who produced the original estimates, and Pamela, who conducted the reanalysis, are members of the work team. Further, when you have had team meetings, it has been clear that Paul and Pamela do not get along. At a meeting just over a week ago, they ended up having a dispute about how data analysis should be evaluated by organizational peers. The other members of the team also talked and debated at that meeting, but there were many times when Paul and Pamela revisited the issue of the estimates of the high school testing plan.

At the subsequent weekly meeting of the work team, neither Paul nor Pamela attended and neither informed the other team members that they would be absent. You hold the same level of seniority as Paul and Pamela. The other two members of the team are junior to you. At the meeting when Paul and Pamela did not show up, it was clear that you could not move forward with the report and guidelines without their additional input. You told the junior members of the team that you would talk to Paul and Pamela about the situation.

Meet Privately with Each Person

To begin the process of mediating a conflict between others, you need to acquire information on the nature of the issues at stake. You also need to work with each of the adversaries, with the goal of getting them both to the point where they can begin to work together to find a satisfactory way to resolve their conflict. In discussing how you might manage your own conflicts with others, I noted the importance of three points:

- Identify and manage sources of triggers and stress,
- Choose your battles, and
- Gain information and perspective.

When you are meeting with others to discuss a conflict that they are in, it can be helpful if you use the initial one-on-one meetings to work through these steps. Often people do not reflect on their stress levels or the ways that stress might lead them to interpret other people's innocent comments or observations as provocations. Also, there might be times when people need to be guided to see that, although there are battles worth fighting, the present situation can be handled in a more positive fashion. Finally, in your initial meetings, it is important that new information is elicited and that the source of conflict is put into broader perspective.

For your initial meetings with Paul and Pamela, you should have two main objectives. First, you should learn how Paul and Pamela view the situation. Second, you should discover what possibilities exist for resolving the conflict between them. To set up the meetings, if possible, you should visit Paul's office and Pamela's office and determine good times to meet with each of them. If e-mail is normally used to set up meetings, you could approach each of your colleagues that way. No matter whether you approach them face-to-face or by e-mail, your basic message might go something like this:

> I would like to meet with you within the next couple of days to talk about the internal-evaluation work team. We missed you at the last meeting. We really need your input into the discussions and the background work to ensure the report and guidelines get completed on time. Please tell me a time when we can talk.

When you have arranged times to meet, make sure that you also find a quiet, private space in which you can have a conversation without interruptions. Because you called the meetings, you should open up each conversation. One way to do this is to review the situation, point out why you think the tensions on the work team need to be appropriately managed, and then ask the other person for his or her thoughts. After Paul (or Pamela) has had plenty of time to talk about the situation as he (or she) sees it, you should begin to direct the conversation toward steps that can be taken for resolving the conflict.

Encourage Direct Dealing

Holpp (1999) has proposed that when conflicts arise among team members those involved should be encouraged to engage in "direct dealing." This requires the two adversaries to work together—not through their manager or a third party—to resolve their differences. According to Holpp, "Direct dealing empowers team members and helps them make informed decisions through individual responsibility, personal growth, and access to decision-making tools. This method is often hard at first, but it can become a part of the way a team handles all of its conflicts" (158).

Following your private meetings with each adversary, you should have acquired sufficient information from both sides to be able to understand the broader issues at stake in the dispute. You should also have achieved some sense of the possibilities that exist for the conflict to be resolved. Following Holpp's advice, the next step you should take is to go back to the people involved and encourage them to meet to discuss their differences and to work out ways that they might resolve those differences and, hence, begin to work productively together again. In some instances, either one of the parties might request that you sit in on and mediate that initial face-to-face meeting. Regardless of whether you attend that meeting, it is essential that you give the adversaries some guidance as to how they might structure the meeting to increase the chances that it will yield positive results.

Facilitate Dialogue

Conflicts among people who typically spend a lot of time together cannot be effectively resolved exclusively through third-party mediation. Face-to-face meetings and dialogue must occur. Thus, as the mediator in a conflict between others, all of your initial efforts should be undertaken with an eye toward making it easier for both sides to sit down together and resolve their differences. In other words, you should view yourself as an agent for facilitating positive dialogue. It is not your role to "solve" other people's problems. Instead, you should strive toward helping others to develop their own solutions. The more rapidly you can place yourself in the background, the better.

Following your initial meetings with each of them alone, there are several steps that you can take to facilitate dialogue between adversaries. These steps closely follow those that you would use yourself to manage a conflict with another person. The most important include

- Separating the people from the problem,
- Defining and discussing the problem,
- Focusing on interests, not positions, and
- Collaborating to design a solution.

In the case of Paul and Pamela, separating the people from the problem should be reasonably straightforward. After all, whereas Paul produced some data analysis that Pamela later reanalyzed, it could just as easily have happened in the organization that Pamela did the initial work and Paul was the one who conducted the internal evaluation. It might be the case that Pamela considers Paul to have been sloppy in his original work, just as Paul might think Pamela was overly eager to find fault with his work. If you can encourage both individuals to look beyond the specifics of their conflict and to think in terms of the implications their conflict holds for the organization, however, the personality side of the conflict should become much less salient. In the present case, further argument over the rights and wrongs of various cost estimates of high school testing would be counterproductive. It is far more important that Paul and Pamela start discussing ways that future data analysis work—no matter who does it—might be managed so that differences over what techniques to use and how findings should be interpreted are thoroughly explored in-house before the work is presented to clients. Paul and Pamela need to understand that the issues to be explored in the work team are not specific to either one of them.

The problem itself might be that, on the one hand, Paul feels he was made to look inept in that episode and, on the other hand, Pamela feels that she was called in to clean up a mess that somebody else had made. Reminding both people that they can change the future but they cannot change the past might be one way to get things moving forward here. The key issue is not how to allocate blame for a past situation. Rather, it is how to develop procedures so there is greater collective agreement in the organization about the best ways to manage the analytical work.

When two people discuss a conflict between them, it is vital that they get beyond the initial problem that led them to be adversaries. Working toward a solution is the most important thing that can be done in discussions. The work team case is instructive here. Paul, Pamela, you, and your two junior colleagues all know what needs to happen. You must quickly get to a point where all of you can work together productively. The outcome you seek is Paul and Pamela getting along with each other again, so they can once more participate fully in the work of the team. Here, separating the people from the problem actually might be the solution that Paul and Pamela need to reach. It would be most productive if they could each agree to find ways to talk about and learn from the issues that emerged in the work on high school testing without actually referring to the specifics of that case.

In general, it is important that people in conflict are able to talk about that conflict in ways that lead them to isolate the nature of the problem. This can be done by each person taking turns to talk about the issue from his or her own point of view. As a mediator at such meetings, you can contribute to this process in several ways. First, you can ensure that each person gets ample opportunity to speak without being interrupted. Second, you can push the discussion along to ensure that all points of disagreement are made explicit. Third, you can list the points as they are being made. Finally, you can encourage the adversaries to reflect on the list of problems and issues with the goal of summarizing the main sources of conflict. As in the broader world of public policymaking, even in conflicts between two people, achieving a clear sense of the nature of the problem represents an excellent start to the development of solutions.

Because conflicts can be emotionally draining, as a mediator you should keep fairly modest expectations of what you can achieve in an initial meeting between adversaries. It may well be that merely getting to the point where the problem is clearly stated and agreed on is quite a victory. If this is achieved, it might make sense for the initial meeting to end. Giving people opportunities to "sleep on" issues can often be helpful, and bringing people back fresh to a second meeting can be a good way to begin discussions of solutions. Here, it is useful again for you as mediator to promote contributions from both people. Even using some aspects of brainstorming (see chapter 7) can be helpful. For example, you might ask that both people offer five possible solutions to the problem. You could even offer this as a task for people to work on when you are wrapping up the meeting where you have taken time to define the problem that is the main source of conflict. With some starting ideas for solutions laid out, it is important that the two people involved then talk together about the key elements of the approach that they will take to resolve their conflict. Again, if you are going to be there, the most important thing that you can do is work as a facilitator. Manage the discussion so that people make their points without interruption, treat each other with respect, and stay focused. You should strive toward having the former adversaries work very hard together in this meeting, so a clear strategy is devised for getting beyond the conflict.

Monitor Progress

As the mediator in a conflict between others, you can play several important roles. First, you can help the adversaries realize that the conflict is damaging to themselves and to others around them. Second, you can lead them to a point where they are ready and willing to meet with one another to talk about the nature of their conflict, what constitutes the underlying problem, and how they might resolve it. Third, you can help those discussions to move along, by either being in the room as they occur or being willing to help the two parties structure their dialogue and to stand ready to receive subsequent feedback from both sides on how things went. Finally, once the parties have designed a solution to their conflict, as the mediator, you can monitor progress. Among other things, this might mean that you will watch out for improvements on the past, be encouraging to both parties about the improvement in their working relations, and watch for signs of the reemergence of conflict.

In team situations, monitoring the resolution of conflict is relatively easy to do. This is because teamwork requires you and those who have been in conflict to continue to work closely together. Hints of problems will emerge rapidly. In the conflict between Paul and Pamela, although it is easy to see how these two might have come to cross swords over the internal evaluation of data analysis, it is also clear that both of them have a lot of recent and highly relevant experience to draw on when thinking about the design of the guidelines for internal evaluation. Their conflict underscores just how important it is that processes for internal evaluation be handled carefully. If you were to succeed in having both Paul and Pamela recognize the broader issues at stake in their conflict, you could potentially draw on their thoughts and insights to support the development of the new guidelines. In fact, pointing out the importance of conflict management as an aspect of internal evaluation could provide a significant conceptual breakthrough both for the members of your work team and for the senior managers who commissioned your report and guidelines.

Managing Public Disputes

So far I have focused on ways that we can reduce conflict in our lives and resolve interpersonal conflicts when they emerge. As policy analysts, however, there are ways that we can help to manage conflicts that occur on a much larger scale. As I noted at the start of this chapter, the making of public policy is an inherently conflictual process. When public decisions are being made, many private interests are at stake. Decisions that could yield a significant net benefit for society might nonetheless impose considerable costs on particular individuals, groups, or communities. Although other people—politicians, lawyers, and professional mediators—often do most of the high-profile work associated with the management of public disputes, policy analysts can help move discussions and debates in productive directions. Here, I will touch briefly on several elements of the work that policy analysts can undertake with the purpose of helping to resolve public disputes. Parallels can be drawn between some of the steps one would take to manage public disputes and those that can lead to the resolution of private conflicts. Thus, I contend that good conflict management skills can improve a policy analyst's ability to contribute to effective public policymaking. Further, in their efforts to help manage public disputes, policy analysts can potentially support greater citizen input into policy design.

Identify Major Players

When you are conducting analytical work on any policy issue, it is important that you build your awareness of the major players involved in

Party	Issues	Interests	Importance of issues (High, Medium, Low)	Sources of power and influence	Positions taken, or options proposed	Interested in working with others?	Comments
A							
B							
C							

Figure 9-1. Conflict Analysis Matrix
Source: Carpenter and Kennedy 1988, 87.

the issue and the positions they hold. This is even more important when those major players hold positions and views that bring them into conflict. Once you have identified the players and their positions, it is useful to conduct a conflict analysis. Carpenter and Kennedy (1988, chap. 4) suggest a variety of techniques that you might use in the development of such an analysis. Perhaps one of the most useful techniques involves constructing a conflict analysis matrix. Figure 9-1 replicates a chart Carpenter and Kennedy suggest using. In their discussion of the need for policy analysts to think strategically about the adoption and implementation of policies, Weimer and Vining (1999, 386) present a similar matrix, which they describe as a "political analysis worksheet." Simple visual displays of this sort can be extremely helpful, for three reasons. First, they provide guidance as to the sort of information you will need to collect to make sense of a public dispute. Second, by working with them, it is easy to see what information you have gathered and where your remaining information needs lie. Finally, once completed, they provide a clear summary of the issues at stake and provide a variety of clues as to how the dispute might be managed to generate a positive outcome.

Develop Appropriate Background Materials

Public disputes often arise because people occupying different positions in society hold different views about where their interests lie and what issues are important to them. We are shaped by the institutions that facilitate and guide our behavior and the organizations to which we belong. For example, members of the property development industry tend to value land based on its potential to generate profits. In contrast, members of government conservation agencies tend to value land based on its contributions to local ecosystems. These are stereotypes, of course, but they serve to illustrate why public disputes often arise over issues of land use. In the words of Schön and Rein (1994), people bring different institutionally based "frames" to the policy process. "We see policy controversies as disputes in which the contending parties hold conflicting frames. Such disputes are resistant to resolution by appeal to facts or reasoned argumentation because the parties' conflicting frames determine what counts as a fact and what arguments are taken to be relevant and compelling" (23). According to these authors, dispute resolution can begin to happen only after the antagonists involved reflect on the frames through which they view issues. For policy actors to engage in "frame reflection," they must have the conceptual ability to imagine what it might be like to stand in the shoes of their adversaries, or to view the world through other people's eyes. Recall that in my discussion of ways to manage your personal conflicts, I similarly noted the importance of viewing situations from the perspective of your perceived adversary.

As policy analysts, we are better placed than most other individuals or groups to promote frame reflection on the part of antagonists in public disputes. By developing background papers and other analytical resources, policy analysts can offer new information concerning an issue. They can also suggest new ways of thinking about problems. The purpose of such work is not to bring a fully developed solution to the table. Rather, it is to provide resources and tools that might help everyone involved to start reflecting on why they have come into conflict, what issues are at stake, and how they might build on any shared interests to begin talking their way through the disagreement. Aside from developing background papers, policy analysts can also contribute to dispute resolution by providing clarifying analytical work as the negotiating parties request it. In addition, by rapidly producing documents or reports that summarize preceding discussions, policy analysts can increase the chances that the future phases of discussions will be highly productive.

Help the Participants Develop a Deliberation Process

In dispute resolution, it is sometimes difficult to separate the process from the final product. Parties to a dispute need to feel that their voices have counted in the crafting of a solution. Nobody likes to have outsiders "solve" their problems for them. With this in mind, there will often be times when policy analysts can help in the management of public disputes by assisting in the design of the deliberation process. Rather than begin with a "grand scheme" for how talks and meetings might proceed—that sounds too interventionist—policy analysts might stand ready to offer suggestions for what issues should be discussed at the next meeting, who should be there, and what information will ensure the discussion proceeds effectively. As with efforts to manage more minor conflicts between just two adversaries, you can make useful contributions by offering advice when called on, by viewing yourself as a facilitator who opens opportunities for others to talk, and by doing your best to maintain a low profile. By keeping a critical distance from the proceedings, by standing ready to offer advice, and by generating timely, insightful analytical work, policy analysts can do a lot to help in the resolution of public disputes.

CONFLICT MANAGEMENT AND OTHER PEOPLE SKILLS

Conflicts of any sort—public or private—impose considerable costs on the immediate protagonists and others around them. How well those conflicts are resolved can have significant, ongoing implications for those involved. Often, even when conflicts are apparently "resolved," people carry with them unpleasant memories and feelings of resentment about what happened. At the level of public disputes, efforts to work out hasty compromises often lead to solutions that, when judged in cost-benefit terms, yield few overall gains for society. All of this suggests that knowing how to manage conflict effectively is a valuable skill for policy analysts. The better able you are to manage your own conflicts and assist others around you to manage theirs, the better able you will be to get on with the business of producing high-quality policy analysis. But experience in conflict management at the personal level can yield important spillover benefits for your work. A clear sense of how to manage personal conflicts effectively provides an excellent starting point for thinking about ways that you might help those embroiled in public disputes to engage in effective deliberation and to design solutions that really do improve social outcomes.

Of course, managing conflicts is hard work. Having a sense of what strategies to use, and how to use them, is important. Furthermore, each conflict is unique, and in each instance you will be required to improvise as you go along. You will notice from this chapter that there are many complementarities between the skills needed to manage conflict effectively and several of the other people skills discussed in this book. For example, if you are able to manage conflict, you will be better able to manage your career, to work with others in teams, and to facilitate meetings. At the same time, if you want to contribute to managing public disputes, then, aside from having good conflict management skills, you will need to be skilled at building expert knowledge, interviewing informants, giving presentations, and writing for multiple audiences. Thus, although conflicts are costly and demanding, they present opportunities for us to practice and further develop our people skills. It is clear that we should not seek out conflicts or promote them, but, when they do arise, we should exercise all our relevant people skills with the purpose of managing those conflicts as effectively as possible.

SKILL-BUILDING CHECKLIST

- When you have a conflict with another person, ask yourself, "Looking to the future, what is the best thing I can do here?" If you are going to address the matter, use your time wisely. Never do things to "get even" with others.
- Avoid actions that provoke conflict. For example, getting angry is a choice. You become angry when you are stressed and you receive a trigger. By reducing your level of stress, you can reduce the potential for a trigger to make you feel and express anger. Further, by acknowledging that you are stressed, you can actively avoid triggers.
- If you feel you have a conflict with another person, you should deal with that person directly, but first you should gain perspective by talking confidentially about the matter with a trusted colleague or friend. Before you act, you should also first figure out whether negotiation is possible and likely to be worthwhile.
- Separate the people from the problem. Try to suspend negative judgments of people's motives. Whenever you are in conflict situations, seek to maintain and improve your relationships with others and, hence, protect your reputation.
- When planning to meet with your adversary, remember that the quality of your discussion will be influenced by such factors as the

timing of the meeting, what each of you has been doing before it, and the privacy of the meeting space.

- Use language carefully when defining problems. When you choose the right words, your talk can point you in the direction of conflict resolution. When you choose the wrong words, harmless misunderstanding can turn into major standoffs.

- Conflict resolution is possible when both sides are able to say, "If I were in your place, maybe I would see things the same way." Try to place yourself in the other people's shoes. To understand their interests, the constraints they face, and the problems they see, ask questions.

- Use shared interests as starting points for conflict resolution. Meetings to resolve conflicts should end with a clear statement of agreed next steps. Those next steps should involve behavioral changes that are easily monitored.

- If you know how to resolve personal conflicts effectively, you can be a resource to others, helping them to resolve their conflicts. As a policy analyst, continuously look for ways that your conflict management skills might contribute to the resolution of broader public disputes.

DISCUSSION IDEAS

- In discussions of conflict management, we are often told to look for ways to separate people from problems. Or we are told to treat anger—our own, or that shown by others—as "data" that can inform our thinking about a dispute rather than as a trigger to statements or actions we might later regret. Yet, in real life, it is easy to fall back on old habits and to react angrily to the things that others say or do. Role-playing is an excellent way for us to build new habits that can make us better at defusing conflict rather than fueling it. Working in pairs, share with your partner a conflict situation you have recently witnessed or been involved in. Then, taking one of these situations, develop two scenes of role-play. As you do so, you might want to change some of the details to make the situation less personal to you and easier for others to identify with. In the first scene, work out how the situation might develop if no effort was made to separate the people from the problem. In the second scene, replay the situation. This time, however, script the scene so that one of the actors makes a concerted effort to avoid an angry exchange and promote productive problem solving. Finally, in the whole group, perform and discuss two or three of these role-plays. On the basis of what you see, does the approach of separating people from problems actually make a difference?

- A freshly minted MPA, Bryan, has joined your organization. You have been assigned to serve as his "buddy," giving him informal guidance on how to get along in this new work climate. After meeting with him once every two weeks over the past three months, you notice a pattern emerging. Frequently, Bryan will tell you how annoyed he feels with one or two of the other policy analysts on the staff. In his view, these older staff are "technophobic" and "squish heads" when it comes to thinking about policy issues. Meanwhile, you have heard others mentioning that Bryan seems to be a "hothead" and a "loose cannon." You know from your conversations that Bryan is smart and energetic and that he has a lot to offer the organization, but his anger toward others worries you, and you think it could get him into trouble. As his buddy, you decide to give him some quite specific advice about his behavior. At the same time, you are concerned that Bryan might take your advice the wrong way, viewing it as a reprimand, and come to demonize you. On the basis of what you have read in this chapter, what would be the gist of your advice to Bryan? Can you construct a simple "recipe for success" to give to him? Having answered these questions alone, working in small groups, share your responses with others. Do you think they will have the intended effect?

- Consider the following statement: "If people are engaged in a dispute, they should turn to a professional mediator to help them resolve it. There are limits to our professional capabilities. Conflict management isn't part of the job description for a policy analyst." Individually, list up to five steps you think policy analysts might take to help other people progress from a situation of public disagreement over a policy issue to the achievement of a mutually satisfactory outcome. Next, in small groups, discuss the items on your respective lists, and decide the three most important ways you think policy analysts can support the resolution of public disputes. How might you reconcile your thoughts about policy analysts and conflict management with the view expressed in the statement above?

FURTHER READING

Carpenter, Susan L., and W. J. D. Kennedy. 1988. *Managing Public Disputes: A Practical Guide to Handling Conflict and Reaching Agreements.* San Francisco: Jossey-Bass.

Dana, Daniel. 2001. *Conflict Resolution.* New York: McGraw-Hill.

Durning, Dan. 1993. "Participatory Policy Analysis in a Social Service Agency: A Case Study." *Journal of Policy Analysis and Management* 12:297–322.

Fisher, Roger, William Ury, and Bruce Patton. 1991. *Getting to YES: Negotiating Agreement without Giving In.* 2d ed. Hammondsworth: Penguin.

Forester, John. 1999. *The Deliberative Practitioner: Encouraging Participatory Planning Processes.* Cambridge, Mass.: MIT Press.

Schön, Donald A., and Martin Rein. 1994. *Frame Reflection: Toward the Resolution of Intractable Policy Controversies.* New York: Basic Books.

10
#####

Professional Networking

I think for some people the term "networking" has a negative connotation. To them, it conjures up images of schmoozing and self-promotion. However, making personal contacts with other professionals is essential to both your success in your current job and to building your future. Being an extrovert is obviously an asset, but it is an asset that you can acquire with practice. Initially, introducing yourself and engaging others in conversation can be daunting. What I've found is that preparation is the key. Plus developing a niche within the policy community. During the years when I was a policy analyst at the National Conference of State Legislatures, I knew that I was in a unique position to monitor trends across the states and to track developments in education policies. Having that information opened the door to many meetings and conversations and made other professionals seek me out to talk with. After those encounters, I always tried to follow up with an e-mail or a copy of something I had written. It's important to view networking as an opportunity to learn from others in the field with differing knowledge and perspectives. This is certainly not just about building up a Rolodex. Being yourself, sharing your thoughts, listening and learning from others will enhance your skills as a policy analyst . . . and you never know when you'll need those contacts later.

—Eric Hirsch, *Executive Director, Alliance for*
Quality Teaching, Denver, Colorado

If you aspire to make a difference to public policy and society, it is essential that you become actively engaged in professional policy networks. As policy analysts, our primary goal is to enlighten and influence policymakers through the development of analytical work and policy recommendations. But the lines of influence between policy analysts and decision makers are rarely direct. Just as public policy is implemented in social contexts and comes to shape those contexts, policy analysis is also developed in social contexts.

During the past few decades, policy scholars have made a variety of attempts to characterize the nature of the policymaking process and the broader social context within which it occurs (Mintrom 2000, chap. 2). Although those characterizations differ in important ways, many policy scholars have come to think of the policymaking process as something equivalent to a group of continuous conversations among interested parties (Kingdon 1995; Majone 1989; Radin 1997; Schön and Rein 1994). The content of those conversations changes over time, as do the people involved, yet the procedures followed in formal political institutions, such as city halls and legislatures, help to structure policy conversations in and around these centers of power and allow for the development of norms of appropriate formal and informal behavior among participants. The set of ongoing interactions among participants in these policy conversations can be thought of as representing ties in policy networks. To increase your influence as a policy analyst, you need to build your awareness of the nature of the professional policy networks operating around you and in which you inevitably participate. As Radin (2000, 168) has observed, "Over the years, many policy analysts have become much less reliant on traditional written documents to communicate their work to decision makers. . . . Often analysts find that they are most effective when they participate in meetings and conferences organized by issue networks and are able to infuse their expertise into the discussion of alternative approaches."

For policy analysts, professional networking involves building a set of contacts in and around the policymaking community. The skills needed to become successful as a networker can be learned. Knowing the value of networking, you can gain many insights into what makes for networking success by watching the behavior of others. Although it is important to be assertive, to take risks now and then, and to always present yourself well to others, you should also try to avoid appearing overbearing or an upstart. A comment once made by Wildavsky (1993) captures the nature of the enterprise. "Creating a network is full of errors and trials. But trying and persisting, absent ability to predict who will be both forthcoming and effective, is the only way" (27).

PROFESSIONAL NETWORKS AS RESOURCES

The social networks we participate in represent resources. This is because our ties to other people serve as conduits for the transfer of valuable information. One of the most commonly noted ways that network ties work for individuals is in helping them identify employment opportunities (Granovetter 1995). It is well known that many people learn of new job openings through word of mouth rather than through formal channels, such as newspaper advertisements and websites. Further, recommendations and referrals from trusted third parties can greatly raise the prospects of a job applicant receiving the attention of recruiters and being invited to interview. The value of the network ties comes from the quality of the information that can be passed between individuals with prior acquaintances. For example, an intermediary holding information about a job opening and who also knows of an individual who is potentially interested in such a job will likely do more than simply point the potential applicant in the direction of the potential recruiter. In choosing whether to alert each party to the possibility of a good employment fit, the "matchmaker" engages in a type of informal screening, revealing a belief that the fit might work. Thus, the very act of suggesting a match infuses important information into the situation. Suggesting a potential match when the fit clearly would not work would be a waste of time for all concerned and could potentially damage the intermediary's reputation.

Of course, our ties in social networks can work for us in a variety of ways, some of which are critical (like helping us to identify employment opportunities) and some of which are ephemeral but that nonetheless improve the quality of our lives (such as advice about places to shop, books to read, or movies to see). The key to understanding the power of social networks is to recognizing the underlying logic of information transfer that allows them to function. In documenting the rise of what he has termed "the network society," Castells (1996, 469) has observed that, countering the logic of information flow in hierarchies, in networks "the power of flows takes precedence over the flows of power." Professional networks represent a subset of social networks, and, hence, we should also be aware of the many ways that our ties within those networks can serve to enhance our professional lives.

For policy analysts, ties within professional networks can be important for several reasons. All have to do with the quality of the information that can come available to you through your contacts. First, through ongoing communication with others, you can gain a large amount of informal knowledge about policy issues, the key players involved in policy debates, and the kinds of arguments that tend to win support in the present circumstances. Policy networks serve as repositories of collective knowledge and know-how that can guide the way you engage in policy analysis and the means by which you communicate your ideas to others. Second, learning who's who in your section of the policymaking community can give you insight into who to turn to for help when you need additional information as you work on a policy problem. As old hands in the policy analysis profession know, a quick e-mail exchange or telephone conversation with the right person can save hours, days, or even weeks of time spinning one's wheels on policy problems. Third, as my comments about employment opportunities would suggest, having a variety of ties within the policymaking community increases the chances that you will learn about developments that could affect your career and about new employment prospects as they open up. Being in touch with others in the policymaking community will give you a sense of the standards associated with particular jobs, the key people you would need to impress to become a contender, and the caliber of the competition you would face.

If, as someone once said, "the meaning of life is to make life meaningful," professional networking is an enormously important activity. Through our ongoing relations with others who share our passion for policy issues and questions, we can come to gain a better sense of our place in the scheme of things and the possibilities we face for making the most of our careers. No matter whether you are a student training to be a policy analyst; an analyst working in a government, nonprofit, or for-profit organization; an academic; or a consultant, making an effort to build and enrich your network ties can be seriously rewarding.

THINKING OF YOURSELF IN RELATION TO OTHERS

When we venture out into the world, and interact with others, we typically continue to think of ourselves as the center of the universe, but that does not mean that we should think of things only from our own perspective. The selfish orientation of going through life is to always ask, either explicitly or implicitly, "What's in this for me?" Networking with others requires a different way of thinking. Call it "enlightened self-interest." One of the best things that you can do to raise your image among others and to have others think highly of you is to think about situations from the point of view of the people you are interacting with, in other words, "What's in this for them?"

"GIVERS GAIN": THE NETWORKING PHILOSOPHY

In books on networking, you repeatedly will find the statement "Givers gain." You will also hear, "What comes around goes around." Give to others and others will give to you, but you might not see the rewards of your giving right away. I once heard the suggestion that you should always give other people a gift when you meet them. On first thought, we might think that this would be very costly and also a form of groveling! On second thought, however, this idea makes a lot of sense. There are lots of ways that we can give to others. Smiling. Being friendly. Giving a genuine compliment. These are nice things to do. We like it when others are nice to us. It makes sense to get into the habit of giving to others in these low-key ways.

More importantly, think about what you would seriously like others to do for you professionally. No matter what your present position, you can do things to help those around you. Think about ways in the past that you might have helped a colleague or a friend solve a problem. These are starting points for networking activity. You can learn from this and build on your good experiences. Wouldn't you just love it if someone else could introduce you to an employer who had a fantastic job that you could fill? Networking can allow opportunities like this to arise. If you get into the habit of trying to help others and make things happen for them, it is likely that, through the connections you make, good things will begin to happen for you, too. People generally like to reciprocate, and, when they can, they often will. So, in short, effective networking starts with a change of orientation. Rather than asking "What's in it for me?" ask "What can I do here to help others?"

Starting Points

There is a lot about networking that will seem intuitive. That is because, in many ways, establishing and maintaining good professional relationships take the same kind of skills that, over the years, we have drawn on to build our friendships and to manage our daily interactions with others. But because professional networking can be so important to our careers, it is vital that we get beyond operating on intuition or instinct and carefully reflect on how we interact with others in the course of our professional lives. In what follows, I have set out a number of steps you can take to increase the likelihood that your efforts to engage in professional networking will prove successful.

Identify Appropriate Venues for Networking

Because so much of what we do is social, even if you have never thought seriously before about your networking activities, you undoubtedly are engaged in a variety of social networks of one sort or another. Of course, your level of engagement in some is likely to be higher than in others. When thinking about yourself as a policy analyst and about your engagement in professional networks, the most important way to start is to think about your activities in the organization where you presently spend most of your time. Through your work or your interest in public policy, whom do you interact with most? What structures allow those interactions to occur? How often do your activities in this organization lead you to meet and engage with new people who also share your public policy interests? Answering these questions can help to give you a sense of the quantity and quality of the professional interactions you currently have. Continuing to think about your immediate situation, list opportunities it offers for you to deliberately engage in more networking activities than you do at present.

As a policy analyst, you will find that there are potentially many structured and unstructured opportunities for you to engage in professional networking. Aside from the opportunities that will arise through your work or your training, occasions for professional networking are offered by the various associations for the advancement of public policy and public administration that exist on the local, regional, and national scale. If you do not belong to a professional association of policy analysts or public administrators, seriously consider doing so. The local chapters of such associations will provide venues for you to meet with other professionals who share your policy interests. They will also offer the chance to engage in voluntary work for the association and, in doing so, become more connected with members of the local policy community. As you become more involved in networking activities and meet with other people, you will find yourself having many opportunities to ask others about the associations they belong to and the kind of regular, structured activities they attend as part of their professional lives. These involvements and conversations with others should eventually allow you to identify the best venues that are open to you and that provide you with fruitful opportunities for professional networking. Ideally, you should strive to be regularly involved in a variety of informal and formal activities that allow you to socialize with other policy analysts and members of the policy community.

Be Goal Oriented

When you are attending events where you think there will be opportunities for networking, you should be goal oriented. If you do not know why you are attending these events, they will probably be a waste of time. Consider the opportunity costs. If you go, make the most of the events. For example, decide in advance that you will seek to initiate conversations with two people during the event. Or, decide in advance that you really want to have a conversation with a particular person. Then make sure that it happens. It is unlikely that these conversations will lead to anything earth shattering for you. But, as RoAne (2000) repeatedly observes in her book on networking, "you never know."

Whenever you are in social settings, strive to make a good impression. This means acting (and dressing) appropriately for the situation. Find ways to make others feel at ease around you. One way to do this is to view yourself in the "host" role as opposed to the "guest" role.

What do hosts do to make others feel comfortable? Often, you can do that too, if you think about it.

Be Enthusiastic

It is difficult for other people to warm to someone who is mildly depressed and does not get excited when talking to others. You do not need to overdo it, but being enthusiastic can go a long way toward improving the impression others have of you. If you are going to show up at an event, mentally prepare yourself. Often, before a variety of events, many people feel nervous and wish in some ways that they could stay home. All the same, you need to go to events with a good attitude. Make a list (mentally, at least) of some of the things that make you feel good about who you are, what you are doing in your work, and where you are going with your career. This will help you to get enthusiastic about being around others, talking, and making new friends. Incidentally, when we enter the world, most of us go out as not just ourselves but as representatives of the organizations we work for or are associated with. Even though we might have some criticisms of our organizations, I suggest that we keep them to ourselves in social settings. When you are critical of your place of work, people might wonder about you. "If the place is so bad, why are you there?" "This person seems critical. What might he or she think of me?" Try to be an enthusiast for your organization. See yourself as an ambassador for it. You want to create a winning impression of both yourself and the organization you spend most of your time working for.

Develop Your Conversation Skills

Networking is about social engagement. We engage with others through our conversations. Being determined to become an effective networker does not mean that you should go to an event, race around to talk with as many people as possible, and tell all of them how fantastic you are. This is, in fact, the last thing you should do.

The trick is to be a good conversationalist, which requires thinking about situations from the perspective of others. Develop a genuine curiosity about other people. Try to ask others open-ended questions that call for more than a "yes" or "no" response. People love to talk about themselves, and so you can get people talking and feeling relaxed around you by the sort of questions you ask. As the conversation progresses, make sure that you also contribute, revealing information about yourself as you go. Try to avoid being like people we have all overheard in airplanes who, by the time they have arrived in New York from Chicago have revealed every detail of every aspects of their lives to the unfortunate people in the seats next to them.

As a policy analyst engaging in professional networking, you will often talk with other people from the policy world, but because the types of things we work on as policy analysts can be numerous, that does not mean that you will necessarily have common interests associated with your work. One way to increase the likelihood that you will be able to have engaging conversations with a wide variety of policy people is to make a habit of reading the newspaper and at least one good news magazine per week. Aside from the intrinsic value of keeping up with current events, knowing what's been happening in the world is great for conversation. Having a good general knowledge will make it easier for you to make intelligent responses to people when they tell you something (for example, "You telling me that reminds me of something I read recently about . . .").

Treat Other People as You Would Like to Be Treated

Suggesting that you view situations from the perspective of others is really the starting point for introducing the golden rule: treat other people as you would like to be treated. In networking, this boils down to several things. First, show a genuine interest in the other person. Listen to what he or she has to say. Second, try to remember people's names. There are certain things that you can do to improve your recall of people's names. (One thing is to immediately repeat the name once you hear it.) Third, try to make others feel at ease and confident around you. At a minimum, when you are talking to others, give them your full attention. Do not look around the room for better prospects as someone is talking to you. You never know who knows who, and you definitely should avoid looking like someone who is only interested in interacting with "big names." Such behavior looks hideous. Further, as a networking strategy, trying to get a moment with big name people is less likely to work than quietly building solid relations with other people at your level or others who you begin to find you have a natural affinity with.

Finally, think about how you might introduce the person you are with to others you have recently met or who you know at the event. (Again, this is acting like a host.)

Keep Track of Who's Who

Before events, it is good to have a sense of who will or who might be there. We network professionally with the purpose of gaining influence in our chosen fields of policy work. Who are the movers and shakers in our policy spheres? Who knows who? It will take a while for you to figure out connections and relationships, but knowing the basic social architecture will help you to better negotiate your way through it.

As I suggested above, one thing that people sometimes comment on is how certain people only want to impress "important" people. You must avoid the appearance of such obsequiousness. Of course, we would all like to make a close connection with important people, but you do not do that by having little respect for "lesser people." If everyone were like that to you, you would never advance in your own career, so keep track of who's who, and be nice to everyone. Again, with some aspects of who's who, "you never know." Over the years, I have been struck by how an occasional chance conversation with someone I previously did not know has been reported back to others I did know. The good news is that the report backs were positive, but this should serve as a reminder to be on guard when you talk with others and definitely do not be critical when you are not sure of the connections that those who you are talking with have to others.

KEYS TO SUCCESSFUL NETWORKING

So far I have reviewed the basics of professional networking. These will get you started, but there are a variety of additional steps you can take to make the most out of your efforts to become engaged in the public policy community.

Have Hard Currency

In professional settings, you will become a more effective networker if you also happen to be excellent at the work you do. It seems to me that we can categorize what we do into two groups of activities. First, we produce policy analysis. Second, we interact with others. Suppose you are very good at what you produce, but you are very shy. If this is the case, some of your good analytical work might not get the attention it deserves. Suppose, in contrast, that you are very good at interacting with others socially, but you cut corners on your work. You may well get a reputation as a good conversationalist, but after a while people will wonder if you are something of a lightweight. You want to be an excellent producer and an excellent networker. That is how you will eventually come to have real influence in the policymaking community. In the end, no matter how good you are at networking, if you cannot demonstrate your abilities through excellent analytical work, all the talk will add up to little. In fact, it could be damaging to your reputation.

Make Time for Networking

Building our relations with other people takes time. Therefore, because networking is about building good relations with others, it takes time. Set aside time for professional networking. This does not mean that you should always be attending events, but it does means following up on the contacts that you have made. No matter what the form of the activities associated with networking, they will require quality time. Making that time will pay off.

Make the Most of Structured Events

Think about ways to make the most of events that others have set up and that you can attend. How can you use these events as opportunities to network and, more broadly, to interact with others? Perhaps there are opportunities for voluntary work. If you have a clear sense of your broader career goals, you can develop a sharper sense of what sort of structured events you should be attending and how you might make the most of them.

Be Visible

When you are at a structured event, make yourself visible. I do not mean that you should make a spectacle of yourself, but you should make an effort to initiate contact with others. Before you attend, think about an effective way to rapidly introduce yourself to others (for example, "Hi, I'm _____ and I work on _____ at _____.") If you have a creative or interesting-sounding introduction, it will provide a "hook" for others to ask questions and strike up conversations with you.

Be Sincere

Networking requires sincerity. People know when others are fakers. Show sincere interest in others. Do not go to an event if you cannot be bothered. In terms of preserving your reputation, it is better that you only go to events where you feel you can be genuinely upbeat and interested in those around you. One way to show your sincerity is to think of yourself as a problem solver. When others tell you about who they are and what they do, think about the sort of things that you could say, or introductions that you could make, that would be helpful to that person.

Evaluate Events and Interactions

After an event where you have met new people, take the time to evaluate how it went. It is always good to reflect on events, to ask yourself, "How did I do? What worked? What did not work? How could I improve things next time?" It is also good when evaluating events to think about the goals you set and how realistic they were. Over the years, when I have attended academic conferences, on occasion, I have found myself driving home feeling a vague sense of disappointment. One way I have come to deal with this is to set quite low expectations, and then, if things go well, to be pleasantly surprised. It is important to avoid being too despondent if your interactions at meetings or events do not seem to have been especially thrilling. Things build up over time. Making a couple of new connections per event is pretty good going. Afterward, think about who you would like to keep in touch with and how you might do that.

Engage in Quality Follow-up

High-quality follow-up is a centerpiece of effective networking. After you have met a new person, think about ways to tighten the connection. Sending e-mail messages of follow-up is a good thing to do, though it takes time. For example, after attending academic conferences, it is not unusual for people to spend a full day on follow-up activities. Is this a waste of time? "You never know!" I suggest that being polite to others, keeping in touch, and suggesting future events at which to meet are very important. If you tell someone that you are going to give them a call, do it. If you promise to send them a piece of your work or your resumé, send it.

Maintain and Enrich Your Relationships

Up to this point, I have talked mainly about how to make the most of social and professional situations where you are likely to meet new people, but a good networker treats those brief encounters with others as just the beginning. Quality follow-up should never end. Think about ways that you can maintain and enrich your professional relationships with others. Begin with e-mail or telephone follow-ups, and then think about ways that you can interact with others so that they get to know more about your work and your interests and you get to learn more about them. Again, you have to be genuinely interested in other people if you are going to be effective at this. Start off with low-key interactions and build up from there.

Bring Others Together

As a networker, one of the best things that you can do is find ways to bring others together. In sociological studies, people talk about actors in organizations as "sociometric stars." These are the people in organizations who have more interactions with a larger number of other people than anyone else. As a sociometric star, you will learn a lot of information about what is going on around you. You are the center of the network. Obviously, a prerequisite to being a sociometric star is to be nice to other people. If you are not, they will stay away. But then you want to show others how you can be a resource for them. One way to do this is to work at introducing people, making connections among them. Bringing others together can be a good professional activity, and it can have important payoffs. This is really an extension of the notion of acting like a "host" rather than a "guest." As you become more involved in voluntary work in professional associations, you will find yourself in positions that require you to interact a lot with other people and to bring other people into contact with one another. This is why putting in effort, and acting like a host rather than a guest, is extremely important if you seek to migrate toward the center of professional networks.

Be Patient

Networking takes effort. There will be many times in your career when you feel as though you have done everything right, you have been nice to people, you have made connections, you have made yourself visible, you have often volunteered and played host, and yet nothing seems to come of all this effort. The final key to networking is patience. Time allows professional relationships to mature. Avoid the temptation of wanting to push things too fast with other people. Mizner (2000) offers the analogy of the farmer who plants crops. You cannot expect to reap your rewards for your efforts until the time is right. If you follow some of the steps that I have suggested here and are patient, you will come to have a lot of influence with those around you. As a policy analyst, a public manager, a consultant, or any other sort of symbolic analyst, being well known and well liked is a huge asset. It is definitely as much of an asset as your expert knowledge and your analytical skills. It is worth taking the time to build your contacts and your reputation. And, by the way, as you put in all this effort, you will find yourself having fun. Networking is about a way of living and a philosophy of work. Remember, "givers gain."

NETWORKING AND OTHER PEOPLE SKILLS

Effective networking requires both time and skill. It is important to have a sense of the structure of the professional networks you wish to be engaged in. It is also important to have the confidence and ability to initiate relations with others who share your interests in public policy. Thus, knowing the rudiments of professional networking will serve you well. But the practice of networking, of initiating and maintaining effective professional relations with others, requires a range of people skills. Knowing how to manage your time effectively will ensure that you make appropriate space in your schedule to engage in quality networking. Having the skills of a good listener and, hence, a good conversationalist is invaluable for those who seek to achieve influence through their networking activities. As well as this, knowing how to give good formal presentations will help you to build the skills needed to present yourself well in a variety of formal and informal professional settings. Finally, if you seek to achieve influence with other members of the policymaking community, you must have resources of your own that you can bring to the table. Engaging in a great deal professional networking will add up to nothing if your work as a policy analyst is not up to the mark. If you are not regularly producing high-quality policy analysis, when it comes to networking with others, you might as well be trading in rubles.

Through professional networking, you can come to share resources and information in ways that will be valuable to your career and to the careers of others. Whenever you are planning to engage in networking activities, take a few minutes to remind yourself of why you are doing this. Networking can help you to get ahead, but only because it provides opportunities for you to allow others to see what you have to offer the policymaking community. Treating other people as rungs on the ladder to your own success is not the sort of behavior that will serve you well when networking. Telling other people at length how wonderful you are will not serve you well either. The purpose of professional networking should be to build a variety of mutually rewarding ties to other people in the policymaking community. Rather than treat networking as a grim task that must be performed so that you can establish a quota of contacts for yourself, think of networking as a socially enriching activity, something that helps you to give more meaning to your work and your career. Actively seeking to use your knowledge, skills, and experience to help others can open opportunities you might never have imagined. Putting in and maintaining a positive, enthusiastic attitude toward your work and the work of others will produce a variety of rewards, not the least of which is a sense of personal fulfillment.

Skill-Building Checklist

- Work to build your understanding of who's who in the organization and the policy community that you are currently associated with. Listen to the broader policy conversation. Seek to attain a clear sense of relations among members of your immediate policy community, and try to figure out why certain people have come to be seen as "movers and shakers."

- Identify and join a few professional associations that will bring you into ongoing contact with other policy analysts who share your interests. Participate regularly in the activities of these associations, such as business meetings, seminar programs, and conferences. Think of effective ways that you could become more involved in these activities and contribute to their success.
- Before attending any professional events, consider who else is likely to be there. Think about the opportunities that might come from attending and how you will introduce and present yourself to others. Remember that showing genuine interest in others and being a good conversationalist is critical for starting relationships.
- Think of your relations with others from their perspective. Remember that "givers gain." No matter what the venue, showing up, contributing your share of voluntary effort, and thinking in terms of what others are seeking is essential to being a successful networker.
- After meeting people, always engage in effective follow-up. If you promise to get in touch, make sure that you do. If you promise to send someone a piece of your work or your resumé, do it.
- Be patient. Building effective network ties takes time and effort and the payoffs may come slowly. But the effort put into developing and maintaining good professional relations with other policy analysts and members of the policy community will enhance the pleasure you get from participating, will help you become better at your work, and will eventually open many career opportunities for you.

Discussion Ideas

- Professional networking can allow you to build productive relationships with other policy analysts. These relationships often exhibit many of the same characteristics as our personal friendships. Individually, list a few of your closest friends and then think about how those friendships started. What were the contexts? In what ways did chance play a role in the first meetings? In a small group, talk with others about how you have made friends, and try to find some common elements to how those friendships started. Having done this, list how your insights about making friends could help you meet and build productive relationships with others who share your professional interests.

- In groups of three or four, brainstorm to make a list of professional associations that could be worth joining as ways to support your career development. Once you have made a list, divide the associations into those that are locally based, regionally based, or nationally based. Discuss why it might make sense for a policy analyst to participate in a mixture of local, regional, and national associations.
- Think about the policy topic that most interests you at present or the policy project that you are currently working on. If there were three people with whom you could talk about this policy area, who would they be? What about these people has led you to think of them as important? What actions could you take to develop your policy expertise and your professional profile so that others might come to think of you as a key policy person to talk with about their work? In small groups, compare your answers to these questions. How important do you think professional networking has been to raising the profiles of the people you identified in answering the first question?

FURTHER READING

Castells, Manuel. 1996. *The Rise of the Network Society*. Oxford: Blackwell.

Garner, Alan. 1997. *Conversationally Speaking: Tested New Ways to Increase Your Personal and Social Effectiveness*. 3d ed. Los Angeles: Lowell House.

Granovetter, Mark S. 1973. "The Strength of Weak Ties." *American Journal of Sociology* 78:1360–80.

Misner, Ivan R., and Don Morgan, eds. 2000. *Masters of Networking: Building Relationships for Your Pocketbook and Soul*. Atlanta: Bard Press.

RoAne, Susan. 2000. *How to Work a Room: The Ultimate Guide to Savvy Socializing in Person and Online*. New York: HarperCollins.

11
- - - - -

Pursuing Excellence

Any excellence I may have achieved in policy analysis owes a debt to the highly capable colleagues with whom I have worked. The most important of these colleagues was Aaron Wildavsky, my mentor and former dean of the Graduate School of Public Policy at the University of California at Berkeley. For him policy analysis started with an idea. His motivation for the idea usually derived from his passionate values about policy outcomes for citizens. His analysis, like a prism refracting light, extended understanding and suggested alternatives that had either been overlooked or did not exist. He opened his rough-draft analyses to criticism, usually in brain storming sessions on Friday afternoons or in class. He believed policy analysts need multidisciplinary skills and abilities and should add value to real decision-making. My multi-year work with colleagues at Michigan State University and the University of Illinois furthered my understanding of excellence. An analysis I conducted with colleagues at Michigan State University, for example, of the effectiveness of state job training programs may serve as an illustration. Our multidisciplinary team met with a select group of policymakers to define a researchable yet politically important question. We also traveled to and met with workers and managers of firms in the communities affected by these programs. The policymakers worked with us in the design and implementation of the analysis. Upon completion, we produced a report, a presentation to the governor's staff, and a published journal article. The policy analysis required an initial idea, research design, original data collection, quasi-experimental methodology, and analysis. It also required team building, interpersonal conflict management, meeting facilitation, community involvement, effective presentations, clear report writing, practical recommendations, and political sensibility. Excellence in policy analysis is often achieved through collaboration and mutual learning, with the ultimate goal to understand better and hopefully improve the lives of citizens.

—Dr. Jack H. Knott, *Director of the Institute of Government and Public Affairs and Professor of Political Science at the University of Illinois, Urbana-Champaign*

Excellent policy analysts are made, not born. The motivating premise of this book is that, beyond displaying well-developed technical skills and deep substantive knowledge, excellent policy analysts display superb people skills. In the past, programs established to train policy analysts and public managers did a great deal to equip people with relevant knowledge and skills in areas such as applied microeconomics, financial analysis, and statistics. Many books have been written to help policy analysts acquire sound technical training. In contrast, little thought has previously been given to the people skills required of policy analysts. Although many policy practitioners and scholars recognize the relevance of people skills, this book is the first to codify how policy analysts might master such skills. I hope my work here will legitimate efforts to give policy analysts systematic training in people skills.

By improving their people skills, as individuals, policy analysts can achieve greater effectiveness in their work. Collectively, the profession has much to gain from a membership that recognizes the complementary nature of people skills and technical skills. As increasing recognition is given to the professional importance of people skills, I believe we will witness a shift in the attributes that spring to mind when we describe someone as an excellent policy analyst. Moving beyond the privileging of narrow technical expertise could have many benefits for the profession, for those who aspire to make their careers in and around government, and for the consumers of policy advice. The enterprise of government is a deeply human one. Policy analysts who know how to work effectively with others, who can make their points clearly to policymakers, and who can reach and inform members of the broader polity hold the potential to do great service for society.

In this final chapter I turn to the notion of pursuing excellence. I use the word "pursuing" advisedly. In situations where continuous improvement is expected of both individuals and whole organizations, those exceptional practices that constitute excellent behavior at one time should subsequently be integrated into standard operating procedures. In accordance with this belief, I offer some suggestions for how policy analysts might work to keep improving what they do. In pursuing excellence, I believe it is important for people to strive to add value, to keep learning, to manage their reputations, to lead by example, and to play the long game. This is advice for people who are restless, for those who know that, no matter how well they perform, there is always room for innovation and improvement.

Strive to Add Value

In most fields of human activity, people who pursue excellence act with the primary goal of creating what others value. For example, throughout his career, the classical pianist Daniel Barenboim has continually strived to produce technically accomplished and intensely passionate interpretations of the works of such composers as Mozart and Beethoven. No doubt, Barenboim has gained enormous personal satisfaction from his decades of effort. Yet, always that effort has been directed toward an audience, toward performing perfectly—and seemingly effortlessly—both in concert and on recordings. Even as they work with musical scores written centuries ago and perform with a deep knowledge of the tradition on which they are building, performers like Barenboim are acutely aware that each performance represents an opportunity to do even better than the time before.

At their best, policy analysts help members of the policymaking community—and, by extension, members of the broader polity—to come to clear understandings of policy problems and to devise and implement effective public responses. Therefore, it is useful to think of policy analysts as people whose entire professional purpose is to add value to the making of public decisions. Of course, public policy issues never exist in a political vacuum. They emerge through processes of discussion and debate. When the socially constructed nature of policy problems is acknowledged, the possible scope and importance of the role played by policy analysts in the policymaking process increases immensely. Policy analysts hold the potential to shape public understandings of problems and their solutions significantly. This exercise, however, can never be narrowly technical. To be truly helpful here, policy analysts must possess a variety of well-developed people skills.

When you begin working on a new project, or when you start wrestling with a policy issue that is new to you, it is important that you think in terms of adding value. Here are some questions that it is always useful to ask:

- Among the things I could do here, which would be the most helpful to my client and to other members of this policymaking community right now?
- Where are the major knowledge gaps, and how could I fill them?
- How could my efforts establish new standards of analytical merit in this policy area?

When you adopt the "value-added" mindset, it is easy to spot areas where you could improve on your own past performances and those of others. As you scan for new opportunities for adding value, however, you must remain mindful of what constitutes your core activities. It is vital that you pursue excellence in your core activities before you branch beyond them. Perhaps this goes without saying. Nevertheless, examples can be found in many areas of activity—business is a salient one—where ongoing efforts to innovate and expand their activities lead people to give less attention to what matters most. That is why Peters and Waterman (1982), have proclaimed, "Stick to the knitting." You must always strive to do the very best job that you can in the areas where people expect and demand you to perform well. Only if you are giving sufficient attention to those activities does it makes sense for you to search for ways to stretch yourself in new directions, adding value as you do so.

KEEP LEARNING

If you want continually to find ways to add value as a policy analyst, you must also be prepared to keep learning. The act of learning contains several components. Among these, the primary component is a will to improve on your present performance. But this will to improve must be accompanied by an understanding of how you might do so. This suggests that, in any given area of activity, you need to be clear about your present level of performance and the kind of performance that you would like to give in the future. Learning involves taking actions, receiving feedback, and making corrections, all with the goal of achieving well-specified improvements in your performance.

There are several ways that you can gain insights into your present performance and learn of ways that it might be improved. First, you can talk to your clients, asking them for feedback on areas where they would like you to do better. Second, you can make a habit of diagnosing your previous projects and engagements with clients. Individually, or as part of a team, you should try to develop a list of things associated with that previous work that you could have done better. This deliberate reflection on past performance can generate a variety of prescriptions for future performance. Finally, you can learn from diagnosing the work that others have done in other areas.

As you work on developing your knowledge and skills as a policy analyst, you should recognize that there are different ways of learning, some of which are more effective than others. I suggest that you try to organize your activities so that you are able to focus on learning and mastering new skills one at a time. For example, suppose that you want to learn to use a new software program. The best way to learn involves combining regular practice with regular reflection on your performance. Therefore, at the beginning of a session with the new software, you might set several goals. During the session, you seek to attain those goals. After the session, you should take some time to reflect on how the session went, looking over the software manual or guidebook. In these times of reflection, be sure to take stock of what goals you have now attained and what goals you still need to work toward achieving. You should plan to have regular sessions with the software, all within a reasonably short amount of time of each other, until you have begun to master it. You will know that you have left too much time between sessions if you find that the start of each session is spent reacquainting yourself with basic procedures rather than focusing on the first of the new procedures you planned to learn. Devoting intensive periods of time to learning a specific new skill might seem like a misallocation of your resources, but when you deliberately set aside time to master a new skill, you can save yourself a lot of wasted time later.

All of the people skills covered in this book cannot be mastered without considerable effort and ongoing practice. In many instances, you will find that you can take an intensive approach to learning. For example, if you are part of a team, you can continuously look for ways to build your skills as a team player. Similarly, if you have been asked to run a regular weekly meeting, you will have a perfect opportunity for building and consolidating your meeting management skills. If you wish, you could also use such meetings as sites for building your presentation skills.

Even when you do not set aside special time for skill building, you can still do a lot of learning in the normal course of your work. I suggest that you get into the habit of thinking of your day-to-day activities as opportunities for learning. The key is to consciously see yourself as practicing and learning, with the goal of pursuing personal mastery and excellence. For example, if you have decided that you want to build your presentational skills, you should deliberately scan your daily and weekly activities, looking for all activities that have even the slightest element of presentation associated with them. (In this case, you will find that all your interactions with other people represent different forms of presentation.) With those upcoming activities listed, you can then think about how you will use each of them to practice your presentation skills. After each encounter, make time to reflect on how it went and think about ways that you could have done better. Keep track of how you are doing.

It is also important to keep in mind that learning can often be enhanced when you do it with one or two other people. That way, each of you will benefit from the shared experience, by observing one another and by giving one another feedback on how to make improvements. Studies of team learning show that learning occurs much faster when skill building is done in an intensive and highly reflective fashion (Edmondson, Bohmer, and Pisano 2001).

Manage Your Reputation

As a policy analyst, you should work to develop a very good reputation in your policy community. We usually hope that other people will judge us solely on the substance and the quality of the work we do. In reality, however, people form their judgments of others based on any information that is deemed relevant. Because this is the case, in everything you do in your professional life, assume that you are always being monitored and that, in all instances, your reputation is on the line.

Continually thinking in terms of your reputation is a way of disciplining yourself to take care in everything you do. What you would most like is for your immediate policy community to operate like an echo chamber, where mention of your name sets off positive echoes in the minds of those who hear it. Over a period of time, if you consistently produce high-quality policy analysis and strive to build effective relationships with those with whom you interact, you are likely to acquire a solid reputation. After a while, people will come to expect a certain quality of work from you. They will hold expectations of how you will behave in any given interaction. When people receive evidence contradicting these expectations, that evidence can potentially do considerable damage to your reputation. If you make a mistake in the work you do or in the way that you handle your interaction with another person, the best thing that you can do is immediately admit your mistake and quickly work to correct it.

In his study of the role of reputation in corporations, Kreps (1990) noted the long-term value of taking actions that might have short-term costs. For example, a corporation that wants to have a highly positive image with customers might implement a "no-questions-asked" returns policy. Such a policy might mean that sometimes the cost of mistakes made by customers are borne by the corporation; however, the judgment is made that, over the long term, a returns policy that assumes competence and honesty on the part of customers is likely to yield a loyal client base. Both as a corporation and as an individual seller, it is always better to have people saying positive things about you and your products than to have any naysayers complaining about how you "nickeled-and-dimed" them. It is also important to note that, in terms of their effects on your reputation, the costs associated with just one negative comment against you can outweigh the benefits derived from many people saying positive things. As policy analysts, we can learn from this. We need to build and maintain good relations with our clients; we need to deliver products of the highest quality; and we should always stand ready to make immediate adjustments and improvements to our work if our clients express concern over what we have done.

So far, I have discussed the relationship between the core work of being a policy analyst and managing your reputation. There are, however, many "second-order" areas of activity and forms of interaction with others where, as a policy analyst, your reputation can be either advanced or diminished. For example, no matter how good you are at producing high-quality policy analysis and building effective relationships with your clients, if you do not get along with your colleagues, or you treat office staff in an arrogant fashion, you can do unnecessary damage to your broader reputation. When you are striving to build good relations with clients, it helps if you have already established good relations with the people with whom you work on a day-to-day basis. If you want a few strangers to think well of you, you should first work toward having those whom you interact with on a daily basis think well of you. Consistently avoiding passing on gossip in the workplace, thinking of ways to be a good colleague, and showing genuine interest and respect for those you work with are important habits for anyone who wants to build a good professional reputation. By acting in these ways, you will not only build a solid reputation for yourself, you will also find that it is easier to deal with ongoing busy work and free up quality time for your bigger projects.

LEAD BY EXAMPLE

As several of my previous observations suggest, the pursuit of excellence is often easier when others around you support you in that quest. In most activities in our lives, our personal performance is influenced by our context. It is much easier to strive to be an excellent policy analyst when you are working in an organization with others who share those ambitions. In contrast, when you find yourself in an organization where many people are satisfied with performing at mediocre levels, it becomes harder to pursue your goal of personal and professional excellence. As you work at building your skills as a policy analyst, it is important that you regularly assess the extent to which your operating context is serving to support or to undermine your pursuit of excellence. In some instances, you might find that the context is unsupportive of your efforts and that there is little you can do to change it. In such cases, you should probably begin to make plans to move on to a more welcoming and challenging organizational environment. It is also important, though, to remember that few organizational situations are ever ideal. Eventually, if you want to be in an organization where the pursuit of excellence is part of the culture, you will have to be prepared to lead by example. Excellent organizational cultures emerge through the efforts of excellent individuals.

Leading by example means first working to achieve personal mastery. Of course, we can never attain the levels of excellence that we would like to reach, but by striving for excellence in our own activities and behaviors, we can send important signals to those around us, indicating what it means to uphold high personal and professional standards. Leading by example means paying attention to your own actions and the messages they send, rather than preaching. When you work in team situations, you will find that there are many opportunities where you can model effective behavior and work with others to help them become better producers of high-quality policy analysis.

As you acquire a reputation for doing high-quality work, people will beat paths to your door, asking for your advice and guidance with their own work. Although you will rarely be able to drop what you are doing immediately to help others, whenever possible you should try to make time to respond to requests of this sort. Helping other policy analysts with their work is a powerful way to help shape the culture of your organization into one that values excellence. In the longer term, leadership by example can have significant payoffs, for both your organization and you. As you lead by example, you further reinforce your positive reputation. At the same time, you create an organizational culture that promotes excellent work. It is difficult to overestimate the ongoing value that individuals can reap from being associated with excellent organizations. Excellent individuals and organizations can do much to improve the quality of discussion and debate in policy communities. Thus, your efforts to provide leadership by example can yield many positive results.

PLAY THE LONG GAME

The policymaking process is complex. Shifting politics and circumstances have the effect of imposing elements of chance on all the outcomes of public policy discussions and debates. Even when we have worked diligently to acquire the broad range of technical skills and people skills needed to offer usable knowledge to members of the policymaking community, there are no guarantees that our work will receive a thoughtful reception. At times, advice is heeded. At others, it is ignored. Yet I am convinced that, as policy analysts, we can increase our odds of attaining influence. That is why I believe it is worth your while to pursue excellence continually; however, I also advise playing the long game. Inevitably, you will come up against moments in your career when your efforts will appear to have been wasted. These are the times when it would be easiest to give up. They are also the times when it is most important that you keep trying. The lessons that you learn at these moments can help you to improve your odds of success in the future.

When you are pursuing excellence—especially in terrain as unpredictable as the policymaking process—you cannot expect to achieve many quick successes. Over the course of a five- to ten-year period, however, you can accomplish a lot. If you keep track of the careers of highly successful policy analysts, you will see that most of them spend well over a decade paying their various dues before their careers take off and they start to have significant policy influence. Describing what it means to be an intellectual, Said (1996, 23) observed that it is "an everlasting effort, constitutively unfinished and necessarily imperfect. Yet its invigorations and complexities . . . make one the richer for it." To my mind, this observation is also suitable for describing the work of the policy analyst. It requires great intellectual and social acuity to think about public policy issues, work with others, and strive to change things for the better. Every time you start work on a different policy problem, you have new opportunities to apply previously acquired knowledge and skills. Over the course of your career, you can accumulate an impressive store of human capital. When you continually pursue excellence, and when you play the long game, you create future possibilities for yourself. It will never be an especially flashy occupation, but patiently striving to be the best policy analyst you can be will yield rich professional and personal rewards.

Further Reading

Covey, Stephen R. 1989. *The Seven Habits of Highly Effective People*. New York: Simon and Schuster.

Edelman, Marian Wright. 1992. "Twenty-Five Lessons for Life." Part 4 of *The Measure of Our Success: A Letter to My Children and Yours*. Boston: Beacon Press.

Knott, Jack H. 1986. "The Multiple and Ambiguous Roles of Profes-
    sionals in Public Policymaking." *Knowledge: Creation, Diffusion,
    Utilization* 8:131–53.
Maxwell, John C. 1993. *Developing the Leader within You*. Nashville:
    Thomas Nelson.
Senge, Peter M. 1990. "Personal Mastery." In *The Fifth Discipline: The Art
    and Practice of the Learning Organization*. New York: Doubleday,
    pp. 139–73.

Appendix

In most of the undergraduate and graduate courses I teach, I require students to engage in teamwork. For example, I often require teams of students to begin a class season by providing a short review and extension based on the topics covered in the lecture given in the previous class meeting and the associated readings. These team efforts are evaluated in two ways. First, there is an external evaluation of the work of the whole group. Second, there is an internal evaluation of the team process. The team members themselves undertake the internal evaluation. Below, I present the guide to the evaluation process. It is designed to give students feedback in a manner that allows them readily to identify the areas of their performance that they should strive to improve before their next presentation.

EXTERNAL EVALUATION METHOD

I will give each team a summary or overall grade for each review and extension. This grade will be arrived at using the template in figure A-1, which contains seven discrete items. A team that pays close attention to doing well on all the items listed here will be likely to give an excellent presentation. This grade will count for 50 percent of your individual grade for the team work. (Note: all team members will receive the same grade for this component.)

Assignment: _____

Student Names: _____ **Overall Grade:** _____

Item	Grade						
1. Knowledge of subject	C	C+	B-	B	B+	A-	A
2. Organization of presentation	C	C+	B-	B	B+	A-	A
3. Effort to convey enthusiasm for subject	C	C+	B-	B	B+	A-	A
4. Use of props (PowerPoint, handout, etc.)	C	C+	B-	B	B+	A-	A
5. Evidence of course-related, cumulative learning	C	C+	B-	B	B+	A-	A
6. Use of provocative or innovative techniques	C	C+	B-	B	B+	A-	A
7. Promotion of class interest and involvement	C	C+	B-	B	B+	A-	A

Figure A-1. External Evaluation Template

INTERNAL EVALUATION METHOD

Students will grade each other on their contributions to the team process leading to the actual presentation. My expectation is that every student will strive to be a model team member. Working to gain a grade of *A* on each item listed in figure A-2 would be consistent with this. After the team work is concluded, each member will fill in one of the following forms for each other member of the team. (The evaluations will never be shared with other students.) I will collate the grades for each student. This grade will count for 50 percent of your individual grade for the team work. (Note: team members will receive different grades for this component.) As far as possible, all team members should work to avoid problems with the team process—the internal evaluations are designed to encourage professionalism; please don't use them to punish each other!

Name of Team Member Being Evaluated: _____

Name of Team Member Doing This Evaluation: _____

Overall Grade: _____

Item	Grade						
1. Attending and participating at team meetings	C	C+	B-	B	B+	A-	A
2. Cooperating with others to specify required work	C	C+	B-	B	B+	A-	A
3. Contributing ideas and relevant materials	C	C+	B-	B	B+	A-	A
4. Taking care to listen to and respect others' ideas	C	C+	B-	B	B+	A-	A
5. Being a friendly, focused colleague	C	C+	B-	B	B+	A-	A
6. Helping others to master the subject matter	C	C+	B-	B	B+	A-	A
7. Meeting deadlines and doing agreed tasks	C	C+	B-	B	B+	A-	A
8. Ensuring the presentation was tight and polished	C	C+	B-	B	B+	A-	A

Figure A-2. Internal Evaluation Template

Bibliography

Alchian, Armen A., and Harold Demsetz. 1972. "Production, Information Costs, and Economic Organization." *American Economic Review* 62: 777–95.

Arredondo, Lani. 2000. *Communicating Effectively*. New York: McGraw-Hill.

Avery, Christopher M. 2001. *Teamwork Is an Individual Skill: Getting Your Work Done when Sharing Responsibility*. San Francisco: Berrett-Koehler.

Axelrod, Robert. 1984. *The Evolution of Cooperation*. New York: Basic Books.

Bardach, Eugene. 2000. *A Practical Guide for Policy Analysis: The Eightfold Path to More Effective Problem Solving*. New York: Seven Bridges Press.

Beam, David R. 1996. "If Public Ideas Are So Important Now, Why Are Policy Analysts So Depressed?" *Journal of Policy Analysis and Management* 15: 430–37.

Behn, Robert D. 1985. "Policy Analysts, Clients, and Social Scientists." *Policy Analysis and Management* 4: 428–32.

Bickers, Kenneth N., and John T. Williams. 2001. *Public Policy Analysis: A Political Economy Approach*. Boston: Houghton-Mifflin.

Carnegie, Dale. 1937. *How to Win Friends and Influence People*. New York: Simon & Schuster.

Carpenter, Susan L., and W. J. D. Kennedy. 1988. *Managing Public Disputes: A Practical Guide to Handling Conflict and Reaching Agreements*. San Francisco: Jossey-Bass.

Castells, Manuel. 1996. *The Rise of the Network Society*. Oxford: Blackwell.

Cobb, Roger W., and Charles W. Elder. 1983. *Participation in American Politics: The Dynamics of Agenda-Building.* 2d ed. Boston: Allyn and Bacon.

Cohen, Herb. 1980. *You Can Negotiate Anything.* London: Angus and Robertson.

Dahl, Robert A. 1998. *On Democracy.* New Haven, Conn.: Yale University Press.

Dawes, Robyn M. 1988. *Rational Choice in an Uncertain World.* New York: Harcourt Brace Jovanovich.

Derthick, Martha, and Paul J. Quirk. 1985. *The Politics of Deregulation.* Washington, D.C.: Brookings Institution.

Dixit, Avinash K. 1994. "My System of Work (Not!)" *American Economist* 38: 10–16.

Dixit, Avinash K., and Barry J. Nalebuff. 1991. *Thinking Strategically: The Competitive Edge in Business, Politics, and Everyday Life.* New York: Norton.

Edmondson, Amy C., Richard M. Bohmer, and Gary P. Pisano. 2001. "Disrupted Routines: Team Learning and New Technology Implementation in Hospitals." *Administrative Science Quarterly* 46: 685–716.

Eisner, Marc Allen, and Kenneth J. Meier. 1990. "Presidential Control versus Bureaucratic Power: Explaining the Reagan Revolution in Antitrust." *American Journal of Political Science* 34: 269–87.

Eyestone, Robert. 1978. *From Social Issues to Public Policy.* New York: Wiley.

Fisher, Roger, William Ury, and Bruce Patton. 1991. *Getting to YES: Negotiating Agreement without Giving In.* 2d ed. Hammondsworth, U.K.: Penguin.

Forester, John. 1999. *The Deliberative Practitioner: Encouraging Participatory Planning Processes.* Cambridge, Mass.: MIT Press.

Fox, Jeffrey J. 1998. *How to Become CEO: The Rules for Rising to the Top of Any Organization.* New York: Hyperion.

Friedman, Benjamin M. 1995. "Principles of Economics." *American Economist* 39: 28–36.

Goffman, Erving. 1956. *The Presentation of Self in Everyday Life.* Edinburgh: University of Edinburgh Social Science Research Center.

Goldhamer, Herbert. 1978. *The Adviser.* New York: Elsevier.

Goleman, Daniel. 1998. *Working with Emotional Intelligence.* New York: Bantam Books.

Granovetter, Mark S. 1995. *Getting a Job: A Study of Contacts and Careers.* 2d ed. Chicago: University of Chicago Press.

Greenberg, Mark, and Michael C. Laracy. 2000. *Welfare Reform: Next Steps Offer New Opportunities.* Public Policy Paper no. 4. Washington, D.C.: Neighborhood Funders Group.

Haas, Peter M. 1992. "Introduction: Epistemic Communities and International Policy Coordination." *International Organization* 46: 1–35.

Hammer, Michael, and James Champy. 1993. *Reengineering the Corporation: A Manifesto for Business Revolution.* New York: Harper Business.

Hara, Noriko, Diane H. Sonnenwald, Paul Solomon, and Seung-Ly Kim. 2001. "An Emerging View of Scientific Collaboration: Scientists' Perspectives on Collaboration and Factors that Impact Collaboration." Technical Report TR-2001008, School of Information and Library Science, University of North Carolina at Chapel Hill.

Holpp, Lawrence. 1999. *Managing Teams.* New York: McGraw-Hill Professional.

Ingram, Helen, and Steven Rathgeb Smith, eds. 1993. *Public Policy for Democracy.* Washington, D.C.: Brookings Institution.

Katzenbach, Jon R., and Douglas K. Smith. 1993. *The Wisdom of Teams: Creating the High-Performance Organization.* New York: HarperCollins.

Kelley, Tom. 2001. *The Art of Innovation.* New York: Currency/Doubleday.

Kingdon, John W. 1995. *Agendas, Alternatives, and Public Policies.* 2d ed. Boston: Little, Brown.

Kreps, David M. 1990. "Corporate Culture and Economic Theory." In *Perspectives on Positive Political Economy.* Edited by James E. Alt and Kenneth A. Shepsle. New York: Cambridge University Press, pp. 90–143.

Leman, Christopher K., and Robert H. Nelson. 1981. "Ten Commandments for Policy Economists." *Journal of Policy Analysis and Management* 1: 97–117.

Lindblom, Charles E. 1968. *The Policymaking Process.* Englewood Cliffs, N.J.: Prentice Hall.

MacRae, Duncan, Jr., and Dale Whittington. 1997. *Expert Advice for Policy Choice: Analysis and Discourse*. Washington, D.C.: Georgetown University Press.

Majone, Giandomenico. 1989. *Evidence, Argument, and Persuasion in the Policy Process*. New Haven, Conn.: Yale University Press.

Mankiw, N. Gregory. 1996. "My Rules of Thumb." *American Economist* 40: 14–19.

Massey, Andrew. 1988. *Technocrats and Nuclear Politics: The Influence of Professional Experts in Policy-making*. Brookfield, Vt.: Avebury.

McCraw, Thomas K. 1984. *Prophets of Regulation*. Cambridge, Mass.: Harvard University Press.

McKay, Matthew, Peter D. Rogers, and Judith McKay. 1989. *When Anger Hurts: Quieting the Storm Within*. New York: New Harbinger.

Mead, Lawrence M. 1985. "Science Versus Analysis: A False Dichotomy." *Journal of Policy Analysis and Management* 4: 419–22.

Micale, Frances A. 1999. *Not Another Meeting! A Practical Guide for Facilitating Effective Meetings*. Central Point, Ore.: Oasis.

Miles, Matthew B., and A. Michael Huberman. 1994. *Qualitative Data Analysis: An Expanded Sourcebook*. Thousand Oaks, Calif.: Sage.

Miller, Gary J. 1992. *Managerial Dilemmas: The Political Economy of Hierarchy*. New York: Cambridge University Press.

Mills, C. Wright. 1959. *The Sociological Imagination*. New York: Oxford University Press.

Mintrom, Michael. 2000. *Policy Entrepreneurs and School Choice*. Washington, D.C.: Georgetown University Press.

———. 2001. "Policy Design for Local Innovation: The Effects of Competition in Public Schooling." *State Politics and Policy Quarterly* 1: 343–63.

Mizner, Elisabeth L. 2000. "The Wise Farmer." In *Masters of Networking: Building Relationships for Your Pocketbook and Soul*. Edited by Ivan R. Misner and Don Morgan. Atlanta: Bard, pp. 261–63.

Moe, Terry M. 1991. "Politics and the Theory of Organization." *Journal of Law, Economics, and Organization* 7 (special issue): 106–29.

Mooney, Christopher. 1991. "Information Sources in State Legislative Decision Making." *Legislative Studies Quarterly* 16: 445–55.

Munger, Michael C. 2000. *Analyzing Policy: Choices, Conflicts, and Practices*. New York: Norton.

Musso, Juliet, Robert Biller, and Robert Myrtle. 2000. "Tradecraft: Professional Writing as Problem Solving." *Journal of Policy Analysis and Management* 19: 635–46.

Myerson, Roger B. 1995. "Analysis of Democratic Institutions: Structure, Conduct and Performance." *Journal of Economic Perspectives* 9: 77–89.

Nelson, Barbara. 1984. *Making an Issue of Child Abuse.* Chicago: University of Chicago Press.

Nisbett, Richard, and Lee Ross. 1980. *Human Inference: Strategies and Shortcomings of Social Judgment.* Englewood Cliffs, N.J.: Prentice-Hall.

Olson, Mancur. 1965. *The Logic of Collective Action: Public Goods and the Theory of Groups.* Cambridge, Mass.: Harvard University Press.

Osborn, Alex F. 1963. *Applied Imagination: Principles and Procedures of Creative Problem-Solving.* 3d ed. New York: Charles Scribner's Sons.

Osborne, David E., and Ted Gaebler. 1992. *Reinventing Government: How the Entrepreneurial Spirit Is Transforming the Public Sector.* Reading, Mass: Addison-Wesley.

Peters, Thomas J., and Robert H. Waterman, Jr. 1982. *In Search of Excellence: Lessons from America's Best-run Companies.* New York: Warner Brothers.

Porter, Michael E. 1979. "The Structure within Industries and Companies' Performance." *Review of Economics and Statistics* 61: 214–27.

Radin, Beryl A. 1997. "The Evolution of the Policy Analysis Field: From Conversation to Conversations." *Journal of Policy Analysis and Management* 16: 204–19.

———. 2000. *Beyond Machiavelli: Policy Analysis Comes of Age.* Washington, D.C.: Georgetown University Press.

Rasiel, Ethan M. 1999. *The McKinsey Way: Using the Techniques of the World's Top Strategic Consultants to Help You and Your Business.* New York: McGraw-Hill.

Rees, Fran. 2001. *How to Lead Work Teams: Facilitation Skills.* 2d ed. San Francisco: Jossey-Bass/Pfeiffer.

RoAne, Susan. 2000. *How to Work a Room: The Ultimate Guide to Savvy Socializing in Person and Online.* New York: HarperCollins.

Rochefort, David A., and Roger W. Cobb. 1994. "Problem Definition: An Emerging Perspective." In *The Politics of Problem Definition: Shaping the Policy Agenda.* Edited by David A. Rochefort and Roger W. Cobb. Lawrence: University Press of Kansas, pp. 1–31.

Rogers, Everett M. 1995. *Diffusion of Innovations*. 4th ed. New York: Free Press.

Said, Edward W. 1996. *Representations of the Intellectual*. New York: Vintage Books.

Schneider, Anne Larason, and Helen Ingram. 1997. *Policy Design for Democracy*. Lawrence: University Press of Kansas.

Schön, Donald A., and Martin Rein. 1994. *Frame Reflection: Toward the Resolution of Intractable Policy Controversies*. New York: Basic Books.

Shulock, Nancy. 1999. "The Paradox of Policy Analysis: If It Is Not Used, Why Do We Produce So Much of It?" *Journal of Policy Analysis and Management* 18: 226–44.

Stone, Deborah. 1997. *Policy Paradox: The Art of Political Decision Making*. New York: Norton.

Strunk, William, Jr., and E. B. White. 1979. *The Elements of Style*. 3d ed. New York: MacMillan.

Sutton, Robert I., and Andrew Hargadon. 1996. "Brainstorming Groups in Context: Effectiveness in a Product Design Firm." *Administrative Science Quarterly* 41: 685–718.

Tropman, John E. 1996. *Making Meetings Work: Achieving High Quality Group Decisions*. Thousand Oaks, Calif.: Sage.

Tufte, Edward R. 1983. *The Visual Display of Quantitative Information*. Cheshire, Conn.: Graphics Press.

———. 1990. *Envisioning Information*. Cheshire, Conn.: Graphics Press.

———. 1997. *Visual Explanations: Images and Quantities, Evidence and Narrative*. Cheshire, Conn.: Graphics Press.

U.S. Congress. 1975. *Civil Aeronautics Board Practices and Procedures*. Report of Subcommittee on Administrative Practice and Procedure of the Senate Committee on the Judiciary, 94th Cong., 1st Sess. Washington, D.C.: U.S. Government Printing Office.

Vaughan, Diane. 1996. *The Challenger Launch Decision: Risky Technology, Culture, and Deviance at NASA*. Chicago: University of Chicago Press.

Verdier, James M. 1984. "Advising Congressional Decision-makers: Guidelines for Economists." *Journal of Policy Analysis and Management* 3: 421–38.

Weick, Karl E. 1995. *Sensemaking in Organizations*. Thousand Oaks, Calif.: Sage.

Weimer, David L., and Aidan R. Vining. 1999. *Policy Analysis: Concepts and Practice*. 3d ed. Upper Saddle River, N.J.: Prentice Hall.

Weiss, Carol H. 1977. "Research for Policy's Sake: The Enlightenment Function of Social Science Research." *Policy Analysis* 3: 531–45.

Wildavsky, Aaron. 1979. *Speaking Truth to Power: The Art and Craft of Policy Analysis*. Boston: Little, Brown.

———. 1993. *Craftways: On the Organization of Scholarly Work*. 2d ed. New Brunswick, N.J.: Transaction Publishers.

Wright, Peter L., Charles D. Pringle, and Mark J. Kroll. 1992. *Strategic Management: Text and Cases*. Boston: Allyn and Bacon.

Index